V.S. Naipaul

An Anthology of 21st Century Criticism

V.S. Naipaul

An Anthology of 21st Century Criticism

Edited with an Introduction by

Ajay K. Chaubey

Foreword by

Manjit Inder Singh

ATLANTIC

PUBLISHERS & DISTRIBUTORS (P) LTD

Published by
ATLANTIC
PUBLISHERS & DISTRIBUTORS (P) LTD
7/22, Ansari Road, Darya Ganj, New Delhi-110002
Phones : +91-11-40775252, 23273880, 23275880, 23280451
Fax : +91-11-23285873
Web : www.atlanticbooks.com
E-mail : orders@atlanticbooks.com

Branch Office
5, Nallathambi Street, Wallajah Road, Chennai-600002
Phones : +91-44-64611085, 32413319
E-mail : chennai@atlanticbooks.com

Reprint 2019

ISBN 978-81-269-1904-8

Printed in India at Nice Printing Press, A-33/3A, Site-IV,
Industrial Area, Sahibabad, Ghaziabad, U.P.

Dedicated to

My parents, teachers and mentors

Foreword

During my rather long and chequered critical engagement with V.S. Naipaul since the late seventies—his fiction, non-fiction, travelogues, memoirs, letters, interviews, and the enormous body of criticism—I have felt that reading and intellectually 'travelling' with Naipaul's alternating views about issues and writing beg many compulsive responses. One of these—and indeed a significant one—is that one has to see his achievement and enviable reputation as a creator of 'worlds' (the ones to which he belongs, and others into which he has peregrined) on his own terms. Any detours, deflections and indirect enlargements, creatively or critically, bring back the reader to the core of what his experiential insights and politics of belonging (or otherwise) have become the stuff of his writing. I had hastened to add in the Foreword to my own book on Naipaul more than fifteen years back, that he becomes a 'companion and a burden' that one carries around everywhere, following his own perception about himself as a writer who belongs 'nowhere and everywhere'. Indeed, what has been remarkable in relation to Naipaul's creation of his fictional universe, and his continuous autobiographical register in his works, is the translation of a unique journey and experience into a discourse that re-inscribes his own, and older, historical journey patterns from India to Caribbean to Europe, and beyond. As a writer from a dislocated, disturbed and itinerant culture, Naipaul has carried within him the scars, memories, the inextricable and intertwined strands of human transitions and the challenges involved in 'enigmas of arrivals', turning them into relationships with wider historical shifts and movements—from Empire, imperialism, colonialism, creation of diasporas and floating communities across the world. Together with this, there are the Saidian contrapuntal movements, strains and troubled affiliations between and in-between, of centre-periphery, colony-metropolis, the powerful and the powerless, the oppressors and the oppressed in addition to many other juxtapositions and connotations resulting from any number of accidents of fate and time—underlining what we have today in the form of global culture of hybridization and hyphenations—a world on the move, accelerating in its speed the mixture of culture, histories, traditions and literary languages as well.

One has only to recollect the undefined journey of Salim in *A Bend in the River*, moving to a central Africa monumentalizing ancient and modern 'passages' of change and incursions, or Ralph Singh's transformative as well as self-critical memoir-writing in *The Mimic Men* about the shipwrecked Hindu indentured community, the memorable cast of characters in *In a Free State*, people struggling and groping for freedom, attempting an abortive autonomy against all odds in alien and hostile landscapes. Or for that matter, his whole painful, meditative and intellectual journey-pattern in *The Enigma of Arrival* in the middle of decay, change and the dialectics of personal and literary development, against the unusual classical setting of a surrealist painting, something Naipaul has stated in different forms and styles elsewhere. His own accounts of a writer's formation, his burdens of experience—personal and impersonal—his sense of weariness and ennui, are in a way, also the trajectories of his developing or shaping vision. The struggle to find a purpose, meaning, order, even a way to understand the impacts of one's biological, ancestral, cultural, communal, religious and ethnic fall-backs, continues to be the thematic and experiential residues of his work, as late as *Half a Life* and *Magic Seeds*. Naipaul's 'legacy', his 'special calling' has arguably affected the post-colonial literary culture, in the sense that contemporary writing oscillates between a quest for interpreting one's diasporic roots and identity, finding one's way in the culturally fragmented world, while writing, more than ever before, reserves a right to narrate, to be heard, to communicate the lives and memories of people forgotten by history, their voices silenced by more powerful and menacing forces. At this point of time when Naipaul's works go back to nearly fifty-five years, and when awards and fame are behind him, there is a Naipaul curiously divided between admirers and detractors—something one can trace back to his unpalatable but truthful statements about societies, nations and communities. There perhaps lies his exclusive place, as a writer, questioned, condemned and interrogated, but admired at the same time for truths and uncompromising stances about life no one can deny. And, as Patrick French writes quoting Naipaul in his recent controversial biography, "The lives of writers are a legitimate subject of inquiry; and the truth should not be skimped. It may be, in fact, that a full account of a writer's life might in the end be more a work of literature and more illuminating—of a cultural and historical moment—than the writer's books."

I congratulate Dr. Ajay K. Chaubey for his efforts to bring out the present volume of Naipaul criticism by young Indian scholars, *V.S. Naipaul: An Anthology of 21st Century Criticism*. I am sure the critical views will contribute and enhance the evaluation of Naipaul's life, career, fictional and non-fictional works to the already existing vast corpus of critical material.

Manjit Inder Singh
Professor of English and Coordinator,
Centre for Diaspora Studies,
Punjabi University, Patiala (Punjab)

Acknowledgements

I take this opportunity to thank teachers, scholarly friends and mentors who have facilitated me to accomplish the academic and intellectual work in the context with an apposite eidetic form. I am especially thankful to Dr. O.S. Pandey (RRPG College, Amethi), my guide and guardian, who brought me to the higher academic success; Prof. S.Z.H. Abidi (former Head, Dept. of English and MEL, University of Lucknow), my mentor, who sharpened my epistemic vision; Dr. P.C. Pradhan (BHU, Varanasi) who gifted me with his gems of intellect; Dr. R.P. Singh (University of Lucknow) for propelling me to this venture and shortening the distance of my destination; Dr. Vishnu Gupta (BBD University, Lucknow), friend and philosopher, whose analysis suffused me with all required energies; and Dr. Sudhir K. Arora (MHPG College, Moradabad), who offered his valuable suggestions from time to time.

There are few friends who have candidly shared their theoretical, philosophical and intellectual understandings which have given to the 'Introduction' to my anthology a speculative contour. They have also obliged me by offering precious suggestions to enrich the excellence of the present book. They are: Veerendra Kumar Mishra (Banasthali Vidyapeeth), Vishnupriya Sengupta (former Post-Doctoral Fellow, Italy), and Dr. Anirban Mukherjee (NIT, Uttarakhand).

I am grateful to my parents—Shree Madhusudan Chaubey and Smt. Kalavati Devi—who are a relentless source of energy and vivacity for me. I also thank all the contributors for presenting their well researched papers.

Ajay K. Chaubey

Contents

Section B: V.S. Naipaul's Travel Narratives: A Post-colonial Passage to the Globe

Section C: Identity, Home, Marital and Gender Discourse through Text/s: Critical Essays on V.S. Naipaul's *A House for Mr Biswas*

Introduction

V.S. Naipaul: An Embodiment of Controversy and Scholarship

> "...Naipaul has become Sir V.S. Naipaul, an extremely famous and, it must be said, very talented writer whose novels and non-fiction (mostly travel books) have established his reputation as one of the truly celebrated, justly well-known figures in world literature today."
>
> —Edward Said

> "Naipaul's particular notion of the value of writing is central to his understanding of the world and himself in it."
>
> —Neil ten Kortenaar

> "Sir Vidia's construction of the Indian nation, his views on certain major episodes in contemporary history, his interpretation of Islam, and the role of minorities in secular India have always been controversial."
>
> —Mushirul Hasan

Sir Vidiadhar Surajprasad Naipaul is one of the prolific authors of the twentieth century and now of the twenty-first. His prowess on history, culture, civilization and ethnicity—a journalistic approach to unearth the past—has been appreciated by his critics too. He has been successful not merely by being a good author but also by producing a diatribe against "third world countries"—Trinidad, a place of his birth and India, a place of his ancestors—both of which he has often described as 'half-baked societies' that have dragged him to be the butt of controversies. Shobhaa De remarks on his velitations, "Naipaul has fed off controversy all his life. He is an 'agent provocateur' and a brilliant one at that."[1] Naipaul's erudition, his faculty of criticism and brush with literary vendetta are *outré*. His willingness to disparage, all that he encounters, has not won him many friends but the simplistic and near-universal assertions of an unswerving heart-felt racism and Orientalist chauvinism seldom undergo close scrutiny. Most of criticism of his works is trivial, hopelessly ignorant to the complexity of his tortured negotiations with his own post-coloniality. Naipaul's permanent estrangement is expressed through a series of surprisingly different and amazingly defective narrators who are placed in an astonishingly similar succession of "chronotopes".

One finds that his novels present "a postcolonial dilemma for us" (Bhattacharya 245). His corpus of fiction manoeuvers his autobiographical information that recounts his historical, socio-cultural and political affairs. He coalesces biography and history in his writings to make his subject matter tangible and substantial. Fawzia Mustafa may appropriately be quoted here, "...Naipaul's use of biographical information in his writing constructs an over-determined relation between notions of the Author and the multiple usage of what is called the colonial subject" (Mustafa 13). The same incorporation has made him a world famous author who juxtaposes eulogy and elegy of the world that gives him countless prizes.

Again, he is the only living author who has bagged almost all the prestigious awards and his "name spells almost endless accolades" (Singh 19) which include a few: the Booker Prize in 1971 for *In a Free State*, the Knighthood in 1990 and the Nobel Prize for Literature in 2001 for his corpus of literary works. He has also received literary awards like the John Llewellyn Rhys Prize (1958), the Somerset Maugham Award (1960), Phoenix Trust Award (1962)[2], the Bennet Award (1980), the Jerusalem Prize (1983), the T.S. Eliot Award (1986) for Creative Writing[3], the David Cohen Prize (the first recipient) given for his 'lifetime' achievement in British Literature (1993). He was shortlisted along with Mahasweta Devi from India and Alice Munro from Canada for The Man Booker International Prize in 2009, which is awarded every two years and given to the living author whose works are available in almost every language of the world. Naipaul, as is well known, was often given grants to travel and document his experiences, as he "writes about a racially complex world with all the compassion and insight which is missing in some of his public pronouncements."[4]

V.S. Naipaul, who was born in 1932 and lived in Trinidad till 1950, is the only author in the world who has mapped the whole trajectory of the post-colonial civilization and has beautifully painted the literary canvas in multiple hues that reflect his ambivalent relationship with the world he lives in. His maiden travelogue, *The Middle Passage* (1962), the upshot of his revisit to Trinidad, his birthplace, was written on a fund from the Government of Trinidad. In this modern travel narrative, he has "created a deft and remarkably prescient portrait of Trinidad and four adjacent Caribbean societies—*British Guiana, Suriname, Martinique, and Jamaica*."[5] Both his fiction and non-fiction usually deal with the individuals trying to preserve their wholeness in terms of individuality while they are "functioning as cogs in the wheels of a social structure" (White 1). His revisit to Trinidad was prolific on the creative front but he is a man divorced from his Caribbean roots—the purist made nauseous by filth and flesh, or the racist who has "forgotten" his own family's sojourn in the cane fields of the New World.

Naipaul's roots lie in the routes of the world. After Trinidad, he looked towards the East to come to terms with the land of his ancestors. His visits to India resulted in the publication of *An Area of Darkness* (1964) that created a hullabaloo in the media and academia. His sojourn provided him with a splendid opportunity to learn about Indian classics that presented him untold tales of Indian legacy that he had often received from his "Gold Teeth Nanee". The "new discovery" of India was a contortion for natives as it was called "an area of 'defecation.'"[6] The non-fiction works of Naipaul are a touchstone for what is happening in every ex-colony of the post-colonial world.

Naipaul did not discontinue writing about India after *An Area of Darkness*. His thirst for the Indian subcontinent was and, to date, remains unquenchable. After the same, Naipaul published two subsequent travelogues on India—*India: A Wounded Civilization* (1977) and *India: A Million Mutinies Now* (1990). The former was Naipaul's dialogue on post-colonial civilization and records "India at the time of Indira Gandhi's State of Emergency" (Nixon 13), while the latter describes his perspectives on contemporary and multicultural politics and in many ways "(the) most ambiguous work" (*Ibid*). His travelogues—from *The Middle Passage* (1962) to *The Masque of Africa: Glimpses in African Belief* (2010)—investigate Naipaul's 'self', map the trail of history, narrate the politics of society but "...totally ignore a massive infusion of critical scholarship...." (Said 53). Thus, one can say that V.S. Naipaul has identified the strange emotional and sophisticated contortions that bind together culturally, in an ambiguously globalized world—as he investigates not only Trinidad, Africa and India but also the countries like USA in *A Turn in the South* (1989) which describes his racialized thinking in the context of the southern part of America.

Naipaul is an author whose works are often the subject of many disputes among the critics of contemporary literary landscape. This controversial writer has divided the critics into binaries—some praise him as one of the most gifted authors of these days; the others blame him for "racial arrogance" (White 2). He is known as an author, who is either loved and admired, or renounced. After all, there is one thing that most of the critics concur on and it is a fact that Naipaul is the master of observation and depiction who always provides his reader with very sophisticated descriptions. He belongs to the lineage of authors whose works are primarily focused on the post-colonial countries, their present situation and the impact of colonialism on identity of individuals. His Indian genesis, Trinidadian nativity and British citizenship allow him to see India and Indian people from a considerably different perspective. He is an "insider" as well as "outsider" to India (Rai 16). Through his Indian ancestry he can see the country from a very intimate point of view; this kind of double perspective makes it more difficult for him to understand his own feelings and reactions in some of the situations that he has to face in India, especially when he realizes his own strangeness. Sometimes he himself seems surprised by the revelation of his merits or demerits that he was not aware of. For him, the cognition of India is simultaneously the discovery of himself. His Trinidadian childhood, Indian origin and the residency in London make his position in the world highly indeterminate. He fully identifies with none of these countries. He rather sees himself as a blend of the three cultures. He feels absolutely alienated and is unable to identify with any of these societies. The innermost notion of his books is "the struggle against the effects of displacement" (Nightingale 6). He intentionally observes what he has expected and ignores what he does not want to see.

Naipaul's literature presents the image of an author who does not receive any sense of belonging to any terrestrial locale but the wide array of his intellect has resulted in many superb books. His works present the image of a person who is constantly in search of a cultural mooring. Although he has a vast repertoire of literary output at his disposal, he is not only a natural writer but also a natural novelist. His vision is his own, unaffected by contemporary social cliché or political bonanza. He has not only autonomy to dictate the 'truth' but also has relevance to subjugate the hideous lies of the societies. He is engaged with the stresses and strains that we recognize vital in our experience now.

Naipaul's scathing and prejudiced circumspection on Islam, his contours on Islamic countries and his pronouncements on Muslims' contribution to India declared him 'voice' of the West. Naipaul's views on Muslim imperialism in India have reiterated his spurious and schematic notion of Indian history. His notion of Indian history cannot be described in nutshell because it begins from an Islamic invasion from approximately AD 1000 which has vandalized a self-contained, essentially Hindu India, followed by an intellectually debilitating Muslim imperialism and rationally regenerative British imperialism; the main victims in all of which have been Hindu Indians. The dilapidation of Indian civilization, culture and history by Muslim invaders has created a hiatus in the classical knowledge system of India. Naipaul's such observation has landed him in utter controversy in the world. He, of late, caught the nerve of controversy as a subject on him and for him. For him, "Islam is worse than most other problems of the Third World" (Said). In Mumbai Literature Festival, Girish Karnad, an Indian playwright of renowned stature, pulped a much awaited criticism on Naipaul for un-favouring Muslims and their contribution to Indian cultural heritage. Karnad was of the opinion that Naipaul has been vocal against Muslims on the racial and religious grounds not on their contribution to music, art and literature. The Karnadian demarche brought Naipaul in the limelight once again. He whimpered that "Naipaul has no idea of how Muslims contributed to Indian history."[7] Adversely, Karnad was trapped in the ruins of controversy because he was not invited to speak on Naipaul but on 'Indian Theatre'. Intelligentsia across the country poured in comments, verbally and in writing. Some favoured Naipaul and some Karnad. But Naipaul remained silent. His silence was not a mere stillness but it was the rubble of an arrogant mind. Through his flabbergasted posture he has deciphered and delineated that he does not care about any comment nor he understands what is said against him. His unavailability on the current scenario has displayed that he need not utter in counter reaction. He says what has been unsaid because he is "sum of his books".

His writing is the fusion of creeds, cultures and continents in him, with his expatriate career, to practice an art in and of totally dissimilar worlds, all giving him peculiar contemporary quality. In this context, Dagmar Barnouw remarks: "A British-educated West Indian, Naipaul has tried to understand and document the difficulties of other cultures through his difficulties at understanding his own multiethnic background". Critics of international repute, even today, present the foray of criticism on V.S. Naipaul in a diverse way. There is no refuting the fact that his travelogues induced various controversies but Naipaul unflinchingly continued his cultural explorations. His multiethnic background, his faculty of mind, his "sophisticated literary strategies" (Barnouw ix) and his creative mission have still been unexplored. This is the reason why "few would dispute Naipaul's status as probably the greatest living writer of Indian origin; indeed some would go further and argue that he is the greatest living writer of English prose" (Dalrymple). Naipaul's "archeology of knowledge", which has the exceptional flair to intermingle murky places and people, makes him an impregnable author in the post-modern world. Younger minds, therefore, differently explore Naipaul's intellectual world which vie with the crusading zeal for the first Nobel Laureate for Literature in the twenty-first century. Hence, this anthology.

About the Anthology

What makes V.S. Naipaul unique is his distinctive way of situating the post-colonial subject matter. He dexterously negotiates the text and context, matter and manner in his fictional and non-fictional corpus of writings. His dichotomy of the 'East and West', dialectics of India and Indian subcontinents, Africa, Trinidad, Islamic countries and the USA present the 'national allegory' of the nations he has visited at regular interregnum. His literary corpus is a matter of serious debate and discussion in academia. The present volume exerts to touch upon almost all his major works. The essays offer diverse perspectives—some eulogizing, others critiquing his perspective.

The volume, divided into three sections containing seventeen essays, offers a fresh critical insight on V.S. Naipaul. The first section, titled "Contexts and Convergences in Naipaul's Fictions", encloses eight essays on the fictional world of Naipaul. The essays included in the same segment closely peruse multiple themes, issues and polemics of desires of Naipaulian protagonists in the 'neo-colonial' world. Prakash Chandra Pradhan's paper "Race, Ethnicity, Sexual Violence and Neocolonialism in V.S. Naipaul's *Guerrillas*: A Postcolonial Reading" is an incisive study of Naipaul's *Guerrillas* against the backdrop of race, ethnicity, sexual violence and neocolonialism, racial tension and political disorder which are indissoluble constituents of 'postcolonialism'. The author contends that "the materialistic society portrayed in *Guerrillas* is a bankrupt one, devoid of the right vision and competence to tackle the enormous doom hanging around it." Pradhan further emphasizes Naipaul's point that 'borrowed' ideas have "no viability and strength to take the country forward to the path of progresses."

Vishnupriya Sengupta's research paper "The Dialectics of Homelessness in V.S. Naipaul's *The Mystic Masseur* and *Half a Life*" follows a line of investigation that Naipaul's power and suggestiveness as a writer lies in the absence of a solution to his problem. Her paper attempts to map Naipaul's mind and its homelessness in a world of dissolving boundaries and expanding horizons. In reading Naipaul, she feels that exile is a fundamental condition of the post-colonial world, one which we must all experience to a greater or lesser extent. She concludes that "cartography and topography are futile concepts in a world that is not our own, and that at any time we may find ourselves homeless in it."

The next essay titled "Invention, Memory, and Place in *Magic Seeds:* A Perspective of Reading" by Valiur Rahman is unique in its way because it studies Naipaul's *Magic Seeds* in the Saidean framework of 'memory' and 'place'. It also tries to deconstruct references and allusions sprung from writer's memory and effects of the place wherever he visits. On this postulation V.S. Naipaul's *Magic Seeds* has been studied with special references to his other works mapping his intertextual habits of writing.

Chandan Kumar Panda's study "Affirming the Different: A Study of V.S. Naipaul's Caribbean Fictions" examines how the second and third generation of Indian expatriates in Trinidad survive by negotiating with the 'peculiarities' of the Caribbean region. He, moreover, addresses the issues of memory, history and identity as they surface in Naipaul's fictions on the region. He further unfolds that "Indians in Trinidad after one generation or two of the traumatic exodus affirm the alien and continue to live conforming to the Caribbean heterogeneities. The land they once left remains for them a land of curiosity and imagination, not the land to return to." The painstaking expertise in the paper foregrounds historical blend in fiction.

Sayantan Pal Chowdhury's exploration "V.S. Naipaul's *Half a Life*: A Study of Powerless Group of the Third World Women" deals with the position of the third world women in the novel. In this paper, he gives more importance to the allocation of power and gender binaries. He borrows the critical framework of Chandra Talpade Mohanty's notion—"homogeneous group of powerless women" and observes that "there is a historical relation between women and power. The allocation of power within the society of men and women is not balanced". The study displays that the group of women is in 'binary' situation—heterogeneity in homogeneity.

Paramita Ghosh's investigation "The Concept of Migration and Exile in V.S. Naipaul—A Selective Study" delves deep to look into what the post-globalized world offers the Naipaulian migrants as a substitute for the 'chaotic' home that they strive to leave behind in course of their exilic journey. She observes that "the quixotic quest for an ideal homeland eludes the travelling narrator as he feels constantly out of place even after arriving in England of his fantasies where he finds a decaying empire that does little to mitigate his sense of homelessness." The exilic situation of Naipaul is a portrayal of self-imposed émigré that displays his displeasure with both—Trinidad and India. On the one hand the former gives him an identity while on the other, the latter renders his mongering situation which tells that he is still in 'liminal' space and feels homeless in the world even today.

Satendra Kumar and Balkar Singh's far-reaching article "V.S. Naipaul: The Quest for Identity amid Deracination" scrutinizes Naipaul's fictional and non-fictional writings that "trace a similar self-conscious symptomatic response to the need of discovering an appropriate literary form to frame a psychic and symbolic sense of homelessness." They map through his protagonists that "symbolises the agony of diasporic and rootless people leading a nomadic life on this Earth". The paper is a sharp criticism of Naipaul's Caribbean novels that reconstruct his 'quest for identity'.

Asis De's article, "An Apology for Failure: Searching Home and Identity…" , studies the theme of identity and belongingness in V.S. Naipaul's novel, *The Mimic Men*. Issues like isolation, displacement, cultural confusion, communal antagonism, etc. have been analyzed through the experiences and reminiscences of the protagonist narrator, Ralph Singh.

The next section "V.S. Naipaul's Travel Narratives: A Post-colonial Passage to the Globe", contains four essays on Naipaul's travel narratives that imaginatively but truly narrate the bona fide events of the post-imperial nations. He innovatively explores the unfledged tales of the world but in ambivalence. His pioneering technique of evaluating a *tête-à-tête* has made him the cosmopolitan traveller and his travelogues a big shot. Amod Kumar Rai's critique "V.S. Naipaul: A Pioneer in Nonfiction Writing" inquires several constituents that make Naipaul's art of nonfiction innovative and unique. Rai argues that Naipaul and his ilk may have realized that fiction alone is not capable of holding the creative explosion of writers who also wished to dabble in socio-economic and political issues of the world in the 21st century. He further holds the view that "Naipaul's nonfictions are beautifully intervened with historical, political and geographical matrix without inclining in anyone direction. He explores history for tracing the root of a particular phenomenon, at times for substantiating his judgment and for showing the contradiction between past and present".

Shashank Shekhar Sharma and N.D.R. Chandra's critical concept titled "Discourse on Travel Theory and Naipaul's Travelogue: *Among the Believers: An Islamic Journey*" focuses on the use of the basic tenets and lexicons of travel theory: tourist/traveller, multiculturalism, colonialism, road narratives, Islamic fundamentalism, pilgrim/pilgrimage, and telescoping historical events in the same text. They conclude their paper by stating that "Naipaul's experiences during his travels and sojourns in copious countries, a novel mode of the narrative technique, which makes his nonfiction and novels most popular and absorbing". The next paper in the section continues the same evaluation but in the Indian context.

Aju Mukhopadhyay's critical discernment "V.S. Naipaul's Reflections on India" dissects Naipaul's views on India in *India: A Million Mutinies Now* (1990). He compares Naipaul's views with the notions of other Western scholars on India like Sir William Jones, Max Muller and Edwin Arnold. He sums his paper up by admitting that Naipaul has concrete "grasp over history and civilization, his viewpoints are true to his personal reactions to the past happenings tinged by his personal experiences, peculiar to his enviable position in life which he achieved and wishes to retain". He offers an Orientalist perspective and draws parallels with Tagore's India.

After India and the Islamic worlds, Naipaul has visited Africa from time to time. The publication of *The Masque of Africa: Glimpses in African Belief* in 2010 brought worldwide *mêlée* once again in the literary sphere and beyond. The editor, hence, takes autonomy to bring/accept a paper on the same. Bishun Kumar's essay "Naipaul's *The Masque of Africa:* Exploring History, Culture and Civilization" delineates a fresh insight on the same book and brings forth that "the colonialism has brought crisis to its ethnic culture that affected historical, cultural and wide changes in civilization but prepared the ground for a cross-cultural and multicultural society". Dr. Kumar sums that "Naipaul's journey from Trinidad to Africa concludes with three other journeys: the first political journey of Africa from rule of autocracy to democracy, the second cultural journey from African rites and belief to enlightenment and humanism, and the third civilizational journey from the Tombs (of Kasubi) to the high buildings, Churches and private monuments making African cities modern wastelands."

Naipaul's several visits to India which have displayed his longing for belonging to the country though he finds it "difficult". But his quest for "home" has been subverted by his Eurocentric visions and visualisations. His aspiration for "home" has already been fictionally narrated by him in his magnum opus, *A House for Mr. Biswas* (1961), the best literary project he has ever produced. The novel not only discusses Naipaul's concupiscence for 'home' but also recapitulates his fissured identity in this post-colonial globe. It gives a pen-portrait of one's endeavour for "home" in urban space where a person, ultimately, realizes that it is not his 'home' which he craved for but merely a 'house'. It has been widely read, critically anthologized and the most debated novel in academia. The present anthology too acknowledges the same. Therefore, the last section, "Identity, Home, Marital and Gender Discourse through Text/s: Critical Essays on V.S. Naipaul's *A House for Mr. Biswas*" has been exclusively devoted to this *tour de force* by Madhu Sharma, Vineet Kashyap, Deepak Kumar, Shagufta Naj, Mujeeb Ali Murshed Qasim and Shalini. Madhu Sharma's paper "V.S. Naipaul's *A House for Mr. Biswas*: An Incessant Quest for Identity and Independence" tries to illustrate the significance of owning a house of one's own to establish a sense of belonging, self-esteem and a sense of freedom in the post-colonial society. She argues that "the search and endeavors of Mr. Biswas to own a house for himself prove to be an absolutely trying journey during which he refuses to accept the ready-made orthodox household imposed on him; rather he aspires more of possessing his own house, his own portion of earth in spite of all troubles and tribulations in the way."

Vineet Kashyap's exposition of Naipaul's diasporic sensibility has been well-described in her discourse titled "Significance of 'Home' in V.S. Naipaul's *A House for Mr. Biswas*" which harmonizes the previous disquisition. It is an attempt to connect V.S. Naipaul's autobiographical feelings of 'home' to the Caribbean island, particularly Trinidad through his character, Mohun Biswas in *A House for Mr. Biswas*. She observes that "Naipaul's postcolonial novels expose the formation of imperialist myths of places, challenge them and deconstruct them." The quest continues but not for 'home' only; it also looks for 'identity' and 'liberation.' The liberation from other's home is conquest, on one hand, but on the other one feels physically 'unhoused' and psychosomatically 'defeated'.

The same agony has been adroitly depicted in Deepak Kumar and Shagufta Naj's research paper "Anguish and Defeat of Unhoused and Unnecessary: A Critical Study of V.S. Naipaul's *A House for Mr. Biswas*". They analyze the psychological forces viz. disgust and anguish which create the feeling of alienation and fragmentation within a person in the colonial world. They attempt to reveal the hardships of post-colonial people, their endurance and search for self-identity and self-esteem in Caribbean society. It foregrounds that owning a house is a not an easy task, rather it's a "Herculean process". It also touches upon the socio-cultural issues by which the individuality of a particular person is affected, decayed and disordered.

'Home' is the place where two souls meet and enjoy the emancipation of their lives. Hence, Mujeeb Ali Murshed Qasim's research article "The Theme of Marriage in V.S. Naipaul's *A House for Mr. Biswas*" aims to spell out the ambiguities of the union of two souls, customs and traditions, which are still adhered to by Hindu migrants in the Caribbean isles. His article traces the thesis of marriage as one of the major themes in Naipaul's *A House for Mr. Biswas*. He foregrounds "Naipaul's vast knowledge on the socio-cultural life of the Hindu migrant community in the Caribbean along with his childhood memories that have been etched in detail in this novel". He also strikes how fair sex is unfairly treated within the ambit of marriage.

The same pursuit is unrelenting in the next paper by Shalini on gender issues as that is tangible in the periphery of marriage as an institution what Qasim has documented in his paper. Despite the fact that the gender issue is a serious one, very few critics have taken critical steps to study Naipaul against the backdrop of gender studies or feminist theory. A few have examined his women in their research papers. But Shalini's paper "Fossilized Folks: Women in Naipaul's *A House for Biswas, The Mystic Masseur* and *Half a Life*" unfurls the same and critically analyzes female characters in a patriarchal stronghold. She holds the view that "the world of a woman ends with her family which reduces her merely to a component in the household machinery. Her world shatters if her family suffers. The women in Naipaul's works are ignorant". Shalini offers comparative criticism on *A House for Mr. Biswas* which has been sandwiched by the earlier and later novels of Naipaul.

The aforesaid critical essays, moreover, produce the gamut of critical insights on multiple issues, themes, and theories as applied to the works of V.S. Naipaul. Each essay in the volume closely follows another. The contributors have critically argued, deliberated and have postulated Naipaul's global perspectives through close quarters which highlight his cosmopolitan status.

Ajay K. Chaubey

NOTES

1. <http://www.mid-day.com/news/2011/jun/040611-V-S-Naipaul-psychiatrist-controversy-Jane-Austen.htm> Accessed on June 3, 2013.
2. V.S. Naipaul was given this award to enable him to write a book on India (Suman Gupta x).
3. <http://core.ecu.edu/engl/deenas/caribbean/naipaul.htm> Accessed on May 21, 2013.
4. <http://news.bbc.co.uk/2/hi/entertainment/1593673.stm> Accessed on May 21, 2013.

5. <http://www.fantasticfiction.co.uk/n/v-s-naipaul/middle-passage.htm> Accessed on June 3, 2013. Emphasis mine.
6. <http://yabaluri.org/TRIVENI/CDWEB/anareaofdefecationoct65.htm> Accessed on June 4, 2013.
7. <http://www.ndtv.com/article/india/vs-naipaul-slammed-by-girish-karnad-for-his-views-on-muslims-288026> Accessed on July 13, 2013.

WORKS CITED

Bhattacharya, Baidik. "Naipaul's New World: Postcolonial Modernity and the Enigma of Belated Space." *NOVEL: A Forum on Fiction*, Vol. 39, No. 2, Postcolonial Disjunctions (Spring, 2006): 245-67. Web. 03 June 2013.

Burnouw, Dagmar. *Naipaul's Strangers*. Bloomington & Indianapolis: Indiana University Press, 2003.

Dalrymple, William. "Trapped in the Ruins." Web. 16 July 2013.

Gupta, Suman. *V.S. Naipaul*. New Delhi: Atlantic Publishers & Distributors (P) Ltd., 2010.

Hasan, Mushirul. "Sustaining the Myth of Hostility." Web. 4 June 2013.

Kortenaar, Neil ten. "Mr. Biswas Finds a Home in the World on Paper." *V.S. Naipaul's A House for Mr Biswas: Critical Perspectives*. Ed. Meenakshi Bharat. New Delhi: Pencraft International, 2013. 168-86.

Mustafa, Fawzia. *V.S. Naipaul*. New York: Cambridge University Press, 1995.

Naipaul, V.S. *An Area of Darkness*. 1964. London: Picador, 2002.

Nightingale, Peggy. *Journey Through Darkness: The Writing of V.S. Naipaul*. St. Lucia: University of Queensland Press, 1987.

Nixon, Rob. *London Calling: V.S. Naipaul, A Postcolonial Mandarin*. New York & Oxford: OUP, 1992.

Rai, Sudha. *V.S. Naipaul: A Study in Expatriate Sensibility*. New Delhi: Arnold-Heinemann, 1982.

Saloni, Dhvani. "Naipaul Needs a Psychiatrist." *Mid-Day*, 04 June 2011. Web. 3 June 2013.

Said, Edward. "Intellectuals in the Postcolonial World." *Salmagundi* 70/71 (1986): 44-64. Web. 03 June 2013.

——. "Unraveling V.S. Naipaul's Islamophobic Imagination: An Intellectual Catastrophe." Web. 03 June 2013.

Singh, Manjit Inder. *V.S. Naipaul*. Jaipur: Rawat Publications, 1998.

White, Landeg. *V.S. Naipaul: A Critical Introduction*. London: Macmillan Press, 1975.

Section A

Contexts and Convergences in Naipaul's Fictions

1

Race, Ethnicity, Sexual Violence and Neocolonialism in V.S. Naipaul's *Guerrillas*: A Postcolonial Reading

Prakash Chandra Pradhan

I

In the early novels, V.S. Naipaul has vividly portrayed post-colonial societies where marginalized people's sufferings perpetuate. However, some of the protagonists face the challenges bravely, and establish their identities. In Naipaul's later novels, more specifically *Guerrillas* (1975), *A Bend in the River* (1979), *The Enigma of Arrival* (1987), *A Way in the World* (1994), *Half a Life* (2001) and *Magic Seeds* (2004) written between 1975 and 2004, the predominant issues are the representations of suppressed histories of the peoples and nations, racial conflicts, ethnicity, sexual promiscuity and neocolonialism as well. In *Guerrillas* and *A Bend in the River*, the external world is "chaotic, disordered, violent and almost deranged" (Kamra 116) just like the mental state of the characters. In these two novels, the political and social realities of the earlier novels have been retained. The concept of power is very much central to these novels because survival of an individual in a democratic set-up is possible only when he is associated with power-groups. These two novels portray racially and culturally complex societies where the cultures are in conflict with each other, although these cultures have already been distorted in the course of history. So the white people's claim of superiority has been altogether rejected. The cultural conflicts between the whites and non-whites are of paramount importance to understand the intricacies of power politics and the concept of "liberation". As in his other major writings, Naipaul here too brings out the dichotomy between the past and the present. Kamra's views on the two novels in the context of exploitation are worth mentioning: "He (Naipaul) shows it in its most ugly form in situations where the third and first world meet deliberately or accidentally to exploit each other, the one culturally and the other economically. This coming together for mutual gain does not constitute a society" (142).

Such a society is rather self-centred to take advantage of each other at the time of crisis. This paper makes an attempt to interpret the novel *Guerrillas*, where Naipaul portrays the multiple problems a postcolonial nation faces on its way for progress. More specifically, Naipaul traces the racial conflicts and black-white politics in rebuilding West Indies in this novel. Bruce King is fairly perceptive when he argues:

> *Guerrillas* (1975) brings together many of Naipaul's recurring themes—the inability of small, underdeveloped nations to be truly independent mimicry; the relationship between whites and blacks in which assertions of black authenticity so often are part of dependency; the ways in which Christianity blending with Black messianism. (99)

In *The Return of Eva Peron*, Naipaul views that Black power outside the United States "perpetuates the negative, colonial politics of protest. It is...deep corruption: a wish to be granted a dispensation from the pains of development, an almost religious conviction that oppression can be turned into an asset, race into money" (1980: 212). It is, therefore, important to illustrate some of the relevant incidents/situations from the novel to elucidate how the negative politics of Black Power results in ethnic violence and political confusion.

II

In *Guerrillas*, Naipaul shows the tension that exists between the whites and the blacks through their mutual deceptions and pseudo-colonial concerns to lift the fortunes of the postcolonial people who are on the margin. However, it is only a showdown. In the Caribbean, there were two types of people: the so-called liberal whites posed to be revolutionaries to uplift the people from their miseries so that they would be their leaders and enjoy power; the other categories were the black people who wanted to be the leaders of the blacks and enjoy power, and control the economy of the country. With such interests, there was always racial tension among the revolutionaries and common people as well. In the process, there were a series of violence, rapes and murders. In his paper "Writers and Readers, the Written and the Read in V.S. Naipaul and *Guerrillas*", Neil ten Kortenaar makes a commendable remark: "V.S. Naipaul's novel *Guerrillas* is about the mutual deception practiced by Black power enthusiasts in the West Indies and white liberals in the West and their sometimes fatal self-deception" (1990: 324). In the very beginning of the novel when Jane and Roche drive on the city roads, they notice a slogan surcharged with racism: "Basic Black, Don't vote; Birth Control is a Plot Against the Negro Race" (*GS* 1). On their way to Thrushcross Grange from their house on the Ridge, they were to cover a long distance of ride across the hilly, barren areas. Some of the foreign investors, getting the affair of tax-holidays, had started projects for their industry and later on moved elsewhere. Jimmy Ahmad was the people's commune leader who had established a commune hut in that of Grange. Sablichs were thinking of buying all the land for investments. However, after jimmy stepped in, "they disgorged this bit. A twenty-five years lease. Gifted just like that" (*GS* 5).

The racial issue, that is predominant on this part of land, is obvious from the reactions of Roche when Jane moves towards the commune hut in Grange:

> When he saw Jane waking up the slight slope to the hut door he felt, as he had feared, that her presence there was wrong, and looked like an intrusion. The flowered blouse, through which her brassier could be seen, the right trousers that modeled stomach groin and cleft in a single, sudden curve: that could pass in the city and in the shopping plaza of the Ridge would be hardly noticeable but here it seemed provocative, over-casual enough to be dressy:

> London, foreign, wrong. And again it occurred to Roche that she was very white, with a colour that wasn't at all like the colour of White people. She was white enough to be unreadable; even her age might not be guessed. (*GS* 6)

Roche rushed to her protectively near the hut when Jimmy Ahmad came. Jane saw that he gave an increasing physical neatness with a slender waist, trimmed moustache, closely-shaved cheeks and all other physical gestures and clothes. Jane however had expected this Ahmed to be more Negroid and awkward in appearance. Jane saw a poster of Ahmad which was looking more Negroid with roughly lettered words below: "I'm Nobody's slave or Stallion. I'm a warrior and Torch Bearer—Haj James Ahmed" (*GS* 10). To her amazement, Jane thought that this Grange was another complete world: "...in that hut, with the junked office equipment on the table, the posters and the black pin-ups from newspapers on the walls with the boys on the metal beds, with the light and the emptiness outside, and the encircling forest. She felt she had entered another, complete world" (*GS* 10). Jimmy had been deported from England on charges of rape and assault. As he himself told he was a *bakwai* Chinese (a nigger Chinese). In his outburst at his home, Jimmy showed off his strength as a leader and claimed that he was a friend to everybody—the investors, the government and the people. He was a worker, who fought for the cause of the Negroes. He was not a street-corner politician to change the government. On the other hand, he was a friend to every capitalist, even to Sablichs and he was not a Guerrilla: "I have no gun. I'm no guerrilla" (*GS* 21). On their return, Jane saw how people were still living like derelicts in the postcolonial scenario: "And Jane thought that that was something else she had stopped seeing. People like the runner, people like the wild men who lived in the hills, among the new developments, or down in the city, in the backyards of certain thoroughfares: derelicts, a whole parallel society" (*GS* 23). It is startling to note the chaos and disorder in the postcolonial society. The government is unable to take care of the distressed people who have no minimum basic needs of life. They still live like aborigines, in rags: "Wild men in rags, with long matted hair; wild men with unseeing red eyes. And bandits. Police cars patrolled these hillside suburbs. Sometimes at night and in the early morning there was the sound of gunfire. The newspapers, the radio and the television spoke of guerrillas" (*GS* 25).

Jane coming from England had a startling experience of the derelicts, people in rags, chaotic law and order situation and self-styled commune revolutionaries. People's sufferings perpetuate. Only there is high publicity of development and fight for the people's cause. But Jane observes: "So bogus…so hidden away. The High Command. All the publicity. All that found. Of course, it's a perfect cover for the guerillas, isn't it?" (*GS* 25).

III

Jimmy Ahmed, the black revolutionary contemplates and urges to Roy, his friend that he is sometimes frustrated to see the dispossessed people's continuous suffering. It is very difficult to change their fortunes. He reflects on how he has been deported from England during the time of crisis. The people who win are the people who have won already: "Perhaps after all Roy the world is only made for the people who possess it now, and there are some people who will never possess anything. The people who will win are the people who have won already and they're not taking chances now, like the liberals" (*GS* 36).

Jimmy Ahmed has been aggressive towards those white liberals who have deported him from England after using him and making him his playboy. They are not sparing him even after deporting him from England: "Even here they are coming after me.... These liberals who come flashing their milk white thighs and think they're contributing to the cause" (*GS* 36).

Then he is also attacking Peter Roche, the Public Relations officer of the imperialistic firm of Sablich's, the great slave traders in the old days. Mr. Roche the great White revolutionary and "torture hero" of South Africa has written a book, the bestseller in Caribbean island. He is working on behalf of the Sablich's, who now pretend that black is beautiful and they think Mr. Roche can prove it. To Jimmy the situation on the Ridge is quite desperate because betrayal has been frequent there: "it's always a case of black faces white masks, you don't know who your enemy is, and the enemy infiltrates your ranks all the time" (*GS*

82). Sometimes he gets frustrated and hopeless because in the night he loses courage and considers that he is fighting a losing battle. When Stephen is vanished, they are sending other agents and he has no means to cope with. His despair makes him a pessimist very often. He therefore expresses his state of mind to Roy:

> Things are desperate Roy, when the leader himself begins to yield to despair, things are bad. The whole place is going to blow up; I cannot see how I can control the resolution now. When everybody wants to fight there's nothing to fight for. Everybody wants to fight his own little war, everybody is a guerrilla. (*GS* 83)

Roche's frustrations, although internal, sometimes disturb him. He thinks about his futile life: "I've built my whole life on sand" (*GS* 87). Though people think that he is working for a cause, he understands that he has neither any political dogma nor vision to go forward: "If he had a system, a set of political beliefs, it might have been easier for him to have set it aside, to have admitted error, as some of his associates had done, to have blamed the system to have blamed the world for not living up to the system, and without any sense of reneging to have made a fresh start" (*GS* 87). He has been disillusioned with his job of public relations officer with Sablich's. He has also been waiting for Jane to leave for England: one failure after the other. Analyzing his life and actions of the past, he feels that he is responsible for his actions by ignoring certain truths about his life in South Africa and Ridge and his relationship with Jane. He therefore now considers his life full of futility and emptiness.

The chaotic situation in a municipal area of the city is rather deplorable. Once upon a time the area had been a "respectable lower-class area" (*GS* 99). The municipalities have not bothered to maintain the civility in this area:

> It was a community now without rules; and the area was now apparently without municipal regulation. Empty house—lots had been turned into steel—band yards or open-air motor-repair shops; cars and lorries without wheels choked the narrow lanes. Where garbage dammed

> the open gutters wrinkled white films of scum formed on the black water. The walls were scrawled, and sometimes carefully marked, with old election slogans, racial slogans, and made-up African names: *Kwame Mandingo* (*Slave Name—Butler*). There was something competitive and whimsical and it seemed at variance with the words of threat and anger. (*GS* 100)

The novel is, therefore, demonstrating that a society without established *inner* structures cannot give stability during transition from colonial to postcolonial stage. Since the society is independent, without a visionary political system, it is dragged to chaos. The revolutionaries have no definite plans and ideas to take the country in the path of progress. They have only fantasies rather than any redeeming movement that can remove the chaotic situation. Jimmy's claims of "back to the land by black people" and the "racial attitude of black consciousness" have the strength of moving forward. Nor even the white liberals' notion of personal power and involvement can redeem these third world situations so effectively.

In *Guerrillas*, there is no treatment of political events directly. Caribbean island has a history of racial humiliations. After independence, there is no viable alternative plan to provide a better life to its people. The political events are thought of being a kind of communal frenzy. The people therefore turn to "quasi-religious notions of racial deliverance" (King 101). Naipaul is not supportive of the outsiders' interference in the distress of the Third World countries after they enjoyed their long-cherished political/economic freedom. He scrutinizes their motivations in the affairs of these postcolonial nations which normally do not welcome the whites who apparently involve themselves to improve their conditions. Naipaul portrays them as the heirs of the Empire, who carry their emotional needs to the former colonies for dramatization of their sexual excitement and access to power after the shrunken condition of their societies during postcolonial period. After the end of Empire, the imperial centre has lost its glamour and the Europeans have therefore turned to these Third World nations for their excitement. But these expatriates, the outsiders have no connections and roots in the local context and hence they are not acceptable. These white liberals however cling to local ethos and activities.

In *Guerrillas*, Naipaul portrays Jimmy Ahmed, a half-Chinese Negro, as Black Power. Jimmy was treated as a playboy in England by the liberal whites. He was made a black-power leader in England and then he was also used sexually for excitement by the whites. Then he was deported to the Caribbean island on the charges of rape and assault. Even in the Caribbean he was not spared. He was used by Roche in order to provoke that he had a cause for the Negroes for their upliftment. Jane, an outsider white woman, tempted him sexually for fulfillment of her excitement. Jimmy Ahmed had always the potential for violence, and Jane had rightly marked that Ahmed had the thrill of playing with fire. Though Jimmy was a Chinese Negro, he was also an outsider in the Caribbean. In spite of his rise as a black-power leader, he was neither black nor a leader and hence he was not protected by any group. Despite his London reputation, he was rather unsuccessful to fulfill the cause of the blacks. His revolution had no vision to inspire, and he had not worked out a political system to expedite the cause of the dispossessed blacks. In England, Jimmy was admired initially for his potential concern for the blacks by progressive politicians but at the time of crisis because of rape charge he was not supported by any group as he was an alien, a non-white. Roche, the liberal white, faced the similar situation in South Africa. For a time, he was highly admired by the left and considered the hero of South African resistance, but he was to flee to England when he was threatened by a South African agent. That was because he was an alien there. Both these heroics are not the true and serious revolutionaries. They have not worked any definite political system to rescue the distressed blacks. Both of them are activists without any ideology or plan. They are associated with the commune in the Caribbean in which they have no trust. They are themselves confused and often reflect upon the credibility of the commune. Both of them as activists attract women because of their reputation as leaders. It is rather difficult to "read" Jimmy who finally indulges in a brutal murder of Jane, the white woman who has tempted him to violent sex. The novel therefore highlights the "black-power rising, killing of a black leader, eruption of violence and the crumbling of the government" (Bhat 94-95). Naipaul thus explores the predicament of the newly decolonized countries. In this context, Kamra's remarks on the postcolonial set-up of the Ridge society are worth-mentioning:

> The various subjective realities of the expatriate society of the Ridge, through whose eyes we see the town and Grange, provide the outsider's view of third world chaos, disorder and subhuman existence. Theirs is the despair of having come as messengers of goodwill to uplift and present a new hope on behalf of the Western World only to find that they are at the mercy of "beasts" and their own similar hungers. Jimmy and indirectly Bryant's consciousness pervade the novel from beginning to end. (132-33)

Jimmy, the so-called half-Chinese Negro, murders Jane after his violent sex with her; then he plans to murder Roche, but fails. If this is the vision of the leader, then naturally he is a lost case. Jimmy is such a black-power leader who is a scheming villain without morality and ethics. He is a guerrilla no doubt; but the question is he is fighting for what, for whom? A leader who fled from England on the charges of rape and assault is indulging here at Grange in rape, murder and conspiracy to murder. He is a leader with no humanity and, having no concern for values. He is not a leader in true sense of the term. He is both perverse and subversive. Despite his tall claim of being a friend to everybody, in his lifestyle there is no such quality and behavior. It is simply impossible on his part to contribute substantially to bring about development and order to that kind of Ridge society. After the end of colonialism what is required at this juncture of a leader is that he should be a man of vision with positive values, design and real concern for the people of the land who are under-living, starving, without clothes and, also uncivilized. A barbaric and racialist as Jimmy is, no change could be possible through his revolution. In other words, he is a secret terrorist who can murder people who have some trust on him. Naipaul, portraying such a character as a black-power leader, is emphasizing that postcolonial societies under the hands of these villains are not safe. The governments are unable to tackle the chaotic situations created by them. Even the white liberals, who claim to have been working for the cause of the blacks, are also unable to counter them because they are working on without any concrete plan based on ideologies to uplift the miserable people and discarded society economically, socially and culturally. Naipaul is scrutinizing the activities of the different groups as well as governments to know if these societies have the potentiality to improve the postcolonial situation in these countries. What is conspicuous in this context is that both these people and the governments are great failures to discharge their responsibilities with clarity, precision and effectiveness. *Guerrillas* supersedes the harsh and black realism that *The Mimic Men* and *In a Free State* establish in Naipaul's fiction. Mustafa's interpretation of the novel is fairly analytical and convincing:

> Its (Guerrillas') unpleasant tale of a doomed quasi-cooperative enterprise on a Caribbean island between the skewed Black Power initiatives of Jimmy Ahmad and his corporate sponsors, Sablichs, is played out amongst a cast of characters confused by their missions and arrogant in their ignorance. The resulting posturing between the expatriates Roche and Jane and the returned "revolutionary", Jimmy, is from the start fated to abort at the level of a gross theatricality because of their failure to grasp anything but their own misplaced vanities. Against a political climate that remains controlled by outside forces, Jimmy's Black Power commune is like the thwarted and stunted vegetables that they profess to cultivate, while the importations of both Roche's anti-apartheid South African resume and Jane's London-chic third-world slumming are similarly misallied. All three characters have in different degrees been molded by a metropolitan liberalism that has utterly failed to discern that its attitude to and understanding of decolonization are necessarily blinded by its own guilt-ridden complicity in the prior colonial enterprise. (125)

The characters in this novel, who consider themselves self-righteous, are deluded and confused and hence are careless "expounders of rhetoric mouthed by the generation of decolonization" (Mustafa 126). Their actions cause more harm to the natives because they are of villainous nature. In the context of inappropriate sexuality and violence Mustafa's comments are worth-noting in relation to such characters as hypocritical Jimmy, his male-lover Bryant and sexually-licentious Jane:

> While she is neither mysterious nor compelling, she nevertheless represents a sexual license that within the island setting is both threatening and inappropriate. Thus, towards the end of the narrative Jimmy's act of sodomy upon her is the novel's twinning of her with Bryant, the foundling of the commune and Jimmy's male lover, and serves as the narrative's impelled sexual mirroring, making sex and sexual promiscuity the novel's frame for political misadventure and misalliance. (1995: 127)

The discussion of Roche with Stephen's mother just before Police gun down Stephens is very important to understand the complexity of the island's political option within a framework of a confined, urban, new-colonial setting. Mrs. Stephens is acutely critical of the lie that Jimmy represents to the community. Mrs. Stephens endorses "the frugal but functional rhetoric of redemption and liberation that still exists among the island's population" (Mustafa 128). Roche's encounter with Mrs. Stephens makes him reflective on excessive role of England on the island to control it, although it is no more under the colonial rule: "England, Roche thought: it was so hard to get away from England here. And there were so many Englands: his, Jane's, Jimmy's, Lloyd's, and the England—hard to imagine—in that old woman's head" (*GS* 104). Mrs. Stephens's hatred for Jimmy is obvious: "That Chinese man I never like that Chinese man. But I am a supporter of this government, Mr. Roche. This government will never fall" (*GS* 106). Mrs. Stephens has therefore no illusions of the commune's objectives guided by London ideas. Britain has no promises for the people of island either. She therefore represents "that silent constituency that helps maintain the *status quo* through its balance between the revivalist faith of the redemption-minded servant-class and a distinct communal identification, despite the harsh realities of poverty and abandonment" (Mustafa 128).

IV

Guerrillas, therefore, reveals that the borrowed ideas from England cannot be applied to the complex situations of the island people, recently liberated politically. Their economic woes still continue because of neo-colonial presence of England. The neo-colonials like Sablichs, and the Black Power commune leader Jimmy do not fit into the set-up of island's design either politically or economically. They are rather inadequate to deal with the complexities of the multiple problems the people of diverse ethnicity and race in the Island face with. Naipaul also discusses the chaos and disorder in the postcolonial African Society in the novel *A Bend in the River.* The African society referred to here is rotten by violence and a mimic civil war because of group clashes. The African attitude towards the whites was based on hatred because of their memory of the past when they were the slaves to these whites. They therefore want to go back to the remote past when their society had not the whites and other outsiders. Naipaul is seriously concerned with the disorder of the postcolonial world in Africa. Both the white forces and the extremist militarism of the nationalistic outfits create havoc and disorder in the country dragging it to the brink of disaster. Naipaul gives us a fearful picture of different historical forces clashing with each other. It has therefore been rightly argued by Bhat:

> A vision of the enactment of historical forces, clashing with one another, gives a fearful picture. It is as dreadful a picture as that of postwar England in T.S. Eliot's *The Waste Land*. Postcolonial Africa torn by the rival and clashing forces of varied types is a new version of "Wasteland", where there seems to be no redemption. (94)

The group clashes are therefore based on narrow racism and conflicts of culture. Naipaul perhaps inquires into a democratic world which explains how an individual's existence is possible only by power groups; otherwise there is always a threat to his existence. Only the man in power enjoys dignity through his power of exercising choice and freedom. In this context, Kamra's comments on the positions of individuals in such societies represented in *Guerrillas* and *A Bend in the River* are relevant to quote:

> In the racially and culturally complex societies of these two novels the narrator enables Naipaul to present a cross-section of a placeless world without intrinsic value in which the self is prostituted into a commodity to purchase "a fix on reality" sex, violence, money, speech—the coins of exchange and communication—are all encompassed by the shopkeeper's jargon of buying and selling the sense of misuse and waste and assessment of this world as a junkyard. (124)

The confrontation of cultures takes place in a third-world society which is an unreal society because of the continuous presence of the dominant whites who try to control such a society economically, though political independence has already been achieved. However, the whites who pose that they have come to do good to such a society impose their "secured" superiority upon them and consider the native culture inferior. This sort of attitude of the whites is altogether rejected by the natives resulting in group clashes and cultural conflicts. Kamra appropriately thinks that the association between "colonial West" and the "colonized third world" have damaged the psyche of the natives to an irreparable loss:

> The significance of *A Bend in the River* can be better understood if the two social situations are contrasted. In these two novels the narrator comes to groups with the psychological reality of the association between the colonial West and the colonized third world. Evoked subjectivity with an ample expression of moods, passions, sentiments and emotions, they leave a deep impression of the far-reaching and almost lasting damage done to the third world psyche. (133)

Although in Africa the sons of the soil like Ferdinand and the young boys trained at the "lycee" question the white man's religion, culture and education regarding their domination and seriously think about the future of Africa, they do not have the vigor, the intellectuality that can counter them. Their ideas and thoughts are rather "borrowed", and therefore have no viability and strength to take the country forward in the path of progress. In the absence of an alternative, viable system of beliefs, the society thus sinks into disasters and disorders. Chaos prevails and hence violence, sexual promiscuity, civil war and bloodshed do occur frequently. These young people have only despair to react to the immediate present rather than having any sense of "nationhood" of the American Negro. Similarly in *Guerrillas* Naipaul portrays such kind of chaos and disorder in the Caribbean society quite vividly that has already been discussed.

The materialistic society portrayed in this novel is a bankrupt one, devoid of the right vision and competence to tackle the enormous doom hanging around it. The so-called leadership, without an idea of its own to deal with the new socio-economic issues of the newly liberated society from colonial rule, is merely indulging in "gimmicks and show-offs". Such insincere attitudes do not lead to bring an order in the society. In the process, the postcolonial situation is further deteriorated increasing the woes of the common folk, and the society is rotten by chaos, confusion, racial tension and ethnic violence. By examining such negativities in a postcolonial society in the novel *Guerrillas,* Naipaul pinpoints that political freedom of a country should go hand in hand with an appropriate socio-economic agenda to deal with the native problems and crises rather than tackling these situations with the borrowed ideas from the former colonial administration.

Works Cited

Bhat, Yoshoda. *V.S. Naipaul: An Introduction*. New Delhi: B.R. Publication, 2000.

Hughes, Peter. *V.S. Naipaul*: *Contemporary Writers*. London and New York: Rutledge, 1988.

Jones, Stephen. *The Journal of Commonwealth Literature*. Vol. 35, No. 1, 2000.

Kamra, Shashi. *The Novels of V.S. Naipaul*. New Delhi: Prestige, 1990.

King, Bruce. *V.S. Naipaul*. Hampshire and London: Macmillan, 1993.

Kortenaar, Neil ten. "Writers and Readers, the Written and the Read: V.S. Naipaul and *Guerrillas*." *Contemporary Literature,* 31.3 (1990): 324-34.

Mustafa, Fawzia. *V.S. Naipaul*: *An Introduction*. New Delhi: B.R. Publication, 2000.

Naipaul, V.S. *Guerrillas*. London: Picador, 2002.

——. *A Bend in the River*. London: Picador, 2002.

——. *The Enigma of Arrival*. London: Picador, 2002.

——. *A Way in the World*. London: Vintage, 2001.

——. *Half a Life*. London: Picador, 2002.

——. *Magic Seeds*. New York: Vintage, 2005.

——. *The Mimic Men*: London: Picador, 2002.

——. *In a Free State*. London: Picador, 2001.

——. *The Return of Eva Peron* with *the Killings in Trinidad*. New York: Knopf, 1980.

Panwar, Purabi. Ed. *V.S. Naipaul*: *An Anthology of Recent Criticism*: Delhi: Pencraft International, 2007.

Trivedi, Harish and Minakshi Mukherjee. Eds. *Interrogating Post Colonialism*: *Theory, Text and Context* (1996). Shimla: IIAS, 2000.

Ray, Mohit K. Ed. *V.S. Naipaul: Critical Essays*. Vol III. New Delhi: Atlantic Publishers and Distributors (P) Ltd., 2005.

Singh, M.I. *The Poetics of Alienation and Identity*: *V.S. Naipaul and George Lamming*. Delhi: Ajanta Books International, 1998.

——. *V.S. Naipaul*. Jaipur: Rawat Publications, 1998.

2

The Dialectics of Homelessness in V.S. Naipaul's *The Mystic Masseur* and *Half a Life*

Vishnupriya Sengupta

> The man who finds his homeland sweet is still a tender beginner; he to whom every soil is as his native one is already strong; but he is perfect to whom the entire world is as a foreign land. (Hugo of St. Victor, a twelfth century monk from Saxony, *Didascalicon*, quoted in Edward Said's *The World, the Text and the Critic* 7)

In view of V.S. Naipaul's corpus of work, it would seem that he is "perfect" in the sense that this epigraph implies: an exile that is familiar with yet chooses to exclude himself from the countries, cultures and communities within which he circulates. The entire world appears to Naipaul but as a foreign land, with cartography and topography rendered irrelevant. Understandably then, Naipaul metes out the same critical treatment to the home of his ancestors (India), the place of his birth (the West Indian island of Trinidad) and his adopted home (England), along with Africa, South America and the Islamic countries of Asia.

Yet the paradox implicit in my use of this epigraph lies in the fact that Naipaul is clearly not the ideal exemplar of non-attachment and spiritual perfection that Hugo of St Victor defines. The perfect man, according to Hugo, achieves independence and detachment by working through attachments, not by rejecting them. Naipaul, on the contrary, is more committed to exclusions and prejudices than to the freedom that accompanies knowledge. His sense of exile, rather than being predicated on the existence of, love for and bond with, one's native place, is linked to a feeling of radical incompleteness, insecurity, restlessness and discontentment with the self.

Homelessness, the recurrent motif that underlies most of his works—both fiction and non-fiction—from *The Mystic Masseur* (1957) to *Half a Life* (2001) and, of late, *The Masque of Africa: Glimpses in African Belief* (2010), proves that for this Nobel Laureate identity denotes not having a home and the awareness of not being at home in a world of expanding horizons and dissolving boundaries. In view of this, I would like to examine *The Mystic Masseur* and *Half a Life* and show how and to what extent his singular preoccupation with the theme of homelessness has shaped his world-view.

For Naipaul, the truth that the world is not our own, and that at any time we may find ourselves homeless in it conditions him, over time, to feel at home with his homelessness in a world of collapsing boundaries. His origin prompts him to raise questions on the process of large scale migration of Indians to the West Indies and its impact on the immigrants, the role of class and race in West Indian culture and how these affect an imaginative discourse; the problem of defining a specifically "West Indian history" and "West Indian culture".

At one level this provides a template for the politics of Naipaul's own individual story, a story that hinges on his patent refrain of not wanting to be like 'them'. On another broader level, by giving voice to the Indian immigrants—the "East Indians" on the Caribbean islands—he succeeds in placing them on a global map as a distinctive group with its own vagaries. Describing the complexities of being an East Indian in the West Indies, Naipaul remarks:

> To be an Indian or East Indian from the West Indies is to be a perpetual surprise to people outside the region.... You don't go to Trinidad...expecting to find Hindu pundits scuttling about country roads on motor-cycles; to see pennants with ancient devices fluttering from temples;

> to see mosques cool and white and rhetorical against the usual Caribbean buildings of concrete and corrugated iron; to find Indians celebrated in the street names of one whole district of Port of Spain; to see the Hindu festival of lights or the Muslim mourning ceremony for Husein, the Prophet's descendant, killed at the Battle of Kerbela in Arabia thirteen hundred years ago.
>
> To be an Indian in Trinidad is to be unlikely. So long as the real Indians remained on the other side of the world, there was little confusion. But when in 1845 these Indians began coming over to some of the islands Columbus had called the Indies, confusion became total. Slavery had been abolished in the British islands, the Negroes refused to work for a master, and many plantations were faced with ruin. Indentured labourers were brought in from China, Portugal, and India. The Indians fitted. More and more came....
>
> But what were these immigrants to be called? Their name had been appropriated three hundred and fifty years before. "Hindu" was a useful word, but it had religious connotations and would have offended the many Muslims among the immigrants. In the British territories the immigrants were called East Indians. In this way they were distinguished from the two other types of Indians in the islands: the American Indians and the West Indians. (Naipaul 33-34)

The experience of exile understandably then is an essential and inescapable element in the histories of colonial peoples. It is not merely a state of being but of becoming, of incessant movement, of repetition and of transformation. It transmutes the perception of place and time, of origin and belonging. In pre-modern times, banishment was a particularly dreadful punishment since it not only meant years of aimless wandering away from family and familiar places, but also meant being reduced to a sort of permanent outcast, someone who never felt at home, and was always at odds with the environment, inconsolable about the past, bitter about the present and the future.

Today, exile has been transformed from the exquisite, and sometimes exclusive, punishment of special individuals into a state of being that can be metaphysical or metaphoric. With refugees, displaced people and mass immigration being a common feature, the term 'exile' is no longer be confined to its narrow lexical definition. It is a state of mind, self-imposed rather than enforced by others.

Edward Said, for one, looks upon exile as a metaphorical condition. He elaborates:

> By that I mean that my diagnosis of the intellectual in exile derives from the social and political history of dislocation and migration...but is not limited to it. Even intellectuals who are lifelong members of a society can, in a manner of speaking, be divided into insiders and outsiders: those on the one hand who belong fully to the society as it is, who flourish in it without an overwhelming sense of dissonance or dissent, those who can be called yea-sayers; and, on the other hand, the nay-sayers, the individuals at odds with their society and therefore outsiders and exiles so far as privileges, power, and honours are concerned. The pattern that sets the course for the intellectual as outsider is best exemplified by the condition of exile, the state of never being fully adjusted, always feeling outside the chatty, familiar world inhabited by natives, so to speak, tending to avoid and even dislike the trappings of accommodation and national well-being. Exile for the intellectual in this metaphysical sense is restlessness, movement, constantly being unsettled, and unsettling others. You cannot go back to some earlier and perhaps more stable condition of being at home; and, alas, you can never fully arrive, be at one with your new home or situation. (Said 35-47)

As an individual at odds with any society he lives in, Naipaul belongs to Said's group of nay-sayers. A permanently exiled writer, his initial novels simultaneously acknowledge his island origins and affirm his present distance from them. Shaped by the geography and history of his circumstances, his status is that of 'willed homelessness'. In transit between three worlds—

the Caribbean isles, England and India—Naipaul wrote as an émigré of the imagination, conveying the feeling of being both part and not part of his culture, of being estranged from the very traditions to which he belongs, of being in exile perpetually.

It is, therefore, not without reason that Naipaul's writings express the ambivalence of the exile, a feature of his own experience as an Indian in the West Indies, a West Indian in England, and a nomadic intellectual in a postcolonial world. That experience of an exile encompasses supreme solitude and Naipaul writes only of the isolation that characterises the lives of his protagonists or his own autobiographical persona, a persona accepted at face value as a permanent exile, a refugee, a homeless citizen of the world. In course of his writings, he helps us realise that in a world increasingly characterised by exile, migration and diaspora with all the consequences of unsettling and hybridisation, there can be no place for absolutism of the pure and the authentic.

For Naipaul, an exile by choice, the exilic condition is a discontinuous state of being resulting in a solitude experienced outside the group in a communal habitation. Homecoming, for Naipaul, is out of question. He feels his distinct difference and, clutching on to it, insists on his right to refuse to belong. And it is this choice to be in exile that has given force to his artistic vision and has helped him rise above national affiliations, above partisan politics to assert a self-contained individuality.

In both *The Mystic Masseur* and *Half a Life*, history conjoins with geography and, in a process akin to that in his other works, the mindscape is mapped as vividly as the physical space traversed by the two protagonists Ganesh from the rural to urban settings of the Port of Spain and Willie, across the continents of Asia, Europe and Africa. Places, then, are no longer considered clear supports of their identities but still play an important role in the formation of the symbolic and psychical dimension of their identifications.

This is a universal truth which implies that home, usually defined in terms of a mapped geographical territory, is more a state of mind. And this is as true of the writer himself, who rejects his place of birth, the place of his ancestors to seek refuge in England. His perceptions are rooted and validated by his own history which accounts for his admission in an interview to Michiko Kakutani in 1980: "I do not have the tenderness more secure people can have towards bush people. I feel threatened by them. My attitude and the attitude of people like me are quite different from people who live outside the bush or who just go camping in the bush on weekends" (Web).

The Mystic Masseur, parable-like in form, already contains the makings of a mimic man Naipaul turned into over the years. At the end of the book, as the good old Hindu Brahmin "Pundit Ganesh" metamorphoses into G. Ramsay Muir, it sets the template for all of Naipaul's subsequent writings.

To start with, *The Mystic Masseur* depicts the larger context of the Creole world in which Indians struggle to retain their distinctive identity. Placed as it is in the East Indian milieu of Trinidad, it symbolises one aspect of the experience of the entire East Indian community, comprising indentured labourers from India, in their move from isolated rural existence to city life and creolization. This ultimately denotes moving away from their East Indian identity. While laughter and wit are part of the lives depicted, there is an authenticity in the work that comes with the intensity of Naipaul's subject, a subject he had visualized in totality way before *The Mystic Masseur* was written. In fact, Ganesh Pundit makes an appearance not only in *Miguel Street* (which was written before *The Mystic Masseur*) but also in an earlier story *My Aunt Gold Teeth* (1954) published later in *A Flag on the Island* (1967) and in *The Suffrage of Elvira* (1958) as the celebrated mystic masseur who has taken up politics. In *Miguel Street*, the first mention is made in the story, "Man Man": "Seeing God was quite common in the Port of Spain and indeed in Trinidad at that time. Ganesh Pundit the mystic masseur from Fuente Grove had started it. He had seen God too and published a booklet called *What God Told Me*" (50-51).

At his next appearance, he has moved from the country to the Port of Spain and is living in the fashionable street of St Clair exactly as will be shown in *Masseur*. *Dhoti-kurta* has been discarded for expensive lounge suits. The narrator of *Masseur* first meets Ganesh in 1939 when the narrator was in school and last in 1954 when he is a university student in England so that the growth of the narrator from childhood to youth implicitly accompanies the story of Ganesh's rise from a struggling masseur to MBE.

The narrator at the outset says "I myself believe that the history of Ganesh is, in a way, the history of our times" (112). The theme, then, is the acculturation of the East Indian in Trinidad, the story of a man's repudiation of his origins, his loss of identity brought to the fore in the change of name from Ganesh Ramsumair to G. Ramsay Muir, the mimic man willing to tow the British line.

Naipaul shows how East Indians try to cling on to their customs and rituals. But the moment they step out of the protective atmosphere of the village enclave, East Indians became immensely vulnerable. Ganesh, for instance, was made painfully aware of his self-backwardness, once he goes to Port of Spain in clothes that mark him as an Indian from the country.

His years at Queen's Royal College are years of awkwardness and embarrassment. "He was so ashamed of his Indian name that for a while he spread a story that he was really called Gareth" (16).

When his father's death forces him to return to Fourways, he is happy to get away from the Port of Spain. He had spent five years but had never felt part of it, "It was too big, too noisy and too alien" (27). But though he is happy to be back where he commands respect, his contact with city life and education has started an undefined sense of alienation in him. His sense of displacement and his groping towards a solution are presented with full understanding of his predicament caught as he is between an Indian past and Creole present.

Even after he has achieved a measure of success and a reputation as a mystic Ganesh shrinks into himself when venturing into the alien world of Port of Spain. He doesn't have the courage to go in his Indian attire and sports English clothes for a visit to the Registrar General's Office. Later at the

Governor's dinner at MLC he finds the whole ritual mortifying. He felt as if he were a boy again going to the Queen's Royal College for the first time.

The move from Fuente Grove to Port of Spain is a wrench too and Ganesh cries out, "I wish the whole thing did never happen" (205). Ganesh knows that he is leaving behind something of his past forever. To survive in the Creole world of Port of Spain, he will have to give up being himself—a process which begins with his giving up his *dhoti, kurta* and turban for lounge suits.

After removal to Port of Spain we see Ganesh, as it were, from a distance. One can sense an authorial withdrawal in this. His nomination to the Legislative Council and an award of MBE are reported in a few lines. When the narrator sees him at the railway station in England, he greets him enthusiastically: "Pundit Ganesh!" I cried running towards him. Pundit Ganesh Ramsumair. "G. Ramsay Muir," he said coldly (214). In that "coldly" is conveyed the loss involved in the transformation.

In *Half a Life,* on the other hand, everything is understood as part of a greater whole, each section has the potential of conditioning others. The 'Half' in the novel's title, refers to, among other things, the 'half and half' people in the book, the emigrants who belong nowhere. It also is a comment on the novel's deliberate incompleteness; although most of Naipaul's earlier preoccupations with his Brahminical origins, his father, and his struggle for recognition as a writer and in the Western world inform the three 'unfinished' narratives in the book.

A brief scene where Willie Chandran encounters "a big light-eyed man"—a tiller born of an African mother and an important Portuguese landowner father—at a restaurant on the coast of the African nation may be regarded as the central motif of the novel. Willie says to himself, "Whenever I remembered the big sweating man carrying the shame of his birth like a brand, I would think: Who will rescue that man? Who will avenge him?" (56).

The question is equally pertinent for Willie and the phrase used to describe the man "who appeared to have no proper place in the world"—clearly describes Willie, as it does, Naipaul.

The insecurity that he had experienced in his formative years remains to date and perhaps accounts for the constant denial of his place of birth, which was his home, which he left or rather felt compelled to leave for fulfilling his objective of gaining worldwide recognition as a writer.

Needless to say, Naipaul succeeds in his objective. So much so that he seems to be at home only when he is writing, patiently stacking sentences with semi-colons until his words, pared to the bone, exactly reflect his circumscribed vision of the world. In fact, the only home available to him, though fragile and vulnerable, is in writing. Elsewhere the house is past though England does provide him a refuge. As he admits in *The Enigma of Arrival*, "In the ancient heart of England a place where I was truly an alien...I had been given a second chance, a new life, richer and fuller than any I had had anywhere else" (156).

In the introductory note to *Half a Life*, Naipaul tells us that "this book is an invention. It is not exact about the countries, periods or situations it appears to describe" (4). Yet while it is true that the periods or locales in India and Africa are nebulous and have been imaginatively constructed in an exotic light, the places in England are easily identifiable. We may deduce that this is because Naipaul lives in England, the place where the bulk of his work has originated. Evidently then, Naipaul's feeling that England, stable and resolute, is still at the centre of the universe as against "areas of darkness" such as India and Africa is foregrounded. India and Africa, in this case, become faded backdrops on which he projects a vision of the West, England in particular.

If one were to assume that, as in some of his previous works, Naipaul is writing back to his father in *Half a Life,* this would, in a sense, be indicative of the author's yearning for home. June Jordan in *Living Room* states, "Everybody needs a home so at least you can have some place to leave which is where most folks will say you are coming from" (28).

For Naipaul, home would then have to be Trinidad, irrespective of his denial of the same. In his very first collection of short stories, *Miguel Street*, this becomes evident in the concluding line/s where the narrator says: "I left them and walked briskly towards the aeroplane, not looking back, looking only at my shadow before me, a dancing dwarf on the tarmac" (222). Also, in the recently published letters between Naipaul and his father, there is a moving section where the young Naipaul wallows in nostalgia. In the cold Oxford winter of 1952, he writes to his father:

> I feel nostalgic for home. Do you know what I long for? I long for the nights that fall blackly, suddenly, without warning. I long for a violent shower of rain at night. I long to hear the tiny tattoo of heavy raindrops on a roof, or the drops of rain on the broad leaves of that wonderful plant, the wild tannia. But, in short, I long for home, or perhaps, the homely atmosphere. And I miss my bicycle rides, and the sea, and the pit at Rialto, and the sort of cigarettes I used to smoke, to everyone's scandal. (108)

But soon after he lashes out at his homeland, perhaps out of sheer frustration:

> Do you know? I got some Trinidad papers, read them, and found them hilariously absurd. I never realised before that the Trinidad Guardian was so badly written, that our Trinidad worthies were so absurd, that Trinidad is the most amusing island that ever dotted a sea. (109)

The paradox, of course, is that without Naipaul's homeland there would have been no body of work. Britain did not produce V.S. Naipaul. True, its literary culture allowed him to become a writer, but it is the Caribbean, a place of double exile for him, a place where he became a culturally inscribed migrant within a migrant world, which gave to him his theme of exile and loss. Moreover, though the much-despised place has long ceased to provide support to his identity, it continues to resonate in his imagination.

In ways reflective of the author's personal life, *Half a Life* shows Willie's attempt to find a place in the world after a collapse caused in part by the difficulties of homelessness. Its significance lies in that it sees the Nobel laureate come full circle both as a writer and as a self-imposed exile trying to come to terms with his Caribbean island origins, Indian roots, his apparent refuge in England and his personal experiences.

For nearly five decades, if not more, Naipaul has been caught in a state of radical incompleteness which cannot be remedied, the world becomes his source of physical and spiritual sustenance and renders him imperfect, one to whom familiarity with the physical world is of acute significance, though never satisfying. Likewise Ganesh and Willie too, wherever they turn, find people whose place is no more certain or secure than their own, but they fail to grasp that this is, in truth, a universal condition.

"Seeing the entire world as a foreign land", as mentioned earlier in the epigraph, makes possible an originality of vision. Most of the people are aware of one culture, one setting and one home. Exiles are aware of at least two, and this plurality of vision gives rise to an awareness of simultaneous dimensions, an awareness that is contrapuntal. Not so in case of Naipaul. For him, all it succeeds in doing is reaffirming the Supremacy of the West which results in a series of interchangeable caricatures of societies depicted as half-made in comparison with Europe. That is why he lacks that sense of achievement in acting as if he were at home wherever he happens to be.

Naipaul's power and suggestiveness as a writer lies in this *absence* of a solution to his problem. In reading him we feel that exile is a fundamental condition of the postcolonial world, one which we must all experience to a greater or lesser extent. Modern man suffers from a feeling of homelessness, exile or no exile. Naipaul's works, in that sense, unite all mankind, though it is a paradoxical unity of disunity whereby we enter a perpetual state of disintegration and renewal, struggle and contradiction, ambiguity and anguish.

But few of us can share Naipaul's bleakly conservative perspective on his condition, nor would we support his rejection of all those elements through which identity is constituted such as family and homeland. Yet in the absolutism of Naipaul's self-exclusion and despair, there is a lesson we can all learn.

It is not the metaphysical truth of my epigraph, but it is a truth, nevertheless, of our fragmented and uprooted postcolonial existences. It tells us that cartography and topography are futile concepts in a world that is not our own, and that at any time we may find ourselves homeless in it. Borders and barriers, which enclose us within the safety of familiar territory, can also become prisons, often defended beyond reason or necessity. In terms of craftsmanship, *The Mystic Masseur* undoubtedly outshines *Half a Life*. As a novel, the latter, to all intents and purposes, is unsatisfactory and unsettling, perhaps one of his weakest books: but it does succeed in communicating the premises on which all his work rests.

Works Cited

Jordan, June. *Living Room 1985*. United States: Thunder's Mouth Press, 1993.

Kakutani, Michiko. "Naipaul Reviews His Past from Afar." December 1, 1980. Web. November 15, 2012.

Naipaul, V.S. *Half a Life*. London: Picador, 2001.

——. *Letters Between a Father and Son* 1999. London: Picador, 2011.

——. *Miguel Street*. London: Andre Deutsch Limited, 1959.

——. *The Mystic Masseur* (1957 rpt.) Oxford: Heinemann Educational Books Ltd., 1971.

——. The Overcrowded Barracoon. London: Andre Deutsch Ltd., 1972.

Said, Edward. *The World, the Text and the Critic*. Massachusetts: Harvard University Press, 1983.

——. "Intellectual Exile: Expatriates and Marginals." *Representations of the Intellectual: The 1993 Reith Lectures*. London: Vintage, 1994.

3

Invention, Memory, and Place in *Magic Seeds*: A Perspective of Reading

Valiur Rahaman

> Over the past decade, there has been a burgeoning interest in two over-lapping areas of the humanities and social sciences: memory and geography or, more specifically, the study of human space. Both of them have spawned an extraordinary amount of interesting work, work that has in effect created new fields of study and inquiry.
>
> (Edward W. Said in *Critical Inquiry*, Vol. 26, No. 2, Winter, 2000).

The invention of memory and place is the 'Discourse of Identity'. The above quoted lines of Edward W. Said, the greatest Orientalist of the present century, about "the study of human space" is the central theme of this paper. The paper is the exposition of Saidean concept of the role of any writer's memory and experiences of place or landscape in the creation of the art of literature.

Willie Chandran in the Frame of Human Space

This study aims at identifying Saidean tools of literary criticism. Edward W. Said, in the study of occident-oriented Orientalism, looked after enormous distortions of the culture of the Third World which was intellectualized and institutionalized in the name of Orientalism in the West. He, then, re-scrutinized, revalued and restored by defining Orientalism in its truest sense. He succeeded in his mission because he understood the history of the world which was the history of memory and geography, i.e. the 'human space'. He did not study literature from formalist or structuralist or deconstructionist points of view. He studied literature with universalist standpoints thinking literature as the expression of the human space. So, while studying literature we also should know the space of characters which has marks of racial, colour, and social identity of characters. Besides rhetoric of language and art, literature is alive for its contents—contents of human space, memory, geography, and history and socio-ethnic remarks.

This idea of 'human space' is relevant to postcolonial theories of subjectivity and violence. The reason is that this phrase has an umbrella effect and implication. It reflects the current scenario of the world about/on which postcolonial thinkers confirm their discourse. It reflects what I call 'space', 'pace' and 'race' of individuals in their society. We should elaborate these terms in their identical manners. 'Space' is identical with human world—residences of characters; 'pace' is identical with direction—movements of the characters of an individual or individuals; and 'race' is identical with color, ethnicity or position of an individual in the society—culture of the character. Thus, 'human space' contains basically three constituents which, after applying literary criticism as the study of the human space, maybe applied for reading Sir V.S. Naipaul's *Magic Seeds* (2004) with references to its prequel *Half a Life* (2001) and to intertextuality of expressed memory and place in his novels. The constituents that I have traced so far in the 'human space' maybe applied for finding out the invention as the result of the process of fictional narrative. The protagonist of the *Magic Seeds* is Willie Chandran. We shall observe how Naipaul has sketched the human space of Willie and how Willie is invented out of embedded memory of the author. We can put Willie in the frame of human space for further discussion:

> Space↔Protagonist roams for home in Germany, India, and England.
>
> Pace↔Protagonist's undecided direction to life.

Race↔Protagonist is an Indian immigrant in societies of the others.

Trace↔homeless loiterer.

I needed to add one more word, 'trace' as fourth constituent of human space signifying what remains in the protagonist identical to his *own* identity—either as social, mythical, spiritual, existential, or political. Now, let us elaborate the above-mentioned analysis in broader sense.

'Identity' is one of the common themes of the Diaspora writings whether it is fiction, poetry, travel narratives, memoir, prose writings, drama or other related genres. It is also one of the foregrounding themes of race, culture, place, memory and gender specific literatures. Edward W. Said's scholarly article "Invention, Memory, and Place", articulates in this context that:

> The concern with memory, for example, has branched out to include such increasingly prevalent forms of writing as personal memoirs and autobiography, which nearly every fiction writer of note has attempted, to say nothing of the outpourings of academics, scientists, public figures, and so forth. The national fixation on recollection, confession, and witness has run the whole gamut from public confession—as in the Clinton-Lewinsky scandal—to various studies of the meaning of collective memory, extended reflection and analyses of instances of it, plus numerous chronicles embodying it. I shall have more to say about that later. In addition, and somewhat on the margins, has been a serious, sometimes bitter inquiry into the authenticity of certain memories, as well as, at the other, calmer end of the spectrum, a remarkable academic analysis of the role of invention in such matters as tradition and collective historical experience.... (Said 175)

He adds:

> Memory and its representations touch very significantly upon questions of identity, of nationalism, of power and authority. Far from being a neutral exercise in facts and basic truths, the study of history, which of course is the underpinning of memory, both in school and university, is

> to some considerable extent a nationalist effort premised on the need to construct a desirable loyalty to an insider's understanding of one's country, tradition, and faith. (*Ibid.*)

T.S. Eliot in his critical stances demonstrated with great emphasis that invention can only be possible when inventor has richness of history and tradition. The invention of tradition can only be possible when the inventor looks at tradition objectively being free from the nature of 'the victim of his temperament' in terms of Eliot in his essay, "The Imperfect Critic" (*Sacred Woods* 35). When Eliot's "Tradition and the Individual Talent", signifies tradition, with the value of 'novelty' which is an outcome of tradition itself. To quote him, "...novelty is better than repetition. Tradition is a matter of much wider significance. It cannot be inherited, and if you want it you must obtain it by great labour. It involves, in the first place, the historical sense (*SW* 43) which is "a perception, not only of the pastness of the past, but of its presence...(which) a sense of the timeless as well as of the temporal and of the timeless and of the temporal together, is what makes a writer traditional." And it is at the same time what makes a writer most acutely conscious of his place in time, of his contemporaneity (*SW* 44). Naipaul puts this sense of tradition of individuals of three countries showing as a fictional world of *Magic Seeds* (2004). He invented a new world out of the world he had seen once in his life.

Descriptions of land are common matters of Diaspora writings. It always has embedded history and ethos. The land has its history, its culture, its ethos, its linguistics which organically reflects narration of an individual, a society, and a nation. It often mirrors the sense of alienation, individual's struggle for existence, societal struggle, patriotic struggle, homelessness, uncertainty of a life, sense of absurdity and unbelongingness. Naipaul's fictional world is the world of such subjective refractions. He unties his memories, rather painful memories, relating them with contemporary incidents taking place in the postmodern and postcolonial societies. *Half a Life* (2001) is the best example of the narration of subjective refractions portrayed with Willie's constant exiled life from India, England, Africa, and Germany. Willie as a loiterer shows the picture of the places wherever he travels in the search of certainty of a stay and self-identity.

In *Magic Seeds*, Willie's memory does not let him to go anywhere that can give him peace of mind and certainty of thoughts. He seeks his belongings knowing nothing about what final destination he will/should belong to. It resulted in the form of travelling which gave him experiences of interaction with people of various places. In this fiction, Willie is very much akin to the character, Tiresias of Eliot's *The Wasteland* (1922). Naipaul had always big words for England, but, he eventuated to criticize the Postmodern England in these two fictions. *Magic Seeds* begins from isolated lifestyle of Willie Chandran, gripped with pessimism and misogynist negative attitude. To him, "It is wrong to have ideal view of the world. That's where the mischief starts. That's where everything starts unraveling" (Naipaul 2004: 280). In his autobiographical novel *The Enigma of Arrival* (1987), Naipaul looks London as 'modern-day Rome' where everybody can live freely and frankly but in *Half a Life* and *Magic Seeds* we find his changed perspective to see London—London of Eliot's days. In these two novels, Naipaul criticized the Western for moral emptiness and lack of people's loyalty. Mr. Biswas, after a lot toils and troubles, succeeded in realization of house he made at last belonged to him. Here, the theme has concerns of the sense of unbelongingness and emptiness.

We may have some examples of how memory and place or description of lands invents a fictional world of the writers. Salman Rushdie's recently published memoir, *Joseph Anton* (2012) is the narration of what T.S. Eliot calls, 'pastness of the past' of his life which tells about the inventiveness and approves that the history of the self becomes the narration of the self, rather say, invention of words or fictional world. Rushdie's *Luka and the Fire of Life* (2010) a so-called children's book,[1] explicates a journey of protagonist, Luka, and his companions to the world where the life, soul or real shadow of his father, Rashid Khalifa is kept under guards of the god of fire. This journey connotes a journey toward finding out the self-identity, self-existence and certain belonging. Rushdie's implicit presence under securities in the real world fostered him to write the 'pastness of the past'.

What my argument is that the literary invention is an outcome of memory and place. The postcolonial literary reading tends to find cultural hegemony in the inventiveness of author's memory and place where he belongs to or looked or observed ever.

The answer to an interviewer's question towards the sense of unbelongingness that V.S. Naipaul has ever felt is akin to the feelings of the protagonist of the *Magic Seeds*. The question stands for the sense of 'looking for'.

> You left Trinidad in 1950 to study at Oxford—setting out across the seas to an alien land in pursuit of ambition. What were you looking for?[2]

Naipaul replies:

> I wanted to be very famous. I also wanted to be a writer—to be famous for writing. The absurdity about the ambition was that at the time I had no idea what I was going to write about. The ambition came long before the material. The filmmaker Shyam Benegal once told me that he knew he wanted to make films from the age of six. I wasn't as precocious as he—I wanted to be a writer by the age of ten.
>
> I went to Oxford on a colonial government scholarship, which guaranteed to see you through any profession you wanted. I could have become a doctor or an engineer, but I simply wanted to do English at Oxford—not because it was English and not because it was Oxford, but only because it was away from Trinidad. I thought that I would learn about myself in the three or four years I was going to be away. I thought that I would find out my material and miraculously become a writer. Instead of learning a profession, I chose this banality of English—a worthless degree, it has no value at all.
>
> But I wanted to escape Trinidad. I was oppressed by the pettiness of colonial life and by (this relates more particularly to my Indian Hindu family background) the intense family disputes in which people were judged and condemned on moral grounds. It was not a generous

> society—neither the colonial world nor the Hindu world. I had a vision that in the larger world people would be appreciated for what they were—people would be found interesting for what they were.[3]

And, now compare with:

> The following quote sums up Willie's identity drama: "I have never slept in a room of my own. Never at home in India, when I was a boy. Never here in London. Never in Africa. I lived in somebody else's house always, slept in somebody else's bed. [...] Will I ever sleep in a room of my own?" (Naipaul 2004: 177)

He furthers:

> .... Counting of beds had become harder and harder with the undifferentiated days of marching, the villages almost all the same. Many months had passed since the life of marching and camping had begun; perhaps a year, perhaps more. What had been painful in the beginning, stretching out the days, had become habit. He felt his memory slipping, like time now, and with that slipping of memory the point of the mental exercise disappeared. It became too strenuous, too frustrating; it caused his head to hurt. He gave it up; it was like shedding a piece of himself. (Naipaul, *Paris Review*, 2013)

Compare it with another question of interviewer that I am willing to quote to accelerate my argument is related with 'place' as the subjectivity of writing.

> You have been to so many place—India, Iran, West Africa, and the American Deep South. Are you still drawn to travel?

The answer has relevance to my argument about 'place' as the subjectivity of writing. Naipaul answers to this question: "The trouble is that I can't go places without writing about them. I feel I've missed the experience" (Naipaul, *Paris Review*, 2013). Here we must refer to the words of Kath Woodward, "constructing the self is made meaningful through mapping practices that select key moments and pivotal points in the narrative of identity" (Woodward 67). Woodward further clarifies, "identity is closely linked to place, to key places and often to the place that we call home. In this sense the map is a useful metaphor for understanding the formation and representation of identity in relation to location and situation as well as movements and translation" (*Ibid.* 65).

Magic Seeds as a Hypertext: The Result of Reading the Human Space in Fiction

Magic Seeds is a sequel to *Half a Life*. It is the story of a forty years old man, Willie Somerset Chandran, who is living an absurd life, suffered for no cause, persuaded and helped and counseled by his sister, moved to his birth-country where they could not adjust finding a reluctant job as a guerrilla—a small group of freedom fighters and finally surrendered to Police apprehending it a fight for futility and unreasoned. He was put in jail and returned to London after he released. He remained vagabond, jobless, friendless, and had to suffer from claustrophobia. So, we may find a lot changes in the perspective of the author.

Salman Rushdie's collection of essays, *Imaginary Homeland* (1991) contains a chapter, entitled, "V.S. Naipaul", in which Rushdie demonstrates how, Naipaul's *The Enigma of Arrival*, depicts the implications of colonial impacts, and how implications, being in the creative process, make a man the creative and an honest author. He puts forth the idea that the absence of belongingness, the sense of alienation, isolation, and emptiness foster a change in a man of creativity and his creation. Rushdie, with reference to emptying and emptiness of Jack's life, the protagonist of *The Enigma of Arrival* says that, "as result of this emptying, the writer becomes the subject; the story teller becomes the tale" (*IH* 148). The sense of darkness and emptiness in the protagonist connotes symbolical sense of the darkness, shadows and isolatory scenes of Chirico's painting 'The Enigma of Arrival'—the source of Naipaul's autobiographical novel, *The Enigma of Arrival*.

The character moves from place to place with desire of inhabiting a pastoral England, but Jack, finally, will fail to find the destination he has ever dreamt of. In his life, he apprehends nothing but a life portraying the 'change and decay'.[4] Such a movement or travelling of the character represents situational metaphor of a writer's struggle for finding out the place for his sustained satisfaction and development of his self as the self of the author. He wants to write his memories. He wants to write about the assortment of memories and places. He describes landscapes with sorrowful and writhing soul of the writer himself. This is due what I call to residual implication of colonial 'deférance'.[5]

Naipaul never wants to get rid of this implication which has become the cause of his creative 'implicature';[6] the cause of his actions and reactions; the cause his portrayal and semantic art. It is his intentional world—area of darkness—where he stands alone to narrate bitter experiences of his life as a migrant. Ganesh, the protagonist, a representative figure of the East Indians in Trinidad, in his first published fiction *The Mystic Masseur* (1957) appeared as trapped in ambivalent condition. The reason of his ambivalence is his physical movement from one place to other places. Being embodied with cultures and habits of Hindu community, he has to adjust with non-belonging culture in Trinidad. We have some confessional lines of Naipaul in this regard: "Conrad's Darkness and Mine",

> It came to me that the great novelists wrote about highly organized societies. I had no such society; I couldn't share the assumptions of the writers; I didn't see my world reflected in theirs. My colonial world was more mixed and secondhand, and more restricted. The time came when I began to ponder the mystery—Conradian word—of my own background: that island in the mouth of a great South American river, the Orinoco, one of the Conradian dark places of the earth, where my father had conceived literary ambitions for himself and then for me, but from which, in my mind, I had stripped all romance and perhaps even reality: preferring to set "The Lagoon," when it was read to me, not on the island I knew, with its muddy rivers, mangrove and swamps, but somewhere far away. (Naipaul 2004: 160-80)

For the double migrant writer the 'place' and 'memory' function as creative forces for establishing the inner subjectivity meshed with personal experiences. Barnouw comments,

> Critical readings of Naipaul's work have generally been divided into two groups: a strongly-focused post-colonialist critique of his indebtedness to western cultural values that does not deal with the textual complexity, and literary studies of his fictional and non-fictional texts that do not deal with representational complexity, the text's connectedness to social and political realities. (Mukherjee 212)

But, if we look at subjects of Naipaulian fictional world, which is much similar to the world of Conrad, we must look at it associating it with 'place' and 'memory' textured in his novels.

Bruce King represents the ideology of Naipaul as a writer of landscape, memory, fractured colonial emotion and experience:

> He hated the narrow, circumscribed brutal life which surrounded him in colonial Trinidad with its limited possibilities, small range of profession, notorious political corruption and social and religious conflict...Indians among whom he was raised lived in a social world of their own uninvolved with the races. The Trinidadian of African descent appeared to have not traditional culture of their own and modeled themselves on the English.... The local whites had produced nothing of lasting values, were drunkards, uneducated and privileged. (5-6)

Half a Life and *Magic Seeds* unties the mystery of "notorious political corruption and social and religious conflict" of nations Willie Chandran visited for his unknown destination. Willie, like Ralph Singh, the protagonist of Naipaul's fictional memoir, *The Mimic Men* (1967), is appeared as a victim of colonial trap, helpless to do anything in favor of him. He says, "I feel a bad hand was dealt me. What could I have done in India? What could I have done in England in 1957 or 1958? Or in Africa?" (Naipaul 2005: 6). He further says with repentance, "I was always someone on the outside. I still am. What can I do here in Berlin?" (Naipaul 2005: 6). Willie attacks pretentions of people of nations and duel characters of politicians, social institutes, and so-called guardians of the society. In *Magic Seeds*, we find many references of history, culture of India, books written to represent Indian nationalism explained in M.K. Gandhi's *Autobiography.*[7] In the first chapter of the novel, "The Rose-Sellers", there is a discussion between Willie and his sister Sarojini who forces Willie to be the part of real life, wants him to see freed from what she calls, 'colonial psychosis and caste psychosis'. Her expression of reality reminds us Ralph's exposition of reality. As Ralph says in *The Mimic Men*, "We, here on our island, handling books printed in this world, and using its goods, had been abandoned and forgotten. We pretended to be real, to be learning, to be preparing ourselves for life, we mimic men of the New World, one unknown corner of it, with all its reminders of the corruption that came so quickly to the new" (Naipaul 1967: 157). Sarojini states about common people and conception of Indian history known to common persons:

> All the history you and people like you know about yourselves comes from a British textbook written by a nineteenth-century English inspector of schools in India called Roper Lethbridge. Did you know that? It was the first big school history book in India, and it was published in the 1880s by the British firm of Macmillan. That makes it just twenty years or so after the Mutiny, and of course it was an imperialist work and it was also meant to make money. But it was also a work of some learning in the British way and it was a success. In all the centuries before in India there had been nothing like it, no system of education like that, no training in that kind of history. Roper Lethbridge went into many editions, and it gave us many of the ideas we still have about ourselves. One of the most important of those ideas was that in India there were servile races, people born to be slaves, and there were martial races. The martial races were fine; the servile races were not. You and I half belong to the servile races. I am sure you know that. I am sure you half accept that. That is why you have lived as you have lived. The Tamils selling roses in Berlin belong wholly to the servile races. That idea

> would have been impressed on them in all kinds of ways. And that British idea about the servile and the martial races of India is utterly wrong. *The British East India Company army in the north of India was a Hindu army of the upper castes*. This was the army that pushed the boundaries of the British Empire almost to Afghanistan. But after the great Mutiny of 1857 that Hindu army was degraded. Further military opportunities were denied them. So the warriors who had won the empire became servile in British propaganda, and the frontier people they had conquered just before the Mutiny became the martial ones. It is how imperialisms work. It is what happens to captive people. And *since in India we have no idea of history we quickly forget our past and always believe what we are told*. (10-11, my italics)

The descriptions of Hinduism, Mutiny, Gandhi's life in Africa, his insult in the compartment of the train, his philosophy, mimicry of nationalistic spirits in common people, the British East India Company, and Lin-Piao's the idea of liquidating the class enemy, are constituents of "place and memory" elucidation. These references are historical textured with the fibers of plamory[8]—the essence of "place and memory". These references are having hidden question of security in the nation, the question of public policy regarding migrants in other nations. Willie says that after marriage, after wasting fifteen or sixteen years in Africa, he began to realize his no-existence reality. His words are, "I began to change. I began to feel that I had thrown away my life, that what I had thought of as my luck was no such thing…I began to feel that because of my insecurity—the insecurity I had been born into…" (*MS* 113). In the chapter two, "Peacocks", there are many geographical references of India and Berlin. Indian Airport, as it is described as "The small, shabby airport building was full of movement and echoing noise." Willie came back to India with feeling of other than Indians, "Twenty years ago I wouldn't have seen what I am seeing now" and visited to countryside, "Riviera Hotel, to the Neo Anand Bhavan, to the guerrilla camp in the teak forest" (59) with his critical eyesight being unaware that this country does also not belong to him.

In this chapter, we come across many literary, historical and political references. Willie refers to Conrad's *Heart of Darkness* (14),[9] Indian caste history. "In fact we are looking at the cruelty of history. And the most terrible thing is it can't be avenged. The old lords oppressed and humiliated and injured for centuries. No one touched them. Now they've gone away. They've gone to the towns; they've gone to foreign countries. They've left these wretched people as their monument" and the cricket people (43).

The chapter six, "The End of Kandapalli" is also full of geographical descriptions; additionally it gives impressions of realization of a self-exiled character's unbelongingness in his country. This chapter revolves around portraits of army architectures with philosophical implications of nihilism (126) and Dalit revolution with reference to Indian Militarism, Marx, Mao, Lenin, and Trotsky. He was arrested, jailed, and left to return to the self-exiled destinations. The chapter seven discloses how people are insecure under public policies and development strategies. The episode introduces a stranger's talk with Willie. The stranger is nihilist in his attitude (126-29). The seventh chapter outsets the scene of the prison of India and a hospital ward. It alludes to Gandhi's capped prisoner period. The chapter eight, "London Beanstalk" alludes to Roger's house, Marble Arch, Wardour Street, Edgware Road, Oxford Street, Notting Hill, St. John's Wood and Maida Vale. But, none of places he belonged to, none of the house was his; none of the bed was under his possession.

Willie realized when there was nothing left to him to do except saying to himself, "I have never slept in a room of my own. Never at home in India, when I was a boy. Never here in London. Never in Africa. I lived in somebody else's house always, and slept in somebody else's bed. In the forest of course there were no rooms, and then the jail was the jail. Will I ever sleep in a room of my own?" (177-78). It refers the thematic discourse of identity which Naipaul has shown in *A House for Mr Biswas* (1961) is fine example of metatextuality. The chapters, "An Axe to the Root", "Suckers", and "Magic Seeds" are significant for their references to the theories of modernity and colonialism, ethnic tapestry, imperialism, socialism and nationalism. The description of landscape is countryside of London. They also have references of literatures of Dickens, Munby, Ruskin, Tolstoy, Henry James, and Morris; and of French Revolution and Indian Mutiny. The novel ends with the sense of half-housed self-exiled life.

These descriptions of places meshed with memory of travelled places embodies creativity which offer a man of letters to say about history, culture, habits, politics, philosophy, above all man's belonging. The above exposition unties the mystery of significance of reading the places and memory in the fiction. It is not the attempt to find the author in the text but what makes the author able to write which is *unwritable*. Naipaul depicts two types of memory: intellectual and common, creative and sub-creative or vice versa. They textured the narration in a way that this writing could not remain a personal diary but a text of historiography of place and memory. Literary invention is incomplete without exposition of these root causes of creative process.

Notes

1. Salman Rushdie's *Luka and the Fire of Life*, published as a children's book, a sequal to *Harun's Sea* but its content, the way it is written, allusions and mythological references make this work complex and difficult to understand its contents. It seems very simple but becomes complex when the reader tries to understand intentions behind words, images and symbols.
2. V.S. Naipaul, The Art of Fiction No. 154, interviewed by Jonathan Rosen, Tarun Tejpal, *The Paris Review*, 2013, http://www.theparisreview.org/interviews/1069/the-art-of-fiction-no-154-v-s-naipaul, retrieved on 7/8/13.
3. *Ibid.*
4. See *The Enigma of Arrival.*
5. Jacques Derrida coined this word to refer to the sense of postponement of meaning after interpretation. I used this word in term of postponement of colonial implication resulting characters in art and art itself.

6. A word used in linguistic, coined by H.P. Grice, referring the sense of unsaid implications or unsigned references in an utterance or writing. It is used here as an alternative to implication.
7. *The Story of My Experiments with Truth* (1925-29) demystifies M.K. Gandhi's life covering early childhood through to 1921, written and published his journal *Navjivan* from 1925 to 1929. Its English translation also appeared in installments in his other journal *Young India*. Later, it was originally published in two volumes, the first in 1927 and second in 1929. The Govt. of India published the complete works of Mahatma Gandhi in 1996. In *Magic Seeds*, Willie was told about Gandhi's way of life in reference to colonial force in Africa and India.
8. I mean to refer the essence of place and memory which functions as creative residual in the mind of the author resulting fictional characters and situation to reflect the reality of colonial truth.
9. In this chapter, Conrad's idea of the materiality of a book in the reference of a African colonial context has been commented both by Naipaul and Homi Bhabha. Such references are called hypertext which represents the narrative technique of Naipaul. See *Magic Seeds*, pp. 43-46.

Works Cited

Eliot, T.S. *The Sacred Wood: Essays on Poetry & Criticism*. London: Faber & Faber, 1920.

King, Bruce. Ed. *V.S. Naipaul*, England: Macmillan. 2003.

Mukherjee, Pablo. *Doomed to Smallness*: *Violence, V.S. Naipaul, and The Global South*.

The Yearbook of English Studies. Vol. 37, No. 1, *From Decadent to Modernist: And Other Essays*. 2007. 209-26. Web. August 27, 2013.

Naipaul, V.S. *Magic Seeds*. New York and Toronto: Alfred A. Knopf, 2004.

——. *Half a Life*. New York and Toronto: Alfred A. Knopf, 2001.

——. "The Art of Fiction No. 154", interviewed by Jonathan Rosen, Tarun Tejpal. *The Paris Review*. Web. August 8, 2013.

Reiss, T.J. "Mapping Identities: Literature, Nationalism, Colonialism." in Vol. 4, No. 4. Winter, (1992): 649-77. Web. August 27, 2013.

Rushdie, Salman. *Luka and the Fire of Life*. London: Jonathan Kape, 2010.

——. *Imaginary Homeland: Essays and Criticism 1981-1991*. London: Vintage, 2010.

——. *Midnights Conversion*. New Republic. Vol. 204, Issue 3. 1/21/91.

——. *Joseph Anton: A Memoir*. London: Jonathan Kape. 2012.

Said, Edward W. "Invention, Memory, and Place." *Critical Inquiry*, Vol. 26, No. 2, Winter, (2000): 175-92. Web. June 05, 2010.

Woodward, K. *Understanding Identity*. London: Oxford University Press, 2002.

4

Affirming the Different: A Study of V.S. Naipaul's Caribbean Fictions

Chandan Kumar Panda

In this paper, I intend to show how Indian expatriates in Trinidad inhabit an unknown locale and how subsequently affirm it. This paper includes a brief background of the Indians settling in Trinidad, India as an absent presence, problem of identity, India as a history, and the affirmation of the other.

With the abolition of the slavery system from Europe and America beginning with the Slavery Abolition Act in 1833 by the British Parliament, blacks were freed from being the enforced and sold labourers in the tobacco and coca fields in Caribbean islands. In the British occupied Trinidad there emerges the urgency to meet the dearth in the number of the labourers. British Government therefore decides to sail Indians to Trinidad as indentured labourers. Naipaul writes in his *India: A Million Mutinies Now* (1990):

> ...I had gone as the descendant of 19th-century indentured Indian emigrants. Such emigrants had been recruited from the 1860s on, mainly from the eastern Gangetic plain, and then sent out from depots in Calcutta to work on five-year indentures on plantations in various parts of the British Empire and even elsewhere. People like my ancestors had gone to Fiji in the Pacific; Mauritius in the Indian Ocean; South Africa; and to some of the territories in the West Indies, principally in Guianas (British Guianas)

> and Trinidad. It was to Trinidad that my ancestors went, starting sometime in the 1880s, as I work it out. (6-7)

On their arrival in Trinidad, a kind of peculiar strangeness surrounds them. Everything seems different to them. A kind of ontological crisis occurs to them. The very idea of survival and the thought of the future badly disturb them. Trinidad is a place which houses people from different races and cultures, prominently blacks, Indians, and Spaniards. Apart from these the rest are the hybrids with different racial connections. The question which comes to the notice now is how Indians survive and settle amid these heterogeneities. The first generation Indians in Trinidad seem to vacillate between two realities—Indian past and Caribbean present. India remains a living present for them because they have lived half of their lives there. India is not a matter of imagination transmitted through hearsay and history. It is where they have already lived but now they are cut off. Here the empirical India turns into a substance of memory. They are uprooted from one reality and placed in the other. The will to leave without the means of leaving becomes the source of their sorrow. The will remains unsupported by the means. This will to return never creates conditions for them to settle. Under a day-long labour struggling with mud and heat and an unknown and inhospitable environ and without a possible future, a hope of a return to the departed haunts them throughout and sustains them for years. Naipaul writes in the same, "We were an agricultural people. Most of us in Trinidad were still working on the colonial sugar estates, and for most of us life was poor; many of us lived in thatched, mud-walled huts" (*Mutinies* 7). A hope against all possible contradictions is the only source for their survival. A thought pertaining to a permanent settlement does not therefore seem to have arisen in their minds. They live more with the memories of the past rather than the realities of the present. The presence of the past in the form of memory inundates the presence of the present. Therefore, a hope of return represses other possibilities. Naipaul narrates in the above book the frustrations of Indians in Trinidad as the promised passage to India was never realised: "In Trinidad, in the late 30s and early 40s, I used to see poor Indian people sleeping in the squares of Port of Spain. These people were peasant emigrants from India; they had served out their indentures 20 years or so before, had not been given their passages back to India, and had then become destitute, abandoned by everybody. In the colonial city they were further isolated by their language; and they were to live the streets until they died out. The idea came to me, when I was quite young, seeing those destitute, that we were people with no one to appeal to. We had been transported out of the abjectness of India, and were without representation" (*Mutinies* 159). A community which had to start from a scratch with no support, strength and affiliation struggles hard to rise under constant sufferings and threats. It is not possible for the first generation of Indians in Trinidad to do anything affirmative and progressive as they were a liminal community uncertain about everything and of course suspicious too. Under such uncertainty the possibility of a settlement of any kind seems very rare. They think nothing apart from the survival and return.

On the contrary the same does not happen with the second generation. India is not a memory for them but becomes history. The lived life is the ingredient of the memory. A return to the past is empirically impossible because the reverse temporality is equally impossible. Memories are temporal because they move with the time, but what constitute them are the products of the temporal without temporality. As time has banished the constituents of memory, an enactment of any kind seems impossible. A play without motion is not feasible. The narrated form of memory is history. Scripting the memory is necessary because it is a means to transmit the lived life to the succeeding. For the second generation Indians in Trinidad, India becomes a topic creating curiosity in them and it is often heard from others or read from the books. It begets fascination in them and creates effects of the exotic. On one hand, it generates curiosity, but on the other creates apprehension. For them who have not seen India only heard and read about it, a return would again be a return to the unknown. The Trinidad Indians know the past but are unaware about the present of India. The return may not guarantee security and happiness. They would ultimately end up nowhere. Their distant relatives might have forgotten them after years of their absence or they may not recognise them. A return in this regard would be to meet more problems or to be outcastes among the known. The exotic may turn banal. The return of the forgotten is not desired by them who have forgotten. They may remember the time of the exodus and may become superficially sad but it would be difficult for them to accept them those once swept by time. The apparition of the ghosts of the time passed into the time passing would unsettle the scheme of the temporal. A return does not only entail a reunion, rather contains a possibility of a claim on the ancestral property as per the norms of the heredity. The idea of return is countered a contradicting idea pertaining to recognition and security. The very fact of forgetting entails the insignificance of the objects forgotten. They become the burden for others and create an unexpected rupture or a sudden disturbance in the existing pattern. Such apprehensions dissuade them from the idea of return; hence the necessity of settlement appears before them as a possible solution towards the disturbing apprehensions. Past continues with present not as it was, because that exodus is a matter of memory now. If time entails both continuity and change, the past suggesting continuity need not neglect the change denoting the present. Past as a residue continuing with the present will cause conflict, if it contradicts the present. This trespass may cause temporal disorder. This leads to the idea of settlement. With the idea of settlement comes the problem of coexistence.

Coexistence is a major problem in the Caribbean societies. Due to colonisation the immigration both forceful and voluntary to those islands becomes rampant. Europeans colonise it for the oil and agriculture. They employ initially blacks from Africa and then Indians in those oil-rich fields and agricultural lands. A kind of continuous excitement pervades in those islands because of this collage of different peoples. Necessity compels them to become neighbours. But they remain culturally different and of course racially. Since race is a matter of biology, it therefore seems apparent and cannot be done away with. The temporary and makeshift arrangements for habitation lead to a collaborative and consolidated attempt towards a permanent settlement. Naipaul continues to write in *India: A Million Mutinies Now*,

> These overseas Indian groups were mixed. They were miniature Indians, with Hindus and Muslims, and people of different castes. They were disadvantaged, without representation, and without a political tradition. They were isolated by language and culture from the people they found themselves among; they were isolated, too, from India itself (many weeks away by steamboat from Trinidad and the Guianas). In these special circumstances they developed something they would never have known in India: a sense of belonging to an Indian community. This feeling of community could override religion and caste. (7)

This sense of community devoid of any religion and caste specifications binds them together to proceed with a view to embrace the alien. The very continuity of such a feeling finally leads them to settle. Naipaul also mentions in the same book, "It was also the India of the great civilisation and the great classical past. It was the India by which, in all the difficulties of our circumstances, we felt supported. It was an aspect of our identity, the community identity we had developed, which, in multi-racial Trinidad, had become more like a racial identity" (*Mutinies* 8). It appears to be a historical necessity for the Indians in Trinidad to come together and to present them as a race to survive in a place where racial heterogeneity is quite common. In such circumstances to progress individually does not seem to be an ideal option, therefore they decide to grow in a group or as a community. The very formation of a community irrespective of interests of any kind of the individuals helps to them to claim residence on a permanent basis. They recover gradually from the sickness of return to the absent and accept the available.

It is with the third generation Indians, permanent settlement becomes indispensable. India is now to be imagined and to be read from the history books. Ralph Singh in *The Mimic Men* (1967) is one of the best examples in this regard. The impossibility of return because of certain obvious reasons creates in them the urge not to lose their Indianness. The love for the ancestral does not diminish under any circumstances. With the affirmation of the alien geography comes the will to live peacefully with other communities and to protect their culture. This takes them into the politics. This also further leads to the formation of political parties and to the nomination of their representatives. Such is the endeavour which makes the voices of the Hindus heard in Trinidad. *The Mystic Masseur* (1957) and *The Suffrages of Elvira* (1958) depict the political life of the Indians in Trinidad. A community in an alien island cannot remain mute for a long tolerating the threats of different kinds coming from different corners. It may take some time as the process of sedimentation takes time but it will one day speak for its security and dignity. It cannot moreover disappear in retrospection. It has to resuscitate from the heaps of the past and to strive for doing something different. Naipaul in his *India: A Million Mutinies Now* writes, "If you get too attached to your roots in the old sense, you might actually become unrooted, fossilised. At least in form, at least in style, you must get into the new stream, get the new roots.... Style becomes substance in one generation" (168-69). To cling to the root in a different environment, where the root of one is unknown and insignificant to the other is quite regressive and such an attitude will dump a community to insignificance. The new never buries the old. The latter remains though not the way as it used to. But on the other hand a transformation in the attitude which one carries from the old world is required for its progress, as transformation is a precondition for progress:

> ...the changes that had come a generation or two earlier to the Indian community in Trinidad, the peasant India that my grandfathers had taken with them, an apparently complete world, with language and rituals and social organisation: an India that had, in its New-World setting, even during my childhood, began to disintegrate: first the language going, then the reverence for the rituals and the need for them (the rituals going on long after they had ceased to be understood), leaving only a group sense, a knowledge of family and clan, and an idea of India in the background, an idea of India quite different (more historical, more political) from the India that had appeared to come with one's ancestors. (*Mutinies* 169)

For the third generation Indians in Trinidad, India does not remain as a strong presence and it fails to impart directly its cultural impressions. They imbibe what they found around. This assimilation, as it was expected to happen for the sake of a safe existence, hardly steal from them the knowledge of their root. Though they have lost much of what is typically Indian as time has demanded from them in instalments, they never discredit their root. The knowledge of the root comes often from its absence. It is mind's jurisdiction and has no physicality. Its proximity is found in distance. Those who are closer to it remain farther from it.

After giving a precise account of the Caribbean lives as a background, I would like to stress on the theme, 'India as an absent presence'. Why does something which is empirically absent remain as a presence in the imagination? Imagination exploits the materials of the memory or the felt or known experiences to reconstruct the dead temporality defying the linearity of the temporal. Why does the temporal lose its regularity and the pattern? With its plastic power, as Kant and subsequently Coleridge have already elaborated on it, imagination 'dissolves' the rigidities and fixities of the temporal in order to integrate them that are separated by time. It gives life to the temporally dead and empirically inert. The absent is the ingredient on which it functions. We imagine that which is not materially available. Something which is absent to the outer faculties becomes the material for the inner ones. This reminds us of Marcel Proust's famous statement "The only paradise is paradise lost". The lost is where we live. The absent is where we are present. The absent is interesting because it contains the possibilities of a different life as a contrast to the given. The lost embodies our essence, therefore the search and the sorrow. For the Indians in Trinidad, India is an absent presence, a presence produced through experience, reading, and imagination. They read to know their roots. Reading unfolds to them the absent and the unknown and induces a fascination for the absent. Ralph Singh for instance in *The Mimic Men* reads the book *The Aryan People and Their Migrations* in Carnegie library in order to reconstruct his identity through identification with the originary epic-moment of the historical community to which one inalienably belongs. He reads to reach the foothills of the Himalayas through the medium of imagination and to participate imaginatively in the heroic deeds of his originary ancestors, "I lived a secret life in a world of endless plains, tall bare mountains, white with snow at their peaks, among nomads on horseback, daily pitching my tent beside cold green mountain torrents that raged over grey rock, waking in the mornings to mist and rain and danger weather" (105). This kind of imaginative flight offers him an esoteric delight and this he does as a response to the racial taunts used against him by his friends. He reads himself into the life of the text. The text does not remain as an object but becomes instead an event and Ralph creatively participates in it. Reading and imagination are perhaps not two different activities. Reading seems to be a form of imagination as they move together. Through reading imagination opens up the realm of the possible which Ralph constantly seeks for. The existence of a possible world however a product of imagination gives him a sense of freedom. That is a possibility to be free from what is given, from what limits him, and from what condemns him to become what he does not want to be. This freedom does not entail a negation of the given but a contradiction to it.

The function of imagination is not merely to offer compensation or consolation. It posits a counter-reality, a virtual world, a created order that runs parallel to the empirically given, the handed down reality. Imagination continues to construct the private worlds beside the arbitrary. They are the subjective constructions compensating the unwanted given. The given is not the product of a choice. It is not chosen by them who live with it. Imagination acts on the demands of the will. Imagination goes on creating what one chooses to. Though the order of the given temporality cannot be transcended empirically, an order of imagined temporality can be made to satisfy at least imaginatively the wishes unfulfilled by the given. The compulsions of the material or the ordeals of the outer and the hostility of the other cannot affect it. Imagination makes the human become the makers to create a counter-universe in the presence of the given addressing the demands of their wishes. However, for the third generation Indians, India is explored through the archival materials. India is imagined along the lines of the knowledge gained through reading. A country which gives meaning to the collective being of a people cannot be forgotten.

The next point to be discussed here is the politics of identity. Caribbean societies are mixed societies accommodating different peoples. Inter-racial marriages make any assertion of identity more complex. Hok in *The Mimic Men* is an example required to be cited in this context. He has some admixture of Syrian or European blood, partly appears African and a little Chinese, etc. When these multiple identities coalesce in Hok, it puts before him a difficult task, what to accept and what to discard. He decides to cling to the Chinese because it has a rich tradition and is respected. He claims to be a Chinese, but unfortunately his physical features do not agree with his claim. This creates problem for him and makes him a target to be easily ridiculed. He does not choose the obvious because it is less respected in the society. Escaping the humiliation for being a black, he spreads stories of his Chinese connection. He admits something which he partially partakes. Taking such a decision he suppresses the obvious. Accepting the identity of a Chinese does not make him a Chinese because he cannot deny the biological. His claim differs from his biology and fails to receive social support. A person with different identities by virtue of the inter-racial marriage finds himself in dilemma. Supporting one would be a suppression of the other. This indecisiveness towards the identity remains unresolved. Identity pertains to the being of a person. Identity is a claim for what you are and for what you feel to be. If your identity is at stake, the very being of your existence is also at stake. This is one case, in other cases sometimes the identity of a person or certain cultural peculiarities of certain communities are looked down upon by other communities which claim to be superior to others. Influenced by the gloss and fashion of the Western cultures, certain people mock at the cultural models of other communities. Hindus are often the victims such mockery. In *The Mystic Masseur*, Ganesh and his father are derided for their dress and typical Hindu manners: "Their dress and manner were no longer drawing looks of respect. People were smiling and when they got off at the railway terminus in Port of Spain, a woman laughed" (20). Even in Dundonald Street, a "tall and plump Negro landlady" (*ibid.*) laughs when she meets both Ganesh and his father. In the school Ganesh being a Hindu, his attire and look induce laughter among his friends. His father is called *Gaddha* (donkey) by the enraged and exasperated principal of the school. He prefers Gareth to Ganesh because the name Ganesh does not seem fashionable. Even towards the end of the novel when the narrator as a boy meets him in London and calls Pandit Ganesh Ramsumair, Ganesh, even after a successful career as a quack and a politician, finds it a little uncomfortable. Ganesh says him coldly to call him G. Ramsay Muir. Writing books on Hinduism and spirituality prolifically and being famous for supporting the cause of the Hindus in Trinidad, Ganesh even fails to resist the influences of the other cultures, especially the white in London. The different around affects the different within. A correspondence is bound to happen when something unavoidably different surrounds him. Ranjit Singh in *The Mimic Men* modifies his name as Ralph Singh because the Hindu name makes him a victim of others' ridicule. He hardly protests the racial taunts of his friends. He instead thinks it better to hide his identity.

Naipaul in his *India: A Million Mutinies Now* also mentions the difficulties on the part of the Indians in Trinidad to continue that which they had inherited from their ancestors: "For the people of that community, separated from the Indian earth, Hindu theology had become difficult (as it had become difficult for people of formerly Hinduised areas of south-east Asia); the faith had then been half-possessed by many, abandoned by many. It had been part of a more general cultural loss, which had left many with no strong idea of who they are" (169). The absence of association causes the cultural loss. Much of ritualism and its external features seem to vanish in course of time as a community stays away from the source and as the effect of the native unknowingly internalised. Here the physical distance entails the cultural distance. The crisis of identity comes from the presence of the other and the absence of that which one belongs. The very idea of identity is caught between two polarities—the own and the other.

Some suppress their identity because some cultural distinctiveness of their race seems outdated on the face of the fashionable cultures. Ganesh and Ralph modify their names to sound a little English. There are also people like Mr. Ramsumair, Ganesh's father, and Duleep Singh, Ralph's father, who remain intransigent to the influences of the dominant and widely imitated cultures. They defy change and therefore disappear. Their struggles do not continue for a long. They are suppressed and forgotten thereafter. The very presence of the other demands transformation. To resist is to disobey the scheme of the temporal. Cultural interfaces and encounters do not lead to a blend or a commotion. Affirming the alien does not necessarily mean a compromise with their essence. The change is bound to occur when the other is around. The presence of the other is the necessary precondition for a change. The suppression of their identity does mean the loss of their identity. The acceptance of the new or the different does not entirely abandon the old that have existed for years or perhaps for the centuries. The new may attempt to make an assertion of modernity but practically the new comes from the known. The new does not descend from nowhere or from the unknown. The known is precisely the tradition which begets modernity. The new is always a departure from the old or often an extension, not certainly the death of the old. The new perhaps demands integration and this integration may be phrased as modernity. In other words, modernity, as Reinhart Koselleck writes in his book *Futures Past: On the Semantics of Historical Time* (2004), alters the nature of temporality from the circular to the linear. It may change the nature of time not the time, because it is as well a product of the temporal. Anything radical may be incorporated into the premise of the modern but conversely the radical does not remain forever. It is always dramatic, it appears with all suddenness and urgency under a violent magnitude in order to destroy and disappear. Human beings are capable of the dramatic but unfortunately cannot sustain it. However, the affirmation of the different does not entirely obliterate their cultural inheritance.

The next point to be explored is 'India as a history'. Here I distinguish between memory and history. Memory is a lived history without chronology, and history is the memory systematised and retold. The impressions of the lived life are the constituents of the memory. The narrations of those impressions are called history. Memory, as Plato in his Dialogue entitled *Phaedrus* (1997) writes, "is a discourse that is written down, with knowledge, in the soul of the listener; it can defend itself, and it knows for whom it should speak and for whom it should remain silent" (276). It seems very apparent that memory is subjective and does the very being one's ontic state—an inseparable other inhabit within. Moreover, memory as a patch or a trace or a slice of a past is a finite eternity. It inhabits a temporal span without a temporality. It is finite because it has a duration and eternal because time cannot return to it. Memory is the empire of known and sometimes of the forgotten. What we forget does not disappear, but remain as inert residue to be recalled at any moment by any associated event. History triggers imagination and induces fascination for the imagined. Memory on the other hand operates through recollection and subsequently generates nostalgia. For the second and the third generation Indians, India is a history not memory because they have not lived in India but only have read about it. They are fascinated towards India reading its history but do not pine for it. For them India is a dream not a delirium.

For the third generation Indians, accepting the different does not necessarily mean a peaceful coexistence amid all differences. The question of security forces them into politics or into the state regulatory mechanisms. With the gain of the political power, social forces can be controlled and social justice can be ensured. This opens the scope for entering into politics. In this context, I would like to mention the life of an upstart named Ganesh in *The Mystic Masseur* and his journey through different professions in Trinidad. Ganesh as a third generation Indian begins his life in Fuente Grove, a deserted and a barren place in Trinidad, after his marriage to Leela. Soon after his marriage calamities shroud him because he is informed that the oil-rich fields purchased by his father is drained off, therefore he is not entitled to receive money as the owner of those fields. He spends excessively on buying books and in that way he spends the money he had received as dowry. He decides to become a massager to earn his livelihood. It is the sheer fluke of his lock which makes him a mystic because he heals a boy suffering from strange hallucinations. This paves his way to politics and to become a writer. This is an example which entails how a third generation Indian lives a successful life through his own effort. A land which is not ancestrally his becomes his land in the course of time. The problems which Ganesh's grandfather and his father faced are not his problems now. The other remains as the other as long as we think it as the other. The other is a projection and the self's contradiction. The self's suppositions about the other is often nothing but a sum total of negations which the former always intends to avoid. Such is the assumption of the inexperienced self. After a short or long proximity, the truth about the other is revealed. The self corrects its preconceptions. Once accepted nothing remains as the other. Nowhere in the novel Ganesh shows any interest to return to India, instead he plans to prosper there. Witnessing the chaotic political conditions in Trinidad he never intends to go back to India but he prefers London to India. Staying in London he also anglicises his name. It would be too naive to say that Ganesh forgets India but it can be stated that the nostalgia of the first generation for the past does not remain with him. He does not see India the way his preceding generations used to see and feel about it remaining away from it.

In *The Suffrages of Elvira* all the male characters are involved in politics because of the forthcoming election. They are not found wrestling with idea of their ancestral homeland. India is no more the topic of their discussion but the Trinidad politics and the election. Chitranjan, Ramlogan, Baksh, Foam, Lookhoor, Mahadeo, and Dhaniram constantly make plans to elect Mr. Surajpat Harbans, their local representative. Their confidence and interest in the local politics indicate their rootedness. The anguish for the absent is not apparent on them. The exodus of the past has become the narratives of history which is only read occasionally to have the knowledge of their root. Trinidad is no more a second home for them. Now they do not search for a house to take shelter in like Mr. Biswas in *A House for Mr Biswas* (1961), they aspire for participating in the governing mechanisms of the state. They have overcome the phase which made them feel insecure. Time offers them different avenues to get preoccupied with. Home is something not to be constantly looked for. It is to be made where you are. Trinidad now becomes their home. Initially, necessity forces them to adjust and subsequently it leads to claiming their rights. They make their way into politics to ensure their stability. Now India not only appears distant in distance but also in prospects. It is just an imaginative presence to be occasionally reflected on. Such instances entail the very affirmation of the other.

Here one can observe a shift from the fulfilment of the basic necessities of existence to the aspiration of the political rights. This evolution of consciousness of a people in the history of Trinidad and by extension of the Caribbean sounds perhaps similar to Hegel's idea of history. He states that the consciousness of a people in history progresses from the inchoate to the complete in an evolutionary fashion. Here it seems apposite to mention Aristotle's statement in *Metaphysics* to substantiate the logic behind the progress of history: "When pressing needs are satisfied, the human being turns to what is higher and more general" (84). However, one can notice here the shift of the Caribbean history from the sentimental and imaginative melodrama to the practical and rational endeavour. This appears to be the evolution of the consciousness and of course of the operation of the reason. Naipaul here seems also closer to Herder who believes in evolution as determined by nature to prepare a people for the next stage. If history, according to Fichte, is the analysis of the present, Naipaul in his description of the Caribbean lives analyses the present. However, if one attempts a scrutiny of his narrative technique, they can find Naipaul's description is implicitly analytical.

Works Cited

Koselleck, Reinhart. *Futures Past: On the Semantics of Historical Time*. New York: Columbia University Press, 2004.

Naipaul, V.S. *A House for Mr Biswas*. London: Andre Deutsch, 1961.

——. *India: A Million Mutinies Now* (1990). London: Minerva, 1991.

——. *The Mimic Men* (1967). London: Picador, 2002.

——. *The Mystic Masseur* (1957). Middlesex: Penguin Books, 1964.

——. *The Suffrages of Elvira*. London: Andre Deutsch, 1958.

Plato. *Phaedrus*. Trans. Alexander Nehamas and Paul Woodruff. Indianapolis: Hackett, 1997.

Ricoeur, Paul. *History and Truth*. Trans. Charles A. Kelbley. Evanston: North-Western University Press, 1965.

——. *Memory, History, Forgetting*. Trans. Kathleen Blamey and David Pellauer. Chicago: University of Chicago Press, 2004.

5

V.S. Naipaul's *Half a Life*: A Study of Powerless Group of the Third World Women

Sayantan Pal Chowdhury

Introduction

V.S. Naipual was born in 1932 in Chaguanas, Trinidad and Tobago. Most of his novels are travelogues and focusing British Empire's colonialism. His view towards the women's writing that he considered inferior to men's, invites much criticism. He also criticised many female writers of the past. Naipaul was of the opinion that women's writing was quite different for their narrow view of the world. In his novel *Half a Life* (2001), he explores women as secondary, sometimes in the hands of the male characters in the novel. The novel has some post-colonial aspects also. The male character of the novel, Willie Somerset Chandran is parented by a Brahmin father and a Dalit mother. His middle name was homage to the writer Somerset Maugham who was for some times familiar to his father. His father was living a life of silence at that time when Maugham visited him. The novel begins with this homage, "Willie Chandran asked his father one day, 'Why is my middle name Somerset? The boys at school have just found out, and they are mocking me.'" His father said without joy, "You were named after a great English writer. I am sure you have seen his books about the house. 'But I haven't read them. Did you admire him so much?' 'I am not sure. Listen, and make up your own mind'" (*HAL* 1).

It was the 1930s when he describes his visit with the writer in his own words: "The principal of the Maharaja's college brought him to me. I was doing penance for something I had done, and I was living as a mendicant in the outer courtyard of the big temple" (*HAL* 1). And again he says about his vow of silence, "I was in a state of nerve because of this persecution, and to calm myself I had also taken a vow of silence. This had won me a certain amount of local respect, even renowned. People would come to look at me being silent and some would bring me gifts" (*HAL* 1). He said nothing to the writer. In front of him the Maharaja and the writer talked, but he remained silent. He did not know anything about the writer at the time he first met him. He read English literature. But to respond in Mahatma's call, he withdrew learning English and unfitted himself for life. But he was surprised when eighteen months later the writer in a travel book wrote the name of Willi's father. Though the account was very small in quantity, it was enough to make him famous.

Willie set for London to study leaving India in the 1950s. He was living a life of an immigrant there. He managed to publish his short story which was read by Ana, a mixed Portuguese and Black African girl. They met and fell in love. Willie followed her in her country somewhere in the colony of Africa. Willie's sister Sarojini in the meantime met a German and accompanied him to Berlin. After staying in Africa for eighteen years Willie moved to his sister in Berlin. Here ends the novel.

The use of the term "third world" has many controversial implications. In *Women in Developing Countries: A Reference Handbook* (2011), Karen L. Kinnear accepts the fact that the terms third or first world is problematic today: "In previous decades, the commonly used term was Third World Countries, rather than developing countries. Third World is still used today, but fewer people, organizations, and governments are using this term because of political and economic changes in the world, as well as the negative connotation of the term to many people" (1). He shows the distinction of the countries as the first or third world countries thus which was hitherto considered:

> First world countries are industrialized, democratic countries, such as United States, Canada, many European

> countries, Australia, New Zealand, Japan and other countries that are not considered communist. Second World countries refers to countries that were part of the communist bloc, including Poland, Hungary, Romania, Bulgaria, the former Soviet Union, China, and Cuba. Today, the line between Second and Third world countries has blurred, and together, many of these countries are considered emerging or developing countries.... (*Ibid.*)

But without going into the controversies I have used the term to refer to the modern world that is touched by every kind of theoretical practices and modern ways of life after the demolition of the colonies. In the title of my paper "third world" is less important than "power". There is a historical relation between women and power. The allocation of power within the society of men and women is not balanced. In the present paper, I have given more importance to the allocation of power and the binary situation of the genders in our present day world or "third world". In the notes to her paper "Under Western Eyes" Chandra Talpade Mohanty expresses her thanks to S.P. Mohanty and Biddy Martin for their discussion about feminine theory and politics. She backs up his use of the term "third world" thus:

> Terms such as third and first world are very problematic both in suggesting oversimplified similarities between and among countries labelled thus, and in implicitly reinforcing existing economic, cultural and ideological hierarchies which are conjured up in using such terminology. I use the term "third world" with full awareness of its problems, only because this is the terminology available to u at the moment. The use of quotation marks is meant to suggest a continuous questioning of the designation. Even when I do not use quotation marks, I mean to use the term critically. (Mohanty 482)

Hence, whenever and wherever the term third world is used here, it always has a critical implication. Even the title of my paper also bears the same. The distinction among the countries as first or third world is still problematical and invites many critical comments.

Lives of Sacrifice: the Sister or the Sisters

V.S. Naipaul's *Half a Life* is more in the form of two biographies—the first tells about Willie's father's life compressed within first thirty pages, and the second is that of Willie's own. Or we can say that these two 'half lives' comprise this complete novel. The two men wanted and tried to lead the lives of sacrifice, but the circumstances prevented them. An ideal of sacrifice never becomes clear to them. Whereas Willie's father's life of sacrifice starts with the burning of *The Mayor of Casterbridge,* though he gives an account of his violence as, "Nothing happened. Nobody seemed to have told my father anything. No message came from the dean" (*HAL* 9) and accepting the woman in his life who was rejected by his father, Willie's sacrifice lies in living the life of Ana in Africa, a foreign country. Both the sacrifices are different in their values. But are there only two sacrifices dealing in this book? If the novel is a complete work of modern art of a collage of different images of Willie's and his father's, what do the importance or relevance of the women characters those who came in touch with Willie and his father? Does the term sacrifice only signify the sacrifices of the male characters? Because a little conversation between Willie and his father give ample instance of such a situation where sacrifice is only on the part of the male members. To quote from the novel:

> Willie Chandran said, "What is there for me in what you have said? You offer me nothing." His father said, "It has been a life of sacrifice. I have no riches to offer you. All I have are my friendships. That is all my treasure." "What about poor Sarojini?" "I will speak you frankly. I feel she was sent to try us. I can tell you nothing about her appearance that you don't already know. Her prospects in this country are not bright. But foreigners have their own ideas of beauty and certain other things, and all I can hope for Sarojini is an international marriage." (*HAL* 35-36)

Whereas for Willie, his father offers a life of sacrifice and all his friendships, for Sarojini he plans for an "international marriage". Her worth lies in the institution called marriage and nothing else. The social system has remained unchanged even in this twenty-first century. Later when an international marriage really took place, his father is worried about "poor Sarojini" even though his prediction comes true. In a letter to Willie he writes, ".... You will know that I always felt that Sarojini's only hope lay in an international marriage, but I must say this took me by surprise...I don't know where this thing will end or how it will work out for poor Sarojini" (*HAL* 113). In a patriarchal society the position of women is decided within and by the group of male members. We have seen that historically women have been tortured by the powerful group of men whether in the family kinship or outside the boundary of family. Their fate is decided by the male members of society. Sarojini's case in this respect is quite similar to the preceding events of women oppression and subordination.

But, with the change of time, situation has changed also. Sarojini is not directly suppressed in the group. She is not *given marriage*; rather, she *goes away* with *a* German, a photographer by profession, "an oldish man with a bad leg" (*HAL* 112). The difference of this event from the early ages is that earlier women as group were oppressed by the patriarchal families who used to choose grooms for their bride girls. She instead of being a member of the oppressed group of the 'third world countries' has walked miles away from the old ideas and broken institutions approaching to the new world. When she writes a letter to Willie from Columbia, her straightforwardness is best revealed. She writes, "I am glad you've at last got the diploma, though I don't know what you will do with it where you are going. Serious work has to be done in Africa, especially in those Portuguese places, but I don't think it will be done by you. You are like your father, holding on to old ideas till the end" (*HAL* 131). She has got revolutionary ideas from her German man with whom she had gone away. She does not wait for any other way to find freedom from male bondage. We have often seen that many women have become vocal to restate their position in the society or as many critics have said that lesbianism have become many times their arm to get freedom from male domain. Sarojini is far from choosing these ways to freedom. She doesn't wait for others' advice or order. Though her father had some plans regarding her marriage, she vanished one day abruptly without informing anyone and started to live a happy-go-lucky life.

But in spite of the revolutionary ideas imbued in her life and proving some of the traits of the modern 'third world countries' by being a free thinker Sarojini still is a sister like Shakespeare's 'imaginary sister' of Woolf. Though Woolf writes,

> ...reviewing the story of Shakespeare's sister as I had made it, is that any woman born with a great gift in the sixteenth century would certainly have gone crazed, shot herself, or ended her days in some lonely cottage outside the village, half witch, half wizard, feared and mocked at. For it needs little skill in psychology to be sure that a highly gifted girl who had tried to use her gift for poetry would have been so thwarted and hindered by other people, so tortured and pulled would asunder by her own contrary instincts, that she must have lost her health and sanity to a certainty. (898)

The condition of these sisters is still objective. They are the objects to the subject brothers. In the later part of the story to the very end the importance of Sarojini is as a passive listener of Willie's life story. Her presence in this part of the novel is not an important one because as a subject she has nothing to do. She is not only *passive* but more accurately she is *inactive*. She remains silent for the rest of the book. Or more exactly her voice has been taken away to be dominated by the male power represented by Willie. She has been objectified by the male voice. The male power is inflicted upon her female voice as it is often done in kinship system of society. As Mohanty has pointed out from Cowie,

> ...women as women are not *located* within the family. Rather, it is *in* the family, as an effect of kinship structures that women as women are *constructed,* defined within and by the group.... Not only is it problematical to speak of a vision of women shared by Arab and Muslim societies (i.e., over twenty different countries) without addressing the particular historical, material and ideological power structures that construct such images, but to speak of

> the patriarchal family or the tribal kinship structure as the origin of the socio-economic status of women is to again assume that women are sexual-political subjects prior to their entry into the family. So while on the other hand women attain value or status within the family, the assumption of a singular patriarchal kinship system (common to all Arab and Muslim societies) is what apparently structures women as an oppressed group in thee societies! This singular, coherent kinship system presumably influences another separate and given entity, "women". Thus, all women, regardless of class and cultural differences, are affected by this system. (Mohanty 470)

In this kinship structure Sarojini's position is objective, though the noticeable thing is that her revolutionary zeal could not bow her as the absence of it has stooped the women characters discussed below. She becomes a victim of private patriarchy, as Kinnear points out that "patriarchy can be both public and private. Private patriarchy generally is practiced in the family environment, while public patriarchy is practiced by the state and within public activities such as government and the economy" (Kinnear 5).

The Woman

Though Ana's presence in Willie's life had much importance, she appears at the middle of the story as an admirer of Willie. She has to be kept so by Willie himself. But Willie's thoughts worried him shortly. "Willie didn't want the woman to be let down. He wanted her to stay an admirer. This line of thinking led him the other way, to worrying about himself. He began to worry that the woman might not find him good enough for the book he had written, not attractive enough or with presence enough" (*HAL* 125). But all his anxieties vanished as soon as he saw her. She became the source for the stories of Willie's books. She told him the story of a school friend, the story of Luisa the adopted child, and next the story of a dowdy and unhappy girl at the boarding school. Willie on hearing the story of the "unhappy girl in the frightening, destructive bush of her African country, was Ana. He thought it explained her thinness, her nervousness. It increased his feeling for her" (*HAL* 129). It is a certain kind of sympathy that attracted Willie towards Ana. Was it love of Willie for Ana, or only an abstract feeling for her that much attracted him to her? The answer to this question is better resolved at the ending of the novel when Willie in his epiphanic moment is impelled to reject Ana and her country and her life that he wished to live to return to his own life. This unhappy girl became the victim of sexual abuses within the family by her step-father who took interest in her and went into the girl's bedroom one night. It not only created much topsy-turvy in their world but once again proved the helplessness of the powerless under the dictatorship of the powerful.

Willie wished to go to Ana's country to live her lie there "for good". Her story that Willie related to her own life-story aroused his feelings for her. The manliness in him got the virility for which Willie had been struggling for years. The girl from Africa gave him the "new feeling of being accepted as a man and being in his own eyes complete" (*HAL* 125) in which he began to luxuriate. He went to Africa with her in her grandfather's house and lived there happily till another woman replaced Ana. Willie engaged in an illegitimate sexual relationship with her without giving a single air to Ana about it. His mind was so immersed in the thoughts of this physical relationship that he could not remember about the betrayal he was going to process for Ana. Later when he retells Sarojini about his life in Africa, he accounts the chain of betrayals made against such women like Ana, "They made me think of everyone who had slept in that carved bed before me: Ana's grandfather, turning away from the African woman who had borne her children; Ana's mother, betrayed by her husband and then by her lover; and Ana's father, who had betrayed everybody. I didn't feel that evening that I had betrayed Ana in any important or final way" (*HAL* 188). The betrayals are going on for many centuries in matters of physical satisfaction in the society irrespective of the colonies and their oppressors. And Willie not only betrayed Ana, but the woman also to whom he engaged in another relationship. Though Ana gave him the first approval of masculinity and made him able to prove his power against a woman, when Willie became quite worthy in it, he tried to free himself from the bondage of Ana to try other women as soon as Ana helped him to identify his own self and his gendered position in the society.

The Women: The Group

After having been failed in intercourse when Willie asked Percy Cato how the latter manages so well in such a situation to take a hold over women, Percy generalizes that brutality is the key to this way.

> When he next saw Percy he asked, "How did you learn about sex, Percy?"
>
> Percy said, "You have to start small. We all started small. Practising on the little girls. Don't look so shocked, little Willie. I am sure you don't know everything that was happening in your extended family. Your trouble, Willie, is that you are too neat. People look at you and don't see you."
>
> "You are neater than me. Always in a suit and a nice shirt."
>
> "I make women nervous. They are frightened of me. That's the way for you, Willie. Sex is a brutal business. You have to be brutal."
>
> "Is June frightened of you?"
>
> "She is scared stiff of me. Ask her." (*HAL* 71)

There are two aspects in this generalization. Firstly, the male power over the women power which is surely lesser than the male power, otherwise Percy could not be able to exercise his power over June and advice Willie to do the same. This is the hierarchy in power where men are powerful and is at the top of the hierarchy and women as the powerless at the lower level. Secondly, on the part of women whose *masochism* allows the male power to be exercised over them? As Mitchell has put it, "'Masochism'—pleasure in pain—which is the turning against the self of the wish for the satisfaction of a drive, typifies the feminine predicament it expresses the wish to submit to castration, copulation or childbirth and to get erotic pleasure out of painful experiences. But feminine masochism is of course inherent within both sexes" (Mitchell 114). But Willie in his first days could hardly exercise this brutality as advised by Percy. He failed with every woman he arranged meetings that led both of them to failure. But as the days went by he became an expert in this act as in cases of Ana or later with Graca. Willie used all of these women to prove his masculinity as opposed to their femininity. When he succeeded in this act, he started to feel good as being accepted as a *man*.

June, Perditta, Serefina, the prostitute, the little girl of about eleven on the days of her first period, Carla, Graca and last but not the least Ana all are used in the novel by their male partners to prove their masculinity. Sarojini is not out of track from this group of powerless women. Her position in her family and later in the novel her silent passive existence objectify her position. The binary of power distribution in developed of developing or underdeveloped countries still remains. Women are oppressed as group that could hardly exercise their power over the male power.

To sum up the long-drawn battle between the two powers in which one is always privileged, I want to quote from Mohanty,

> What characterizes women as a group is their gender (sociologically, not necessarily biologically, defined) over and above everything else, indicating a monolithic notion of sexual difference. Because women are thus constituted as a coherent group, sexual difference becomes coterminous with female subordination, and power is automatically defined in binary terms: people who have it (read: men), and people who do not (read: women). Men exploit, women are exploited. Such simplistic formulations are historically reductive; they are also ineffectual in designing strategies to combat oppressions. All they do is reinforcing binary divisions between men and women. (Mohanty 473)

This binary of men/women is not satisfactory in our practical world. The allocation of power has not only made men the privileged, a division within women is also privileged. In the hierarchy of gender men are not always established on the higher position then women. Women also inflict torture upon women in our social milieu. There are two groups within the group of women: one is powerful that is constituted with those women who torment the other group of women who are tortured. In such case, the binary becomes women/women, not men/women. If we take 'Women' for the powerful group and 'women' for the powerless, Mohanty has shown for instance, how Western women are powerful or becomes the subject and the third world women are powerless or the object.

> What happens when this assumption of "women as an oppressed group" is situated in the context of Western feminist writing about third world women? It is here that I locate the colonialist move. By contrasting the representation of women in the third world with what I referred to earlier as Western feminisms' self-presentation in the same context, we see how Western feminists alone become the true "subjects" of this counter history. Third world women, on the other hand, never rise above the deliberating generality of their "object" status. (Mohanty 479)

When Willie becomes more attached to Graca and doesn't bother about Ana any more at the end of the novel, the binary becomes woman vs. woman; in the hierarchy one woman is privileged and another is subjected to deprivation. The allocation of power is not balanced within the same group. For Willie's lack of self-confidence and identity crisis in the gendered world, he uses women as the touchstones of his masculinity. And in doing so he has always privileged one woman over the other. He says, "I began to arrange my life around my meetings with Graca, and I didn't care who noticed. With one part of my mind I was amazed at myself, amazed at the person I had become" (*HAL* 206). Again when he first met Graca, he discovers,

> The first thing I noticed about her light-coloured eyes; they made me think again about her husband. And the second thing I noticed was that, for a second or two, no more, those eyes had looked at me in a way that no woman had looked at me before. I had the absolute certainty, in that second, that those eyes had taken me in not as Ana's husband or a

> man of unusual origin, but as a man who had spend many hours in the warm cubicles of the places of pleasure. Sex comes to us in different ways; it alters us; and I suppose in the end we carry te nature of our experience on our faces. The moment lasted a second. It might have been fantasy, that reading of the woman's eyes, but it was a discovery of me, something about women, and something to be added to my sensual education. (*HAL* 198)

Though I have extracted from the novel a long passage, it is not merely to show how Willie discovers himself or his identity. We cannot reject the fact about his self-discovery. But more important to me here is the fact that unknowingly Willie through his self-discovery has distinguished women both as a powerful group and a powerless group within the same group. Each time he met with a woman he accepts her and rejects the other. June, Perditta, Serafina, Carla and even Ana also fall in the group of deprived. And at last when Graca is privileged, this position is not static. When the guerrillas took over and life in the colonies was changed, Graca was quite despaired. Willie was becoming disillusioned. He ventured to state that, "I didn't think I could live through another war. I could see that it would have a point for Ana. I didn't see that it had a point for me. For some weeks I was perplexed. I didn't know what to do. I suppose I didn't have the courage to tell Ana" (*HAL* 227).

The "another war" is not the war that was going in the background. The guerrillas and the Portuguese and the tribal war has very little to do in the life of Willie or Ana. But it is the war that was going in the psychology. The choice of life and its illusion gripped Willie's life at the end very dramatically. He states exhaustively, "I am forty-one. I am tired of living your life" (*HAL* 227). Both of them discovered that they were not living their own lives. Ana also realizes, "Perhaps it wasn't my really my life either" (*HAL* 228). But from an overview in this half-living the women characters become only the puppets in the hands of power, as if power itself is individualised.

Works Cited

Kinnear, Karen L. *Women in Developing Countries: A Reference Handbook*. California: ABC-CLIO, LLC, 2011.

Mitchell, Juliet. *Psychoanalysis and Feminism* (1974). USA: Basic Books, 2000.

Mohanty, Chandra Talpade. "Under Western Eyes." *Media and Cultural Studies Keywords,* Eds. Durham and Kellner. USA: Blackwell Publishing, 2004. 462-87.

Naipaul, V.S. *Half a Life*. London: Picador, 2001.

Woolf, Virginia. "Shakespeare's Sister." *The Norton Anthology of Theory and Criticism*. Ed. Vincent B. Leitch. New York: W.W. Norton and Company, 2010. 892-905.

6

The Concept of Migration and Exile in V.S. Naipaul—A Selective Study

Paramita Ghosh

Born in Trinidad in 1932, the descendant of indentured labourers shipped from India, Vidiadhar Surajprasad Naipaul himself admits to be immensely shaped by his experiences of the material and cultural deprivations in his colonial birthplace. Naipaul has not only produced actual travel narratives that have become in/famous for various reasons; he has also effectively incorporated travel writing in a large number of his novels in a significant way. *In a Free State*, his 1971 Booker Prize winning novel, presents the themes of cultural incommensurability and the broken symmetry of colonial relationships from the traveler's point of view. The plight of the uprooted former colonial becomes a metaphor for modern restlessness here, and homelessness and exile are seen as a contemporary state of mind afflicting all in this novel. *A Bend in the River* (1979) vividly describes the disorder in the wake of imperialism and the problems of emergent but underdeveloped Third World people caught between old tribal ways and the new technology of dangerous arms and tinsel consumer materialism in a small town in 'New Africa' through the eyes of a Muslim migrant, Salim, who journeys to the interior of Africa in search of a new life, is uprooted from there and undertakes another journey to an indefinite future. *The Enigma of Arrival* (1987), a partly autobiographical novel by Naipaul, describes the narrator's exodus from Trinidad to England. The quixotic quest for an ideal homeland, however, eludes the travelling narrator as he feels constantly out of place even after arriving in the England of his fantasies where he finds a decaying empire that does little to satisfy his sense of homelessness.

Half a Life (2001) presents the life of Willie Chandran who moves to London from India, marries a woman of African origin and then moves to Africa where he witnesses the breaking down of the colonial system there. He, however, remains an outsider in the crumbling society while his existential search continues as he leaves Africa and goes to Germany. Naipaul's last novel, *Magic Seeds* (2004), takes over this existential search of Willie from *Half a Life* and presents his adventures which shift between the post-war Britain and India. As these novels testify, Naipaul, born of Indian ancestry in Trinidad, appears unable to form any tender association as a global/cosmopolitan traveller with his heritage, be it Trinidadian, Indian, or even British. Partly owing to this status of his as a rootless wanderer, as a man without heritage to guide him, Naipaul consistently refuses the idealized views of the places he/his protagonists journeys to, be they England, Trinidad, Africa, or India and appears in search of a truth that is complex, bitter, and even contradictory as the novels mentioned above demonstrate.

In *The Empire Writes Back* (1989) Ashcroft, Griffiths and Tiffin touch upon this significant and much talked about aspect of post-colonial literature when they note the element of the crisis of identity in it to be concerned with the "development or recovery of an effective identifying relationship between self and place". But as they also observe, this post-colonial 'self' has become fragmentary because of displacements by migration, enslavement, transportation, or the much common imperial practice of indentured labour (8-9). While contemporary theory and literature have never failed to address this essentially dispiriting aspect of the post-colonial world, critics like John Phillips, on the other hand, find that the rootless colonial/decolonized migrant is "nomadic in essence, begins in travel, or with a lost beginning, an essentially irreversible trajectory, and has nowhere to return" (Phillips 65). In V.S. Naipaul, the controversial literary master, we can expect to find the reflections of all these sentiments to enable us to investigate the layers and varieties of meanings associated with the subjects of migration and exile in the post-globalized world that many find to be striving towards a single cosmopolitan identity.

As it appears, in almost all other contemporary writers like Salman Rushdie or Amitav Ghosh, migration and exile are found to negate the notions of 'home' and fixed positionality in the post-colonial world. They also situate the diasporic subject as a representative protagonist rather than a marginalized exile with her/his ever-renewing constructions of a homeland or home throughout the course of migration/exile. Naipaul's protagonists, on the other hand, though as rootless, are often led by the event of migration/exile to a bitter disappointment at being unable to find the idealized place they cherish in their mind as their home/homeland. And although Naipaul, like these other contemporary writers, presents his protagonists to be enforced migrants in a chaotic colonial and post-colonial world, they like Salim in *A Bend in the River* (*Bend*), Willie in *Half a Life* (*Half*) and *Magic Seeds* (*Magic*), or the unnamed narrator of *The Enigma of Arrival* (*Enigma*) are almost always found to enter the role of a migrant to escape from a spiritual or social disorder that threatens their sense of identity and desire for self-realization.

In Naipaul, thus, migration and exile appear to be much more a result of a conscious and deliberate choice of the migrants to avoid remaining in or returning to a home that they consider discreditable and pitiful to the extent of stifling their desire for self-actualization. Salim or Indar in *Bend*, for example, migrate to other places to escape what they think an unavoidable disintegration in every sphere of life. As in the words of Salim: "I had to break away from our family compound and our community. To stay with my community, to pretend that I had simply to travel along with them, was to be taken with them to destruction. I could be master of my fate only if I stood alone" (22). Willie and Sarojini in *Half* and *Magic* and the narrator of *Enigma* too choose to migrate, leaving the ties of their home land behind to search for or arrive at a place that can sustain their ambition for self-realization that their respective homes cannot offer. But alongside the migrant's desire to search for the

Promised Land in Naipaul is also present the migrant's hatred for a home that he desperately tries to disown. As for example, in *Half*, we find Willie becoming depressed even at the slightest contact with home, like getting a letter from his family while living abroad: "Willie could easily imagine himself back there, without hope. For that reason the first sight of these letters from home was depressing, and the depression could stay with him, its cause forgotten, after he had read the letter" (111-12).

The narrator of *Enigma* too shows the same desperation to disown his past when on the ship to England he finds himself surrounded by other migrants travelling to the West, sharing a journey similar to that of his: "in each there were aspects of myself. But with my Asiatic background, I resisted the comparison; and I was travelling to be a writer. It was too frightening to accept the other thing, to face the other thing" (137-38).

However, perhaps because of the idealized nature of the adopted country that the traveller in Naipaul presupposes while completely rejecting his homeland, the first moment of contact between the eager migrant and the new country never confirms his preconceptions about the new land and almost verges on disappointment. As the narrator of *Enigma* remarks after his first view of London and its grandness: "I grew to feel that the grandeur belonged to the past; that I had come to England at the wrong time; that I had come too late to find the England, the heart of empire, which (like a provincial, from a far corner of the empire) I had created in my fantasy" (141). In *Half*, Willie's first reaction after arriving at his cherished 'fairyland of splendour and dazzle' (England once again) is also of disappointment: "he felt let down. He didn't know what he was looking at.... He was disappointed by Buckingham Palace. He thought the maharaja's palace in his own state was far grander, more like a palace.... His disappointment turned to something like shame—at himself, for his gullibility" (52).

Nonetheless, it is also these first moments of contact that introduce to us the persona of the migrant that is constructed completely by a Eurocentric system of education. Thus, as the narrator of *Enigma* realizes: "But in spite of my education, I was under-read. What did I know of England? The London I knew or imaginatively possessed was the London I got from Dickens. It was Dickens—and his illustrators—who gave me the illusion of knowing the city" (144). But as the adopted country—though only if it is the West—gradually grows on the migrant in Naipaul; it is suggested that the first note of disappointment was actually triggered by the untrained and raw, thus inherently flawed, perception of the newly arrived migrant. But later, as the traveller begins to experience a new sense of liberation in his adopted country, he also comes to admit the infinite and universal greatness of the foreign land that not only makes him a better and wiser person but at times also heals the old wounds—spiritual, emotional or intellectual—inflicted on his psyche by his deplorable homeland. Thus, although Salim, coming from "the bush" in *Bend* finds England as "something shrunken and mean and forbidding" (269) immediately after setting foot on it, cannot but admire the great city before leaving it: "There you really did have an idea of the city as something made by man, and not as something that had just grown by itself and was simply there.... It was so easy for people like us to think of great cities as natural growths. It reconciled us to our own shanty cities" (272).

A migration to a non-Western place, on the other hand, can disintegrate a person in Naipaul. Salim in *Bend*, for example, realizes that his passionate, but immoral affair with Yvette was possible only because he was in the central Africa and away from home where his life in his family and community was 'full of rules' and where "Adultery was horrible to me. I continued to think of it in the setting of family and community on the coast, and saw it as sly and dishonourable and weak-willed" (224). What therefore initially appeared to Salim as liberation from rules, soon leads both him and Yvette to a disgraceful separation thus reflecting his anxiety accompanying his initial sense of freedom: "I had stripped myself of the support the rules gave. To think of it was to feel myself floating and lost" (*ibid.*).

The situation is however quite opposite in the event of a migration to a Western country, where the traveller finds that s/he has to pay a very small price to be allowed into a land of infinite wonder. Willie in *Half*, for example, has to accommodate himself to an altogether new way of living once he migrates to London that at first seems hugely unsettling to him: "He had to learn how to eat in public. He had to learn how to greet people.... He had to learn to close doors behind him. He had to learn how to ask for things without being peremptory" (59). But the price seems to be too insignificant once Willie becomes overwhelmed by the benefits his new life showers on him, when he discovers that the old rules of his home were in reality "a kind of make-believe, self-imposed", and finally observes "with great clarity that the old rules no longer bound him.... The possibilities were dizzying. He could, within reason, re-make himself and his past and his ancestry" (60).

Migration liberates not only Willie, even his otherwise unremarkable and conservative sister Sarojini also becomes a new woman—more confident, authoritative and attractive—once she is married to a German and leaves India to settle down in Germany. As Willie is surprised to find this new woman in his sister in *Half*, he also realizes that "None of this would have come out if the German hadn't come and taken her away. If he hadn't come, would she and all her soul have just rotted to nothing? She was attractive now—something impossible to think of in the ashram days..." (138).

Willie, however, appears to be quite oblivious to the price Sarojini has to pay for this new woman in her. Wolf, Sarojini's German husband, becomes such a towering person in her life that she remains nothing but an intellectual slave to him—while he, as she admiringly admits throughout *Half* and *Magic*, fashioned the ignorant Sarojini into her present attractive form by his own world view. Even later, when Willie and Sarojini miserably fail in their attempts to revolutionize Indian society while following Wolf's visions, it is the irreversible disintegration of the Indian society that they blame, not Wolf's unrealistic, Eurocentric notions. Unwilling to acknowledge the fact that their Eurocentric world view has left no other place but the West for them to live in, Willie leaves for England while Saro goes back to her intellectual master and husband Wolf who, as she writes to Willie, "without one word of rebuke has promised to do what he can for me in Berlin. It will be nice to make a few documentaries again" (*Magic* 237).

But it is in *Enigma* where Naipaul not only carefully elaborates on the price the migrant has to pay to arrive at and stay in the land of his life long fantasy—England; but also on how the migrant's adopted country, in spite of his raw nerves and hesitant apprehensions, time and again heals the wounds of his colonial past and present. As the narrator feels, he could never stop carrying within himself the anxieties and apprehensions of a colonial migrant into an imperial centre: "I still had that nervousness in a new place, that rawness of response, still felt myself to be in the other man's country, felt my strangeness, my solitude" (5-6). That the narrator, even after a long time of arrival at England still experiences the apprehensions of a rootless, colonial migrant is again apparent in his constant anxiety about his stay in the country: "What accidents had given me my life in the cottage! What accidents protected it! How little it would have taken to alter the whole feel of the place, and to drive me away!" (72). Another price that the narrator has to pay at arrival is however an inevitable one: "I lost a faculty that had been part of me and precious to me for years. I lost the gift of fantasy, the dream of the future, the far-off place where I was going.... Now in the place that for all those years had been the 'elsewhere', no further dream was possible" (146).

The narrator, however, prefers to live as a migrant in England even at such a cost, as the slightest possibility of going back to Trinidad makes the narrator realize in utter panic that "the only thing I could do, the only way I could look after myself, was to be in England—no longer now a country of fantasy, but simply a place where as a writer I might make a living" (163). Likewise, when the time to leave his manor cottage arrives, it remains one of the most tender moments he shares with his adopted country; while in another moment of poignant admission the narrator reasserts the nature of his relationship with his adopted country where "I felt protected, isolated, far from every wounding thing I had known" (184).

Related to the way the migrant is looked at by the world around her/him is the way the migrant looks at the world around her/him. Thus, the squalor of the town Salim migrates to in *Bend* is pointed out to him by another migrant, Indar, "looking at the place with his eyes, I was amazed at the little I had been living with. And I had stopped seeing so much...I had thought of the town as a real town; I saw it now as an agglomeration of shack settlements" (134). It is Indar once again who looks at the India—his ancestral homeland—through the India House in London and finds a different world altogether than the one that has been handed down to him by his family: "I studied the large framed photographs of Gandhi and Nehru and wondered how, out of squalor like this, those men had managed to get themselves considered as men. It was strange, in that building in the heart of London, seeing those great men in this new way, from the inside, as it were" (171).

Nazruddin in *Bend* too finds a different London than the one he had expected to find once he migrates to it: "London is destroying itself for its tourist trade—you can see that here. Hundreds of houses, thousands of flats, have been emptied to provide hotels, hostels and restaurants for the tourists" (277). Quite in the same vein the narrator of *Enigma* too finds himself as part of a dereliction process at the heart of the formerly imperial England: "the process of contraction, though begun twenty or twenty-five years before, had recently accelerated; and that my own presence there was a part of that accelerating process" (240). Willie in *Magic* too finds himself among strangers when he joins the guerrilla movement to fight for social justice, but finds half-lives instead of revolutionaries who make him wonder "what weakness or failure had caused them...to leave the outer world and to enter this strange chamber...some kind of sexual perversion...hard or abused childhoods and tormented adult lives..." (52).

The im/possibility to return home for the migrant/exile, however, receives a completely different treatment in Naipaul who is less concerned with the deferred possibilities or impossibility of return to a homeland and more with the enigma of arrival. This enigma of arrival in Naipaul, on the other hand, negates the possibility of an absolute separation of the traveller from his past to enable him to arrive at the first place, and thereby leaves the traveller suspended in the process of migration/exile itself. Thus, Willie, who could not make Africa his home even after living in there for eighteen years, reflects his inability to arrive at the very first moment of reaching the country in *Half*, "I don't know where I am. I don't think I can pick my way back. I don't ever want this view to become familiar. I must not unpack. I must never behave as though I am staying" (135). The migrant, caught between a home he had disowned and a destination that eludes him, finally tries to reconcile himself with his role as an eternal migrant, as Salim realizes in *Bend*: "There could be no going back; there was nothing to go back to. We had become what the world outside had made us; we had to live in the world as it existed" (286). But the way this 'world' existed to the characters in Naipaul was always the one where the 'home' was lost even before the traveller could conceive the possibility of a journey, thereby complicating the concept of arrival in its turn.

The attitude towards the mass immigrants is even more notable in Naipaul. As compared to the description of the transportation of labourers in the novelists like Ghosh (in the novels like *The Glass Palace* or *Sea of Poppies*), Salim's views on the slaves being transported from the heart of Africa to the European countries in *Bend* is surprisingly different and rather focuses on the element of travel than on the defenseless traveller:

> The further away they got from the centre and their tribal area, the less liable they were to cut loose from the caravans and run back home, the more nervous they became of the strange Africans they saw about them, until at the end, on the coast, they were no trouble at all, and were positively anxious to step into the boats and be taken to safe homes across the sea.... The greater the discouragements of the journey, the keener...to press on and embrace...new life. (4)

Naipaul not only erases the imperial presence in the background of the middle passage in the days of Empire; even in the post-colonial England to the mass migration to him acquires an altogether different meaning—something that throws the spotlight on the grand centre and not on the immigrants:

> Cities like London were to change. They were to cease being more or less national cities; they were to become cities of the world, modern-day Romes, establishing the pattern of what great cities should be, in the eyes of islanders like myself and people even more remote in language and culture. They were to be cities visited for learning and elegant goods and manners and freedom by all the barbarian peoples of the globe, people of forest and desert, Arabs, Africans, Malays. (154)

And even when the mass migration does not follow the cultural route but rather an economic one to search for livelihood in the former centre of imperialism, Naipaul is quite cynical as far as the outcome of such a mass migration on both the migrant and the great cities—of 'great stores, great buildings, great universities'—are concerned. Consequently we find in *Bend* Salim pondering on the issue of economic migrants in England:

> Where hundreds of thousands of people like me, from parts of the world like mine, had forced themselves in, to work and live.... They were cut off from the life of the great city where they had come to live, and I wondered about the pointlessness of their own hard life, the pointlessness of their difficult journey. (269)

At times in the novels of Naipaul these immigrants are also reduced to the level of parasites that threaten the great life force of the city that they live on; as Nazruddin expresses his apprehensions to Salim on Arabs and how their leaving Arabia only spells doom for the world at large:

> Persia, India, Africa.... Now Europe. They're pumping the oil in and sucking the money out.... They want the goods and the properties and at the same time they need a safe place for their money. Their own countries are so dreadful. But they're destroying money. They're killing the goose that lays the golden egg. (274)

Moreover, although the migrants in Naipaul like Salim, Indar, Nazruddin, Willie, and the narrator of *Enigma*, travel from the colonies to the Europe and eventually settle down there; they feel themselves different from the other non-Western migrants who they find to be mostly parasitic and a disgrace to the grandness of their host country/city. Thus, whether it is Nazruddin on the Arab immigrants in England, Salim on the faceless migrants in London, Indar on the disgraceful Indians at the India House in London, Willie on the immigrants from Indian subcontinent who seem to gobble up London, or the narrator of *Enigma* who comments on how "the barbarian peoples of the globe, people of forest and desert, Arabs, Africans, Malays" travel to cities like London to learn about model civilizations (154)—all these Naipaulian travellers find the hordes of parasitic immigrants responsible for the degeneration of the cities like London with their barbarous manners and customs that they refuse to leave behind even when crossing the threshold to enter these great cities.

Although critics like King, Nixon or Weiss have never failed to point out the migratory nature of the characters in Naipaul's fiction, the attributes and effects of this migration on these characters' observations of the societies they come from or travel to have always remained a matter of debate. For example, the usual effect of dislocation, as it results in the loss of identity in the traveller, is quite problematic in Naipaul. And so, while Naipaul's characters like Salim, Willie, or the narrator of *Enigma* appear to suffer from a loss of identity even before they undertake their journey; they also seem to have a pre-determined notion of the societies they observe which their travels only re-confirm. Salim's initial observation of the self-destructive nature of the Africans and the civilizing presence of the Europeans in *Bend* is eventually confirmed by the time a traumatized Salim finally leaves Africa for England.

Willie and the narrator of *Enigma* too go through similar journeys, as their disappointment with their colonial homeland of half-lives and the adulation for the European civilization since their childhood are eventually validated by their later travels. Thus, the characters in Naipaul in a way remain trapped between their colonial past and the allure of a future life in Europe, as symbolized by Salim's most valuable documents in *Bend*: "my birth certificate and my British passport" (78). This is the fractured identity that they inherit as colonial subjects and that precedes their travels and displacement; as in Weiss's words, "None of these characters truly belongs in his community or society; each tends to observe rather than act, and through those observations of others, experiences new territories of seeing and feeling". But as the 'observations' offered by these travellers in Naipaul are highly controversial, Weiss also goes on to add, "Whether Naipaul's characters do see clearly is moot, but a character like Salim does seem to choose to be nothing, to live without a fixed social identity, in order to be a watcher and an evaluator of others and thus to know them (or have the illusion of knowing them)" (217).

Undoubtedly, as Weiss and others to find, the clarity of vision in Naipaul's travellers remains questionable; but even the observation by these critics that these Naipaulian travellers decline a "fixed social identity, in order to be a watcher" might as well appear misleading as the migrant in Naipaul like Salim, Willie, or the narrator of *Enigma* undeniably try to belong to a 'fixed social identity'. Naipaul always presents his migrant as an upholder of the civilization and culture of the imperialist Europe, although the migrant's efforts to integrate into this imperialistic civilization always turn out to be a lifelong pursuit. Anyway, what we should note here is that whether it is Indar, Salim, Willie or the narrator of the *Enigma*, Naipaul's migrants too want to view themselves as a cosmopolitan traveler with a penetrating vision and "a man without a side"—traits that they believe to have acquired following their dislocation and migrancy (*Bend* 178).

The preconceptions that the characters in Naipaul are shown to possess are further related to their choice of destination of their self-directed course of migration and exile. Salim, Indar, Nazruddin, Willie or the narrator of *Enigma* are all shown as predisposed to leave their colonial land of birth as they are eager to arrive at the imperial centre of Europe—the great city of London—that they believe will provide them with a life of dignity instead of the half-lives that their colonial land of shame and defeat had destined them to. But as it appears, caught in the no-man's-land between their colonial past disowned by them and the elusive world of the West that they try to 'rejoin' as a former colonial; the migrant/exile in Naipaul is an eternal traveller on a journey between his past and future. He is a soul permanently self-exiled in his present state of movement in the continuity of time and experiences. The migration and exile in Naipaul is thus never able to produce any significant effect on the traveler as his is a travel that begins with a set of preconceived, fixed notions and never finishes its course as the destination remains ever elusive. Consequently, the unfinished course of journey remains unable to challenge/change those fixed notions in the migrant.

The traveller in Naipaul, however, also demonstrates that the initial effect of a migration brings out the worst in the non-Western migrant's nature, as can be seen in Willie's fabrication of a factitious identity for himself or in Salim's adulterous and degenerate relationship with Yvette. Therefore, as Indar describes a non-Western traveller at his first moment of contact with the West in *Bend*: "When we land at a place like London Airport we are concerned only not to appear foolish.... We are concerned only to let people see that we can manage and are not overawed. We might even pretend that we had expected better. That is the nature of our stupidity and incompetence" (165).

Another aspect of the issue of migration and exile that differentiates the travellers in Naipaul and in his contemporary diasporic writers like Ghosh or Rushdie is something that has become inseparable from the post-colonial scene the mass migration involving within its ambit the political refugees, economic migrants and the occasional scenes of an epic exodus. The literary genres and criticism have also come under attack by many post-colonial critics on this particular issue as can be seen with Kaplan who has pointed out how the concept of the individualized romantic exile still dominates the arena of literature and criticism. She also points out how in the post-colonial world of flux and displacement, where "the modern experience of forced or voluntary movement has been widespread and diverse, the metaphors and symbols used to represent displacement refer to individualized, often elite, circumstances" (4).

As Kaplan believes that "considering the material histories of immigration is only one way to destabilize modernist myths of travel" (5), we find that such a perspective is quite absent in Naipaul. While Angela in *Enigma* had led a young Naipaul to attempt a naïve and romantic portrayal of economic migrants; an occasional look at the hordes of mass immigrants—Arabs, Indians, Pakistanis, Bangladeshis and Sri Lankans—in England and Berlin in *Bend* and *Magic*, and the African immigrants like Percy Cato and June in *Half* by the central characters in the novels leads them to be labeled as parasitic. In Naipaul they are often portrayed from a Eurocentric perspective that shows them as greedy opportunists beckoned by the benefits of a Western society. Moreover, the mass immigrants are often found by the characters in Naipaul to carry their barbarous customs and culture into the host country in the West that not only prevent their successful integration with the European culture and society but also negate the possibility of their harmonious and enriching co-existence with the Western world view.

Furthermore, as it appears, Naipaul does not believe in the concept of the subaltern or the marginalized; to him there are only two terms for the citizens of the Third World, one being the 'pure natives'/the 'primitive'—who are "insufficiently improved, hopelessly backward" and the other being 'the mimic'/the '*évolués*'—who "ape the metropolitan values, rather than absorbing them, and so become living parodies of civilization" (Nixon 110). This in turn leads Nixon to observe that "Naipaul thus couches primitivism and mimicry as antipodes that, between them, contain the spectrum of Third World cultural identities. By resorting to this imperial catch-22, Naipaul forecloses rhetorically all possibility of affirmative cultural identities, self-respect, and productive cultural interchange" (110). As Naipaul finds only a static society in the former colonies, Nixon points out that the sheer act of putting up a resistance to the colonizer while striving for a new cultural and national identity on the part of the colonized not only proves it beyond doubt that the post-colonial societies are not static, but also that the 'scope and validity' of the category 'primitive' is no longer valid in the post-colonial world (114).

Anyway, it cannot be denied that Naipaul's acerbic description of the former colonies has led many critics to laud what they think is a penetrating insight into the neo-colonial forces at play in the former colonies—in their socio-political, cultural or economic lives. As for example, Manjit Inder Singh finds that in Naipaul the "questions of power and authority once directed at the classical empires of Britain and France are now thrown at despotic successor regimes" in Africa or Asia (172). Nixon however disagrees with this view on Naipaul as he remarks: "On a superficial reading, his emphasis on the continuities between the colonial condition before and after formal independence might appear to support the theories of neocolonialism advanced by Fanon, Kwame Nkrumah, and Julius Nyerere, among others, in the 1960s." But, as Nixon goes on to add: "examined more closely, Naipaul's "colonial" comes back to look more like neocolonial's antonym. Naipaul points repeatedly to the "colonial's" abdication of responsibilities as a fundamental cause for the ailing condition of many Third World societies" (139).

And so to Nixon, the metropolitan Naipaul as a travel writer "has contributed little to the tradition of inverted travelogues produced by Third Worlder or colonial subjects who have sought to write up the foreign peculiarities of Britain and United States" (57). Rather, as Nixon later points out, "while Naipaul has written extensively about the Caribbean, stressing the psychological legacy of colonialism and the persistence of mimicry, he has never documented (far less protested) the United States' economic and military subordination of the region" (140-41). Nixon, in fact, repeatedly accuses Naipaul of displaying a most biased, or in other words, an imperialistic outlook in his travel writings that appear to be predetermined in their observations while travelling: "Dividing cultures with Manichean rigidity, he assumes that there is virtually nothing of cultural worth outside the West." As he adds further, "Behind this categorical rejection there are really two assumptions: first that the values of the globally marginalized and the 'primitive' are not even functionally valid in their own contexts and, second, that such cultures have nothing to offer the West" (115).

Caren Kaplan, on the other hand, directly accuses Naipaul of joining the league of the travel writers who continue the traditionally imperialist practice of travel writing in their "travels through a postcolonial construct of oppositional binaries" in their texts where "the 'Third World' is always located in a clearly defined periphery, the colonial relations have shifted from military/economic to cultural/economic, and stereotypes serve as explanatory legitimations of foreign policy" (84). Likewise, although Bruce King suggests that Naipaul is as critical of the European civilization as of the non-Western ones (204); Nixon thinks otherwise on this too: "Naipaul's angle, ingenious yet perverse, screens out the violent decrepitude of London and Birmingham's inner cities as well as...of the north.... Ruin, in its unpopulated, bucolic English mode, becomes a ruminative, poetic affair, where in the Third World it made him irascible and accusatory" (163).

Naipaul, thus, remains a brilliant example of a post-colonial writer who displays all the possible contradictions involved in the scene. While the master narrator unfolds the sweep of a colonial history in his grand narratives, he also displays his Eurocentric vision in the process; while he never fails to note the defeat and humiliation in the life of the colonized, he seems to hold him responsible for his defeat; while his Eurocentric, migratory self yearns to 'rejoin' the panacea of civilization, he never feels at home in the West. As Singh observes, Naipaul has not only introduced us to an "original and ground-breaking method of archaeological and intellectual perceptions and dimensions to study a pattern of history, the order of things, civilizations and their break-up, a post-colonial agenda of re-working the subtle operations of power and freedom, the fate of revolutions", but most importantly, has also shown us "the hybridized realities of a new world order in the ongoing debates and strategic political shifts in what promises to be a post-globalized scenario" (242).

Works Cited

Ashcroft, Bill, Gareth Griffiths and Helen Tiffin. *The Empire Writes Back*. London & New York: Routledge, 1989.

Kaplan, Caren. *Questions of Travel: Postmodern Discourses of Displacement*. Durham: Duke University Press, 1996.

King, Bruce. *V.S. Naipaul*. New York: Palgrave Macmillan, 2003.

Naipaul, V.S. "Two Worlds: Nobel Lecture December 7, 2001." *V.S. Naipaul: Critical Essays*. Ed. Mohit K. Ray. Vol. 1. New Delhi: Atlantic Publishers & Distributors, 2002. 1-15.

——. *A Bend in the River*. 1979. London: Picador, 2002.

——. *Half a Life*. 2001. London: Picador, 2002.

——. *Magic Seeds*. 2004. London: Picador, 2005.

——. *The Enigma of Arrival*. 1987. London: Picador, 2002.

Nixon, Rob. *London Calling: V.S. Naipaul, Postcolonial Mandarin*. New York: Oxford University Press, 1992.

Phillips, John. "Lagging Behind: Bhaba, Post-colonial Theory and the Future." *Travel Writing and Empire*. Ed. Clark. London: Zed Books, 1999. 63-80.

Singh, Manjit Inder. *V.S. Naipaul*. Jaipur & New Delhi: Rawat Publications, 2002.

Weiss, Timothy F. *On the Margins: The Art of Exile in V.S. Naipaul*. Amherst: The University of Massachusetts Press, 1992.

7

V.S. Naipaul: The Quest for Identity amid Deracination

Satendra Kumar and *Balkar Singh*

Sir Vidiadhar Surajprasad Naipaul was born on 17th August, 1932 in a small country town Chaguanas, two or three miles inland in the gulf of Paria in Trinidad. Chaguanas was a strange name, in spelling and pronunciation, and in many of the Indian people who were in majority in this small island town preferred to call it by Indian name of Chauhan. Trinidad which was developed as a 'New World Plantation Colony' had a population of about 4,00,000 in 1932 of which 1,50,000 were Indians, including Hindus and Muslims, mostly of peasant origin and from the Gangetic plain. As reported by the writer himself, his grandfather was brought from India in the 1880s and, he 'carried his village with him'. Naipaul writes, "Half of us on this land of the Chaguanas were pretending—perhaps not—perhaps only feeling, never formulating it as an idea—that we have brought a kind of India with us, which we could, as it were, unroll like a carpet on the flat land" (Nobel Lecture). Thus, Naipaul grew up in an extended Hindu family of India bound by customs and conventions, rites and rituals and always trying to, jealously guard the Indianness against the possible contamination of an alien culture. His father Surajprasad, a sensitive man and journalist and, his mother Dropatia Capildeo, a genteel lady, fostered their seven children affectionately and tried their best to provide them all sort of things for education in Port of Spain, Trinidad.

Naipaul was indifferent to this house and he liked the move to the house in Port of Spain because of the pleasures and sights of the city—the squares, gardens, and the children's playground, the street lights and the ships in the harbor. Naipaul was fed up of constricted houses in Chaguanas, and always longed for a life in the city. He liked to observe appearance and behavior of people and the things around him. On the other hand, Naipaul's inability to form spiritual connections with his heritage dominates his thought, be it Trinidadian, Indian, or even British. He, in fact, was a non-believer because the religious rituals and ceremonies appeared to him repetitive and monotonous. He could not understand the language of prayers; neither did anybody care to explain the significance of prayer or ritual to him. Naipaul's lack of faith and distaste for rituals led him to atheism. As his father's inclination towards Hindu speculations was great, it was a case of denial of heredity on Naipaul's part. So, Naipaul followed the principles of Charvaka's school of Hindu philosophy found in theological domains.

Naipaul's fictional and non-fictional writings trace a similar self-conscious symptomatic response to the need of discovering an appropriate literary form to frame a psychic and symbolic sense of homelessness. A need to write constantly about 'unhousing', while still remaining unhoused, to find a way of inhabiting an inherited language and 'tradition' which, simultaneously alienated him because of his 'colonial' education and childhood as a twice-removed descendant of an indentured Brahmin family in Trinidad. Before his departure from Trinidad to England in 1950 to study at Oxford, as a 'scholarship boy', Naipaul nurtures the romantic vision of being a writer. But soon he discovered that writing was a sign of disease, a sickness, a sign of anguish and despair. He admits in a revealing essay 'Jasmine' that it was not easy, whatever the blinkered power of colonial fantasy, to extricate oneself from the predetermined plot of an imperial history and, to let his memory, rather than his pretention, speak. He never made a conscious effort to write on a particular theme rather he looked into the labyrinths of his experiences and wrote. While delivering his Nobel Acceptance Speech on 7 December 2001, he observed:

> When I became a writer, those areas of darkness around me as a child became my subjects. The land; the aborigines; the New World; the colony; the history' India; the Muslim world, to which I also felt myself related; Africa and then England, where I was doing my writing. That was what I meant when I said that my books stand one on the other, and that I am the sum of my books. (Nobel Lecture)

His uniqueness lies in his full devotion and dedication to the art of writing. As a result of his remarkable writings, in 1989, Naipaul was bestowed with Knighthood by Queen Elizabeth. In 1993, he was awarded the David Cohen British Literature Prize by the Arts Council of England. He holds honorary doctorates from the universities of Cambridge, London and Oxford. He also got the highest tribute for his uniquely imaginative and authorial skills, i.e. Nobel for Literature in 2001.

As we know that '*Search for I*' or '*Search for self*' has been the pivotal and perennial question for all the philosophers during all the ages and therefore modern times are no exceptions, in this regard. Since, Sir V.S. Naipaul is termed a modern philosopher; therefore, we are supposed to evaluate his literary works and ideology in philosophical terms. Here, we find that in the major works of Naipaul the most important concern from humanistic perspective remains 'The quest for identity amidst the maze of deracination'. In other words, we can describe it as an interesting study of exile and alienation vis-a-vis double consciousness. The feeling of not belonging to a place yet trying to relate while being torn apart with a longing for home is found to be a predominant feeling experienced by an exile. The exilic condition can be best summed up as being suspended in the middle space like *Trishanku*. Hence, we have a classical question of philosophy, i.e. "Who am I and where do I belong to?"

Consequently, the exile always faces a duality of experience. In case of Naipaul, this feeling is witnessed in his fictional characters, most of whom inhabit an alien space and culture. The pains of acculturation are poignantly portrayed by Naipaul. In all expatriate writers, the dilemma to choose between the adopted land and homeland is the central driving force around which move other issues such as racial discrimination, cultural conflict, the persistent sense of loss and desire for a 'home'. This inevitable conflict has its own ramifications at individual as well as universal level. Naipaul visited India several times in his life. When he began his journey to India in February, 1962, he had hoped to find at least a society in which his wandering spirit could find its moorings. India was the land from which his grandfather had been brought to Trinidad as a baby and from which his maternal grandfather had come as an indentured labourer. In spite of his early detachment from ritual and religious beliefs, Naipaul could not remain untouched by Hindu attitudes. He grew up surrounded by mementoes from India, for in its artifact, India existed as a whole in Trinidad. This kept India alive in his mind, even if only as a mysterious land of darkness from which his ancestors arrived. India, the background to his childhood, was in fact, an 'imaginary homeland'. The journey to India was undertaken as an exploration of this imaginative space which later became the 'area of darkness'. There is an incessant quest for finding the homeland among the people of Indian origin. They create beautiful landscape of imagination. But, as it happens everywhere, landscape of the mind, where his ancestral 'area of darkness' or literary and intellectual utopias, usually shock and disenchant, when confronted with stark reality. Such experiences, where utopias in reality are found non-existent, the seekers of homeland are shocked as Naipaul himself was, on coming to India. Despite being disillusioned, the craving for the mythical homeland remains alive.

While in his early novels, *The Mystic Masseur* (1957), *Miguel Street* (1960), *A House for Mr Biswas* (1961), he used the familiar milieu of the land of his early upbringing, Trinidad, he shifted the setting of his future writings to India, Africa and Latin America, both in fictional and non-fictional narratives. It is not that Naipaul is torn only between the two lands of Trinidad and India. The doublings of his consciousness continuously changes. He has always been looking at London as the ideal place to settle. So, he is not torn not only between India and Trinidad but also India and London. This tripartite pull finds expression in fiction and non-fiction, where the theme of fatalistic deracination and double-consciousness of the expatriate is fully explored. The quest for identity or search for the roots has acquired myriad connotations and gets manifested in various ways, e.g. in the will to survive and exist despite all odds. The literature of Diaspora focuses on the dislocation of an individual or a race and the consequent alienation. Alienation leads to a sense of loss but life consists not in the loss alone but in the rediscovery of the self. Naipaul seems to champion the issue of rediscovery of the self and this becomes a recurrent theme in his writings.

Naipaul's first novel, *The Mystic Masseur* (1957) itself shows in good measure this element of deracination and quest for identity. *The Mystic Masseur* is placed firmly in the East Indian milieu of Trinidad. This protagonist, who had been apparently taking shape in Naipaul's mind since he was a child of eleven, is a representative figure. The narrator in *The Mystic Masseur* expresses the view of the writer that the history of Ganesh is the History of the people of his times. Though he is happy to be back where he is known and respected, his contact with city life and his education created in him an indefinable sense of alienation. He knows the four ways people, and they also know and like him much but he feels mentally and emotionally cut off from them. The novel is set in Port of Spain and the rural area of Trinidad where the Indians lived and worked, and is a comic study of life in Trinidad in the face of the rise of postcolonial politics. The central concern of the narrative is the meteoric rise and metamorphosis of Ganesh, the protagonist. *The Mystic Masseur* is in a way the equally painful story of a man's negation of his origins. It tells the opposite tale of the process not of recovery, but of loss—of how Ganesh Ramsumair, a Brahmin of Indian origin becomes G. Ramsay Muir—a mimic man. Even in their carefully preserved and reconstructed Indian village-life, these men and women are quite aware of the fact that they are not in India. Their way of life is altered from their lives in India by the pressure of the environment, no matter how much they cling to customs and rituals.

Ganesh's rise from a masseur to a mystic and then to M.L.C. may have elements of farce about it but the episode which launches Ganesh as a mystic, has nothing farcical about it. Ganesh prepares for his first case seriously and with full dedication, like a school boy. There is nothing of the impostor or trickster in his attitude. Both Ganesh and Leela are humanly involved and the commercial aspect is quite forgotten in their sympathy for the distressed people. Leela tells Ganesh, "Man, I hope you could help the lady out. I feel too sorry for her. She just sits down quiet all the time, not saying anything, she face small with sadness" (*TMM* 131). Ganesh adopts an intelligent and effective psychological approach and sympathetic identification with his client. His treatment of Bissoon, a tragic figure, also speaks of his generous nature. He perceives Bissoon's poor circumstances and tries to help him with a gift of money. Ganesh's is a success story while Bissoon's being the other side of the coin, hinting at the grimmer alternative.

Even after he has achieved a measure of success and a reputation as a mystic, Ganesh shrinks into himself when venturing into the alien world of Port of Spain. He does not have the courage to visit the Registrar General's Office. He still finds himself to be an alien. Later, at the Government dinner as an M.L.C., he finds the whole ritual mortifying. He feels alien and uncomfortable. He grows sulkier and sulkier and refuses all the courses. The meal proves to be a mental torture to him as he finds it as traumatic as going to the Queen's Royal College for the first time. The move from Fuente Grove to Port of Spain is equally torturous. He wishes painfully that the whole thing should not have ever happened. Beharry's effort, at consoling him, that he could understand the pain of leaving a place after eleven years of attachment, implies his failure to understand the true reason for the grief of Ganesh. It is not only leaving Fuente Grove that is distressing for Ganesh. He also knows that he is leaving behind something of his past forever. To survive in the Creole world of Port of Spain, he will have to give up being himself. He has retained Indianness even in Fuente Grove. But, now he is attempting to fit himself in the alien atmosphere.

The moment, the East Indian stepped out of the protective atmosphere of the village enclave, he became immensely vulnerable. He was made painfully self-conscious about his backwardness. At the railway station of Port of Spain, the Indian outfit of Ganesh and his father evokes laughter of a woman for their sartorial incongruities such as *dhoti*, *koorta*, with cap and an unfurled umbrella of the old man and new outfit of Ganesh which marks him as an Indian from country. Ganesh's years in Queen's Royal College are years of awkwardness and embarrassment. He felt awkward on account of his Indian name Ganesh. He was so ashamed of it that for a while he spread a story that he was really called Gareth and not Ganesh. This hiding behind an anglicized name is his incipient struggle to circumvent an identity crisis which is qualitatively different from the one at the end of the novel when he assumes another anglicized name, G. Ramsay Muir. In Ganesh's instinct to hide behind the name Gareth, the author is sympathetically aware of the pains of adjustment to an unfamiliar environment.

Since dislocation is a recurrent phenomenon, therefore the adaptation happens to be the key to survival. This remains an important theme in Naipaul's work, a way in which he has explored the challenges to the preservation of identity in an alien environment. That many Indians felt the compulsion to take an anglicized name, does suggest that they found it difficult to preserve their cultural identity in the Creole world. Quite ironically, even when they surrendered their names in a move to identify with their environment they met with a measure of contempt and hostility. When father's death forces Ganesh to return to Fourways, he is happy to get away from Port of Spain. He had spent five years there but he had never become used to it or, felt a part of it. It was too big, too noisy, and too alien for him. His humiliation at the Port of Spain school where he worked for a brief period as a teacher and, his giving up his job after his dispute with Miller, compounds an already aggravated crisis. As a teacher in Port of Spain, he had to face irritating and humiliating comments from his Creole colleagues when one of them sarcastically remarks that teaching is an art which is beyond the talent of man coming from cane fields, Ganesh loses his temper and leaves the school. This episode shows that the hero's assimilation into an alien culture is not easy; his Indian self revolts against the humiliation. Ganesh is Naipaul's symbolic depiction of the psyche of an exile struggling for recognition. It implies that he is aware of himself being a misfit in the present. His mind always functions in the present with the memories of the past. The realities of the new world now force him back to the country to try his luck on the home turf.

Though Ganesh is trying to make his impact clear and distinct in the emergence of the new nationhood of Trinidad, he along with Harbans and RRK Singh suffers from self-deception. Inwardly, he contrasts Trinidad with the larger consciousness of sophisticated London. There is obviously a physical and intellectual poverty and a bankruptcy in the midst of plenty for Ganesh and his ancestors lived in a very circumscribed life as labourers doing sub-standard work. Set in the West Indies, on the eve of independence, *The Mystic Masseur* highlights the displaced and mediocre individuals in pursuit of recognition and success. The reason for Naipaul's discourse of aspiration in *The Mystic Masseur* is his own dilemma over the question of home. He has his own irreversible feeling of disaffection for Trinidad with its reality of maladjustment in a colonial multicultural society. On the one hand, there was the colonial West Indian picture of slavery, exploitation and squalor, on the other, the East Indian's anxiety for acculturation into the Creole world. On one hand, there was Naipaul's Hindu ancestry blocking a full assimilation with the Trinidadian society of mixed culture and on the other, his hatred for the insensitive materialism of the West Indians. His identity is problematical under dissimilar socio-cultural forces, which occasioned his escape into the metropolitan centre of London for the pursuit of a writing career, but, even there he felt himself castrated. In fact, his predicament is that of one caught in a double bind—that of an insider-outsider, who finds no home and therefore, gropes for identity everywhere.

The Mystic Masseur presents in Ganesh an intensity of desire to change his social reality from the initial stage. Ganesh is determined to bring about a change in the life and confidently tells Leela that really great things are going to happen in Fuente Grove in future. His anxiety for appropriation of the British culture through language is another facet of his aspiration for social upward mobility. The following words of Ganesh to his wife and squalid reality of their life have a deeper significance. Ganesh wants to learn and practice better speech than his own dialect in which he speaks, "Leela, is a high time we realize that we living in a British country and I think we should not be shame to talk the people language good. Leela was squatting at the kitchen chulla, coaxing a fire from dry mango twigs. Her eyes were red and watery from the smoke" (*TMM* 71).

Secondly, in Ganesh's feeling of shame at using his spoken dialect in a British country lies the seed for his final metamorphosis into the colonial mimic man at the end of the novel. The image of Leela squatting at the kitchen chulla and cooking under difficult conditions is emblematic of the Trinidadian reality from which he seeks to escape. Naipaul satirizes the Trinidadian society, the setting of Ganesh's success, rather intensely through such specific pictures as Ganesh's father cursing Port of Spain in eloquent Hindi, Mr. Stewart dressed as a mendicant, the Negro woman with white powder on her face, the American serviceman providing gum to the children of Fuente Grove, where they have come for spiritual advice and, Leela's fridge packed with Coca-Cola and visible from road. These scenes dramatize the confusion of origins and loyalties, customs, and aspirations. A sense of dislocation is noticed here. There is a perennial quest for identity and a struggle to maintain relation with both the cultures.

The *magnum opus* of V.S. Naipaul, *A House for Mr Biswas* (1961) happens to be a collaborative creation between a son and his father's life and writings, which depicts communities being transformed by larger socio-cultural forces. From East Indian village to an urban atmosphere of the Port of Spain, it documents the transition of a colony from a rural to an urban-cum-industrialized society. It is the tale of an exile's desire to strike roots and attain an authentic selfhood. Mr. Biswas's life is a perpetual struggle between desires and obligations, inner motivations and circumstantial necessities. Besides focusing on the personal life of the protagonist, the novel also tells the ethnic and social history of a community, its acculturation to an alien society and acquisition of a social identity. Naipaul takes the reader into the dimly-lit corridors of Mohun's inner world, "the laughter broke but Mr. Biswas could take no part in it...the rain encouraged him to stay, silent and unlistening on a tall stool" (*AHMB* 560).

Mohun Biswas and his family drift from country to town, from Hindi to English and from sprawling joint family system to a nuclear family. Hence, the novel traces Mr. Biswas's search for order and identity amidst socio-cultural change. Mr. Biswas's identity crisis springs from his agonizing historical experience of slavery and his psychic encounter with the people who constitute a forlorn culture. His is the fate of despairing and the agonizing lot who "carry about them the mark, in their attitudes, sensibilities and convictions, of the slave, the unnecessary man" (Walsh 71).

Naipaul writes about a society that is chaotic and centre-less, a society of customs, rituals and superstitions that drive the individual away from his roots. Mohun is branded unlucky by the horoscope, a catalyst, which drives him away from Indian world. He becomes the lonely expatriate seeking a new social role in a world of cross-cultural connections and encounters. Mohun's crisis of identity manifests itself in self-assertion and self-affirmation. Mr. Biswas continues to maintain an uncanny consistency in his struggle to possess a house, which forms the focus of the novel. The Hanuman House serves as an integrating and unifying symbol in the novel. Mr. Biswas's stories with their recurrent fantasies of escape from marriage trap has genuine link with its relevance to the building of the house. The house represents not only a recognizable location and identity for the displaced second generation colonial out of sympathy with his Indian roots and unable to identify with his new surroundings. It also stands for the acceptance of the roles of husband, father and the breadwinner which, both circumstances and temperament invite Mr. Biswas to resist for so long. It is only when this resistance is abandoned that Mr. Biswas succeeds in attaining a home which survives him and can become a point of growth for the new generation of Savi and Anand. For Mr. Biswas, writing represents the channel for the realization of the self, for the fulfillment of his quest. Throughout the story,

Mr. Biswas continues desperately searching for his identity in an agonizing milieu.

Mohun's relation with the Tulsis is also debatable. Between the Tulsis and Mohun, there is no proper form of relatedness and it results into his alienation from them. Whatever work he undertakes he feels indifferent from it. He seems to be drawn away from centrality of his experience by some inscrutable centrifugal force. As a Braham, he does not get the becoming treatment from the Tulsis. Instead, he is pushed to a low rung in the Tulsi family's hierarchy because he is the son of a labourer and because he is a financial liability and burden to the family enterprise.

The hierarchy of the inhabitants of the Hanuman House mirrors the stereotyped and hackneyed caste attitudes of the East-Indian community where Mohun Biswas is a 'have-not', an outsider. Mohun develops an ideal image of himself so different from his self-image that there exists a profound gap between his ideal image and his real self. The Tulsis' treatment of Biswas is in sharp contrast to what Biswas thinks about himself, belonging to a higher social ladder. The Tulsis are frustrated at Biswas' declining to work either in their store or in the sugarcane estate. Biswas, on the other hand, is hurt by the Tulsis' utter indifference to his Brahmin status and their reluctance to treat him as an educated, civilized person.

To Biswas, the Tulsi household is an object of dislike and hostility. He abhors the Tulsis and delights in imaginatively upsetting the family hierarchy. Hence, he sarcastically mocks at the family members by renaming them. Thus, Mrs. Tulsi becomes the 'old cow', 'old hen', and 'old queen'; Seth, the elder brother-in-law and business manager, 'the Big Boss'; Tulsi's pampered sons, Owad and Vidiadhar, the 'Young God'. Mohun is a stunned houseless wanderer, who on the one hand, wants to be treated as a Brahmin and, on the other, wants to destroy the class and caste system. He sounds at once Indian and a Trinidadian both. Dependant on Tulsis for his bread and butter, at the expense of the self-mortification, he becomes ridiculously irritating to Tulsis. His mockery of the Tulsis leads to his expulsion from the

Hanuman House. The reason for his expulsion, as Seth makes clear, is not his refusal to work in the store or on the estate but his arrogant ways of ridiculing the very people who provided him a shelter.

Biswas's conflict with the Tulsis symbolizes the thematic conflict of the novel between desire and necessity. Mohun lives in a world of fantasy. He dreams to be somebody in the Tulsi household but his desires and expectations only lead to his utter humiliation at the hands of Tulsis. He leads a double life—life of what he is and a life of what he desires to have. Biswas tries to escape from the traumatic world of Tulsis by taking recourse to philosophical musings in the form of reading the romances written by Hall Caine, Marie Corelli, and Samuel Smiles whose exotic tales nourish his fantasy and makes him despair of finding romance in his own dull green land. Out of necessity, he comes to the Tulsi household but he exists merely as an exile. He lacks genuine involvement in the Tulsi household and, hence his estrangement. He does not truly belong to the Tulsi enterprise. "Real life was to begin…soon and elsewhere" (*AHMB* 147) is what Mohun believes. His search for a profession and his dream of a house of his own symbolizes his desire for a sense of identity and belonging. He never really owns his house and feels at home in his work or in any group within Trinidadian society. He dislikes working as an agricultural labourer what his ancestors had to do.

He does everything in his power to escape his inherited class identity, that of an indentured labourer. Unreality overshadows his desire to be somebody in the Tulsi household. His attitude towards the Green Vale workers mirrors his shame at his own class designation and his dependence on Tulsis. Biswas longs to escape from the degrading conditions of being an agricultural labourer, who belonged to the lowest rung of the socio-economic ladder. Throughout his life he remains sensitive to his class and caste designation. In Tara's house he became once more only a labourer's child-father's occupation:

> Labourer was the only entry in the birth certificate-living with a penniless mother in one room of a mud hut. And

> throughout life his position was like that. As one of the Tulsi's son-in-law and as journalist he found himself among people with money and sometimes with graces; with them his manner was unforcedly easy and he could summon up luxurious instincts, shabby room. (*AHMB* 49)

The crowded, shabby room to which Biswas returns symbolizes his class designation and dependency. He is not what he seems to be. In his sense of inverted reality there is an effect of his enslaved ethnic community and his colonial society. His is a Creole culture. He declines to submit to the traditional practices and many times in the novel takes a solitary stand against unacceptable social practices. Mohun Biswas symbolizes the expatriate experience of a minority culture adapting to a cosmopolitan society and the painful scenario of shifting socio-moral values. As in the other works of the author, change is the complex motif carrying two ambivalent and contradictory representations and evaluations. Naipaul views change since it is through change that Mohun breaks out of his inherited identity as the son of a labourer and the suffocating hierarchy of the traditional Tulsi family.

Through socio-economic changes, Mr. Biswas steps out of his caste-identity and tenuously joins the middle class. Thus, change gives an identity to his fleeting self by unshackling him from the stifled authoritarian caste-order symbolized by the Tulsi family and pushes the agricultural East Indian community into the centre of Trinidad society. Like an exile, Mr. Biswas is a stranger to himself, a fragmented self, almost drifting: "as a boy he had moved from one house of strangers to another and since his marriage he felt he lived nowhere..." (*AHMB* 8). An observer from the margins, Mr. Biswas is in search of his centre which is 'here and anywhere'. Being alienated from society, he is a passive spectator who only sees but never feels. He is sandwiched between an old identity in a traditional community and a new identity in a post-colonial society. Mr. Biswas becomes an exile, trapped in the cultural collisions of his conflicting societies in transitions. He lives without a stable social identity. Empty and fragmented, he simply drifts in the cross-cultural current of a transitional society. He lives because life has to be lived and there is no alternative.

Although, the novel focuses its attention on the community of Hindus from India, the community is considered a part of the colonial society of the West Indian islands. The story of Biswas's career from being a fatherless, homeless child of six to becoming a father of four children with a house of his own at the time of his death is a reflection of the social history of the Indian community in Trinidad. Their way of looking at life has not changed substantially from what was in India. Like any ordinary Indian; the Trinidadian Indians also desire to have a house of their own. Though, they physically belong to the community in West Indies, they seem to have failed to inculcate the carefree nature of the native community on their adopted land.

Biswas is only about fourteen and has just lost the job for which he was paid two dollars a month. He shares with his penniless mother his condition of living as a poor dependant in one room hut belonging to her sister Tara, "I am going to get a job on my own. And I am to get my house too. I am finished with this. He waved his aching arm about the mud walls and the low, sooty thatch" (*AHMB* 67). Like Ganesh, Biswas too moves away from his Hindu past but is unable to cut off completely from his religion and cultural past. Without repudiating his name or his religion, he concentrates on the task of carving out a place for himself in the Creole world. His search ends with shaky, jerry-built house, he comes to own at the end of his life. For Biswas himself, this is a matter of great triumph.

Biswas always feels as an outsider even though the people he is acquainted with surround him. V.S. Naipaul is very much aware of the different psyche of the people of two culturally different groups. He consciously attempts to prove his point by presenting the difference. In the barracks at Green Vale, in a period of increasing mental stress, Biswas feels a black cloud billowing into his head. He is living in one room of the barracks of a sugar estate surrounded by hostile labourers. His situation, besides being a strain on his nerves, seems to trigger off some kind of subconscious recollection of the terror of those childhood days when after his father's death the family is every night held at bay within the hut while the garden outside is dug up and destroyed by the village men looking for his father's money. Biswas also suffers from a subconscious guilt because he could not help his family when needed. The tradition of caring for old parents is of course ingrained in the Indian value system.

In the background of the story of Mr. Biswas's transition from the isolated rural Indian community of Parrot Trace, where he was born to the 'Miguel Street' world of Port of Spain, Naipaul has recorded the slow but relentless erosion of the Hindu social order in Trinidad. In Parrot Trace, the first indentured labourer's seem to have established a community life that appears to be no different from that of a village in India even though Trinidad does not intrude here as well. When Biswas's father Raghu dies, he cannot be cremated, he has to be buried something unheard of for an adult Hindu in India. The Indian people have become hybridized, as there is intermingling of cultures. Because of this intermingling the people of Indian origin in West Indies remain split between two cultures.

In such hybridized society, Biswas grows up with little attachment to the Hindu way of life. When he was sent to be trained as a Pundit at Jairam's he performs the rituals without feeling and sits without religious fervor before the elaborate shrine. The Hindu rituals appear to him not only strange but disagreeable and incomprehensible. He copies out Sanskrit verses mechanically even though he could not understand as in Hanuman House, the Hindu deities seem unsightly and the Hindi books ungainly. But Naipaul with a deep understanding of the dilemma of those with a divide cultural past shows that Biswas's attitude to his past is ambiguous. Since his roots are in the Hindu culture, he mocks the Tulsis for their Roman Catholic affinities. In Green vale, at a time of deep distress, he seeks solace by making elaborate tags full of religious sentiments. When discovered by Tulsis these placards "were considered to be beautiful; though the sentiments, from a man long thought to be an atheist, caused some astonishment" (*AHMB* 299).

During the storm he falls back on the chanting the names of Hindu deities—'Rama, Rama, Sita Rama' telling Anand to do the same. When his first child is to be born he thinks up a long and assertively Hindu name Krishan-dhar Haripratap

Gokulnath Damodar Biswas. Meanwhile all around him in Trinidad things are changing, Bhandat, his aunt Tara's brother-in-law, takes a mistress of another race and after his wife's death goes to live with her in Port of Spain. Bhandat's eldest son too was having an affair with a woman of mixed Negro-Spanish blood and was the proud father of an illegitimate child—a peculiarly Creole attitude as we have seen in Miguel Street. The Tulsis enthusiastically celebrate Christmas as an exclusively family festival. The elder Tulsi's son not only goes to a Roman Catholic College but, also wears a crucifix. Years later, an old and cantankerous Mrs. Tulsi makes further compromise, "She sent Sushila to burn candles in the Roman Catholic Church; she put a crucifix in her room; and she had Pundit Tulsi's grave cleaned for All Saints' Day" (*AHMB* 522). The feeling of the loss of cultural moorings that the people of Indian origin undergo is at the focus when Biswas says:

> The elder god did wear a crucifix. It was regarded.... Exotic and desirable charm. The elder god wears many charms and it was thought fitting that someone so valuable should be protected. On the Sunday before Examination he was bathed by Mrs. Tulsi in water consecrated by Hari, the soles of his feet were soaked in lavender water, he was made to drink a glass of Guinness stout, and he left Hanuman House, a figure of awe, laden with crucifix, sacred thread and beads, a mysterious sachet, a number of curious armless consecrated coins, and a lime in each trouser pocket. (*AHMB* 11)

Naipaul himself had an ambivalent attitude to these changes. He knows they are inevitable, even necessary, but, he also regrets the passing away of an ancient way of life. In *An Area of Darkness*, he talks about the absorption of the Indians into the Creole world: "we knew there had been change, gain, loss. We knew that something which was once whole had been washed away. What was whole was the idea of India" (*AAD* 187-88). Biswas comes to a gradual appreciation of what he had blindly discarded earlier. Even his attitude to Hanuman House undergoes change. When Savi is born, Biswas watches Shama display an extraordinary gentleness through her work torn hands rubbing the baby with coconut oil and exercising its limbs exactly as Mr. Biswas's had been by Bipti. This conveys a deeply nostalgic feeling for recovering the ancient traditions that constitute the Hindu way of life that is lost in Trinidad. It also shows that it is quite impossible to drive away the feeling of being a Hindu from anywhere in the world.

Biswas is very well aware of his limitations and his own chances of survival if he rebelled against the Tulsi household. Beneath the grotesque mask one can perceive the fear of the future of objects, of people, of time, place and mankind. He constant seeks to negotiate a free space for himself wherein he can overcome the degenerating and suppressing tendencies of the Tulsi environment. In this cruel, comic world, both crowded and solitary, bullying and servile, Mr. Biswas keeps alive a mere sign of independence and selfhood by refusing to be a mild victim. He is weak but nourishes his irritability and keeps his malice going. He is a bundle of contrasts. When it is necessary to be solemn he was a clown, when pious he was a blasphemous, when he was supposed to be appreciative he was graceful. Very soon after his marriage he realizes that life, even after a love marriage is not romance but an act of responsibility and duty for the other. Since he has no money or position, he is expected to become a Tulsi. This cornered position of Biswas instigates him to be a rebel against the Tulsis. Pretending not to know what is expected of him; he leaves Hanuman House and goes back to Pagotes. And when social pressure compels him to return, to acknowledge his obligations to Shama, his return is marked by express contempt for the Tulsis. "He was troublesome and disloyal, and could not be trusted. He was weak and therefore contemptible" (*AHMB* 102). And a determination on his part makes him defy them and assert his identity by such comic acts as parading himself in pants made by Bipti from flour-sacks bright with letters and even whole words. He presents Savi with a personal gift, a doll's house which is against the norms of the Tulsi system. He further goes to the extent of challenging the Tulsi's religious belief by aligning himself to the Arya Samaj which sought to make Hinduism a philosophical system rather than a ritualistic one.

He first asserts himself by putting forward his motto as, "paddle your own canoe" (*AHMB* 107) and by refusing to do any estate business. As a result of his disobedience of Tulsi household rules, he is put into service at Chase. The journey to the Chase puts an end to his rebellion for all practical purposes and now begins the most significant chapter of his life—his quest for a house of his own. House is the most consistent metaphor of his aspiration, his intense desire to escape from homelessness to home and identity. It also releases him from the stasis of suffocation in the Tulsi household to the dynamics of struggle in the world outside. Of course, his rebellion facilitates his journey and emancipation. His first independent encounter with real life, i.e. running a Tulsi shop in the Chase ends in failure and he valorizes the protective safety of the Tulsi refuge. The novelist observes, "How lonely the shop was! And how frightening! He had never thought it would be like this when he found himself in an establishment of his own. It was late afternoon; Hanuman House would be warm and noisy with activity. Here he was afraid to open the door of the shop, to step into the light" (*AHMB* 145).

Biswas does not become a rebel suddenly. The role as Robert Hammer clearly points out, "slowly grows upon him and is never his dominant attribute" (Hammer 226). When he begins to become aware of his limitations he gets dissatisfied with himself and consequently considers flight to be the only resource from this sense of imprisonment. Biswas does not like to fit himself into any given pattern. When he fears insecurity, he runs to the Tulsis' house. When he feels his individual identity threatened, he is once again prepared to face the uncertainties of the disorganized world outside. Unable to find a stable mean between these two he takes to the ambiguous path. His option to live at the Chase on his own is one of his attempts to escape from the suffocating servility of the Tulsis. When at one place, his longing for the other place reactivates. He keeps on shifting longing from one to another. His escapist tendencies are manifested in what he does at the Chase in free time. As observed by the novelist, "He painted cool, ordered forest scenes, with gracefully curving grass, cultivated trees ringed with friendly serpents and floor bright with perfect flowers; not to the rotting, mosquito infested jungle he could find within an hour' walk" (*AHMB* 183).

These attempts of escape through writing and reading lead towards something positive which makes him gain independence through journalism. In his attempt to better his condition he adopts different strategies to reach his goal. The protection and care of Tulsi household cannot solve his acute problem of rootlessness. The care that he receives at Hanuman House provides temporary reprieve, but his condition is actually emblematic of "psychological nowhereness" (Chakrabarty, 42) of the second generation Hindu in a poverty-stricken colonial Trinidad. His journalistic spell achieved through his skill in sign writing gives him economic sustenance, which leads to his final achievement—the Sikkim Street House. The Short hills interlude in which he makes another house is very brief but illustrates the profundity of his passion for getting his domicile.

After recovering from nervous breakdown, consequent upon the disheartening adventure of *Green Vale*, Biswas gets a job in Trinidad Sentinel and moves from rural Short hills to the urban Port of Spain. With this new assignment his liberal Hinduism gets tainted because he is in no way less hypnotized by Western modernity than other members of the family. However, at sub-conscious level he still has faith in Hinduism. The religious confusion of Hanuman House is no longer displeasing to him because now his own son, Anand chants hymns from Bible. This is the peculiar cultural plight of Mr. Biswas sandwiched between two generations—older people as usually seen engaged in talking nostalgically about India and Hindu rituals and feel themselves lost in the new setting, younger generations might go to Europe for higher studies on scholarship. To Mr. Biswas "the old already look 'forlorn' and 'romantic'.... He spends his whole life crossing from East to West" (White 99).

Thus, we find that all his major protagonists suffer the tragedy of displacement and separation from their land. Separation from land leads to disorder and the forlorn spirit's search for land is associated with its search for order. There is a host of writers who revolve around the anguish and pain of the

Diaspora but what makes Naipaul truly great is his sensibility. His fictional characters are moved not as much by anguish as by anxiety. Naipaul's works derive its strength from his first hand experience of life. Though, he is dispossessed and disillusioned but goes much beyond his personal pain and anxiety. In fact, through his protagonists, he symbolizes the agony of diasporic and rootless people leading a nomadic life on this Earth. The Swedish Academy for the Nobel Prize has very correctly recognized this dimension of his literary acumen in its Nobel citation that author's authorities as a narrator is grounded in his memory of what others have forgotten the history of the vanquished.

Works Cited

Bingham, Nigel. "The Novelist V.S. Naipaul Talks to Nigel Bingham about his Childhood in Trinidad." *The Listener*. 7, September 1972.

Chakrabarty, Santosh. "Naipaul's Discourse of Aspiration: A Study of The Mystic Masseur and A House for Mr. Biswas." V.S. Naipaul: Critical Essays, Vol. I. Ed. Mohit K. Ray. New Delhi: Atlantic Pub. & Dist. (P) Ltd., 2002. 30-44.

Ezekiel, Nissim. "Naipaul's India and Mine." *New Writing in India*. Ed. Adil Jussawala. Harmondsworth: Penguin, 1977. 193-205.

Hamner, Robert D. Ed. "Introduction". *Critical Perspectives on V.S. Naipaul*. London: Heinemann, 1977.

Mason, Nondita. *The Fiction of V.S. Naipaul.* Calcutta: The World Press Pvt. Ltd., 1986.

Naipaul, V.S. *The Mystic Masseur.* London: Andre Deutsch, 1957.

——. *Miguel Street*. London: André Deustch. 1959. Penguin, 1971.

——. *A House for Mr Biswas*. London: Andre Deutsch, 1961, Penguin, 1969.

——. *Nobel Lecture*. December 07, 2011. Web. March 3. 2012.

Ramadevi, N. *The Novels of V.S. Naipaul: Quest for Order and Identity*. New Delhi: Prestige, 1996.

Walsh, William. *A Manifold Voice: Studies in Commonwealth Literature*. London: Chatto and Windus, 1970.

White, Landeg. *V.S. Naipaul: A Critical Introduction*. London: Macmillan, 1975.

8

An Apology for Failure: Searching Home and Identity in V.S. Naipaul's *The Mimic Men*

Asis De

The Mimic Men (1967) is chronologically the sixth novel in the Naipaulian canon and his first one about the devastating lure of politics and sex, where his hero Ranjit Kripal Singh or Ralph Ranjit Kripal Singh as he likes to be known—a forty-year-old Indian from the Caribbean island of Isabella (the name is fictitious), once a rich and idealistic man in Caribbean politics, now disgraced and exiled in London, is writing his memoir in a London suburb hotel. As Gillian Dooley finds, this novel is quite bleak in vision and "Naipaul's least comic novel to date" (Dooley 2006: 55). In this novel, the protagonist, unlike Mr. Mohun Biswas in *A House for Mr Biswas* finds no home and secures a hotel room at the last phase of his life. Like Jimmy Ahmed in *Guerrillas* or Salim in *A Bend in the River*, Ralph Singh is "forced to mobile without necessarily having any place to go" (Mustafa 1995: 17). Ralph's stay at a hotel due to homelessness implies an absence of all the positive elements like warmth, companionship and family associated with a house. But nevertheless the yearning for a personal space remains within him. His autobiography becomes this personal space where he discovers himself in absolute seclusion, finds his own follies, and examines himself thoroughly trying to secure an identity.

In *The Mimic Men* Naipaul seems to be interested "in the nature of subjectivity of the exile" (Dascalu 2007: 98). Here the protagonist is placed at a distance from any clear-cut national identity or any particular notion of home. The issues of 'home' and 'identity' are two poles of subjectivity and these are very much in a dialectical relationship with each other in the fictional world of *The Mimic Men*. The novel significantly emphasizes on the issues like isolation, displacement, race and origin, history, cultural confusion, communal antagonism, mimicry and the dangers of Americanization. The experiences and the reminiscences of the protagonist-narrator find a dramatic exposure and offer an empty excitement finally ending up in a chaotic disorder. Cristina E. Dascalu sounds quite right as she comments: "Ralph Singh plays *roles in a drama*, and the landscapes that create his agency are *imaginary*" (*ibid.* 105; original emphases). The absence of real power, a solid tradition or the bondage of national culture and myths results in a tendency to mimic, and a feeling of rootlessness and identity crisis.

The novel begins and ends in the present time with the narrative flashing back and forth in time between Singh's childhood in Isabella, student life in London, his return to the island after securing a university degree and an English wife, his marital strife, his political career and lastly an ultimate exile again in London. The deliberate destruction of a linear, chronologically ordered narration "in correspondence with the starts and swerves of the recovering memory, his instrument of self-examination" (Walsh 1973: 62) helps the reader to recognize Ralph Singh's attempt to reconstruct some meaning out of his melancholic and muddled experiences. This autobiographical exploration becomes a recovery and retrieval of a blighted individual and transcends from the level of a confessional report to an allegory of survival of modern man. Naipaul's protagonist only "seems to have achieved equilibrium at the time of writing, away from the excitement and difficulty of striving for success" (Dooley 2006: 56). What is important is Singh's various roles. The older figure represents his former younger selves in different stages of life.

In his 'auto-critique', Ralph Singh writes elaborately on the postcolonial society of the Caribbean islands with all its pains and panics that produced him. In his book *Contrary Awareness* (1982), K.I. Madhusudana Rao comments: "The writing of his story becomes the very means to endure the terror, 'shipwreck', abandonment and loneliness of his situation" (Rao 1982: 126). S.F.H. Deena finds Ralph Singh in his book *Situating Caribbean Literature and Criticism in Multicultural and Postcolonial Studies* (2009) as someone, who "remains the most dramatic portrayal of the shattering and shipwrecking effects of colonization" (Deena 2009: 90). To be precise, Naipaul's *The Mimic Men* upholds the precarious nature of the transition from colonialism to independence, when power is fraught with danger. The important thing Naipaul shows here is the inevitable failure of man due to his inability to attain a higher vision of reality, a proper understanding of his own situation. Ralph Singh, like Mr. Biswas does not fight with a system or social code; rather he treats his withdrawal after his failure as a politician, as an opportunity to sum up his experience creatively through the act of writing a 'history'. In this novel, Naipaul relates modern man's experience in the light of his historical circumstances with an air of disenchantment and total surrender.

The first section of the tripartite novel mostly consists of memories of Ralph Singh's days as a student in London presented alternatively with his exilic experiences in London. Chapter four to six, shows his marriage to Sandra and return to Isabella. The second section of the book deals with Singh's memories of childhood and education shifting more backward in time. The third section upholds the memories of his political life in Isabella against his present exilic experiences and observations. The time covered in *The Mimic Men* is about thirty years—from 1930, when Singh is about ten years old to 1960, when he is forty, and writing his memories at a hotel in a London suburb. The novel straddles the Caribbean island of Isabella and the metropolis of London. The Isabellan scene, as reflected in Singh's reminiscences is representative of the chaotic Caribbean condition shortly after the war. The disastrous impact of the past, the appalling lack of tradition, the heterogeneity of races and communities, the failure of political vision in a newly freed country—all these issues contribute to Singh's limitations and mistakes. In dealing with the political reality and moral poverty of ex-colonies like Isabella, Naipaul's approach, though negative and pessimistic, is decisively therapeutic and analytical. He finds little hope in the Caribbean transition from slavery to independence, for freedom has only brought further violence, confusion and disorder. As Naipaul's narrator-hero says: "To be born on an island like Isabella, an obscure New World transplantation, second-hand and barbarous, was to be born to disorder" (*MM* 118).

Naipaul's narrator-hero Ralph Singh sets the tone of his narrative by projecting a bird's-eye-view of the Jewish landlord Mr. Shylock's boarding house in the Kensington High Street and his first London-days of student life there. Singh also introduces us to Lieni—the Maltese housekeeper of this boarding house and to the London weather—its snow and light: "Snow At last; my element.... But the greater enchantment was the light" (*MM* 6). After walking down the memory-lane in the first ten paragraphs, the protagonist-narrator realizes that he has already made a good start—"a somber beginning. It could not be otherwise" (*MM* 7), and shifts back to his present with his observations:

> The career of the colonial politician is short and ends brutally. We lack order. Above all, we lack power, and we do not understand that we lack power. We mistake words and the acclamation of words for power; as soon as our bluff is called we are lost. Politics for us are a do-or-die, once-for-all charges.... For those who lose, and nearly everyone in the end loses, there is only one course: fight. (*MM* 8)

In making such observations and in analyzing his own past actions, Ralph Singh is now trying to achieve universality and objectivity. It would be somehow misleading to identify the narrator-hero's observations with Naipaul's. Bruce F. MacDonald rightly remarks: "...through Ralph Singh's generalizations, observations, and even through his failures, Naipaul has revealed much about the nature of Ralph's generation and about his island society" (MacDonald 1979: 249).

The Isabellan scene consisting of the various racial, cultural, communal segments to which Singh and his school-mates

(Deschampsneufs, Browne and Hok) belong has hardly achieved any cohesive social order. The protagonist-narrator Singh finds the origins of his ennui and emptiness in the environmental influences of his childhood and student days, and also in the education he received at 'Isabella Imperial'. In both *A House for Mr Biswas* and *The Mimic Men*, Naipaul makes the colonial educational system the butt of his satire—a system which succeeds only in alienating the scholar from his environment. Victor Ramraj proposes that this colonial educational system serves as an important "reason for Ralph's alienation from his society" (Ramraj 1979: 132). Even in his childhood, Ralph realizes the inadequacy of the educational system of Isabella and becomes eager to get education in London. His search for a new space begins, though the actual fulfillment of his dream journey to London comes quite later. Designed by the colonial masters, this sort of education does not help the children to realize their own situation. It usually superimposes upon the schoolboys' imagination yet another dream of a different society and landscape. The schoolboys think of visiting their teachers with an apple instead of an orange of their own orchard: "My first memory of school is of taking an apple to the teacher. This puzzles me. We had not apples on Isabella. It must have been an orange; yet my memory insists on the apple. The editing is clearly at fault, but the edited version is all I have" (*MM* 90).

Ralph comes to London, the "centre of the world" (*MM* 18) for higher education and "to find the beginning of order" (*Ibid.*). Now his identity is that of a non-European scholar and he secures a place in a room of a boarding house which is his first shelter outside Isabella. But here his role is very much like an aimless wanderer who simply observes the glamour of the city and moves from place to place. He feels like a nomad or gipsy. From the boarding house at Kensington Street, he moves to the lecture halls, the canteen, and the halls of the British Council. He meets girls of different backgrounds ranging from Norwegian to Swedish French and Maltese. The growing indifference to his scholarship and his purpose makes him a dandy: "In London I had no guide. There was no one to link my present with my past, no one to note my consistencies or inconsistencies. It was up to me to choose my character, and I chose the character that was easiest and most attractive" (*MM* 20). And it is Lieni, who strikes the matchstick to the situation: by suggestion and flattery and "with the woman's limited view of the world" (*MM* 21) she creates in him the character of the rich extravagant colonial. The displaced Ralph enjoys and even sometimes exaggerates his newly-assigned role.

Lieni makes Ralph conscious of his appearance—his "dark, luxuriant and very soft hair" (*MM* 20). She accompanies Ralph to the departmental stores and chooses his garment and thus, as he confesses unhesitatingly, he becomes her pupil: "I became her apt-pupil" (*MM* 21). She also expects Ralph to bring women to the boarding house and wishes to "witness my [his] conquests" (*MM* 21), and thereby vicariously share his pleasure. In this phase of his life in London, Singh actually attempts "to remedy the double deficiency of situation and temperament by indulging in a most bizarre kind of sex" (Mason 1986: 69). His "hunting grounds" (*MM* 22), the vast intercommunicating rooms of the art galleries and the excursion trains to provincial centers of culture, provide him with ample opportunity to find girls to flirt with. The older Singh now diagnoses his relationship with Lieni as one of "son-lover-brother' (*MM* 27) and a few pages earlier he is seen making a sordid confession: "I never wanted our darkness, our auras, to mingle. Understand the language I use. I am describing the failure, a deficiency; and these things can be so private. I had spent all my life among women; I could not *conceive of an existence away from them* or their influence" (*MM* 25; my emphasis).

At this stage of his life, Singh confesses his inability to 'conceive of an existence away' from women. Without the company of girls Ralph becomes less confident and cannot realize his personality, probably his masculinity wholly. Women, in several stages of his life, contribute substantially to build up his identity as a man. This cry of helplessness comes from a peculiar dilemma of a displaced sensitive young man who yearned for earning an identity: "But there was my 'character'" (*MM* 25); "I had tried to give myself a personality" (*MM* 26).

Ralph's brief relationship with Beatrice significantly upholds the irony of situation. After surrendering himself to her mood, Ralph receives an envelope from her containing a small note and the Isabellan dollar note given by him the previous day. The clear-sighted older narrator now attempts a clinical analysis which is no less correct: "She had sensed more than the absurdity of our relationship; she had sensed its wrongness. And, perhaps, she had seen the absence of virtue" (*MM* 24).

The narrator-protagonist fails to find the roots of the misdeeds of his own younger persona who had then just come from the margin to the metropolis: "Though even now I cannot understand why I began keeping a sexual diary" (*MM* 25). Now his experience ripens his observation and the narrator's voice asserts with a confident judgment—"Intimacy: it was violation and self-violation" (*MM* 25). In his student life in London, Ralph is surrounded by people who seem to be hollow men without any integrity or principles. His close connection with these people and his meeting with several girls, which he calls 'intimacy', lead him to a kind of 'self-violation'. He comes to London with a certain goal of being educated, to earn an identity for himself, to give himself "a personality" (*MM* 26). But these people misdirect him and compel him to violate his own self, and his good intention. This 'self-violation' ultimately leads him to a kind of aimlessness.

Ralph, at the very moment of his absorption in such 'auto-erotic' enterprise becomes confused and a peculiar feeling of non-existence crystalizes his psychological predicament. He finds himself "longing for the certainties of my [his] life on the island of Isabella, certainties which I [he] had once dismissed as shipwreck" (*MM* 27). As there is the positive and comforting image of a 'house' in *A House for Mr Biswas*, similarly in this novel, here is the equally negative and threatening image of 'shipwreck'. Singh's situation in *The Mimic Men* is virtually dominated by this dark metaphor which both describes his Isabellan predicament as a kind of Indian castaway and his sense of abandonment in London. His search for home in the island of Isabella is never fulfilled, for he always finds himself as an uprooted person, an immigrant Indian there. Instead of a man comfortably lodged at his home, he finds himself as a voyager in the sea of life. Possibly, Singh wanted to be a free-moving ship on the open ocean of a developed human society with a lot of cargo—his dreams and desires and 'dramas'. But the dilemma of a diasporic man, stemming from his internalized habits of 'self-violation' and his love of mimicry destroy him. In *The Mimic Men*, Ralph becomes very much influenced by the Western set up and often tends to imitate or mimic them blindly without thinking deeply. All this leads to his deterioration and disintegration which Ralph himself sees as 'shipwreck'.

Naipaul's skill and accuracy in delineating perfect replicas of men, women and their manners is unquestionable. But in *The Mimic Men*, it is quite difficult to establish a feeling of reciprocity with them since most of them do not behave like perfect human beings. The vital areas of human interaction—society, family, human relations—are in most cases reduced to simple mechanistic ritual or to the material level. Ralph Singh's disastrous marital life with Sandra which he himself considers as a mere 'episode' in the active period of his life is only an instance of his further alienation from flesh and carnal desire: "In the active period of my life, which I have described as a period in parenthesis, marriage was an episode.... It seemed a textbook example of the ill-advised mixed marriage" (*MM* 41).

As their marriage itself symbolizes an experimental attempt on Naipaul's part to establish a bond between two different cultures, so their relationship is just a channel of playacting to get lost in the aristocratic, moneyed social whirl. Like his dynamism and the later political life, this too is a charade that falls apart.

Ralph first comes across Sandra, the tall, bony-faced English girl, while reading the badly-typed notice of some Turkish League. Ralph, breaking the silence, begins the conversation and hears about the series of quarrels Sandra had with her father just that morning. Her helplessness and vulnerability and also her possessiveness attract him. Her language also substantially fascinates Ralph: "Language is so important.... With Sandra ...the mere fact of communication was a delight" (*MM* 44).

But only language cannot bridge the basic gap between them, originating from their widely different background. Ralph submits to Sandra's wishes, and in doing so, allows himself to be guided by an alien culture. The West now exercises a greater influence on him. Both of them get involved in a sexual relationship and Ralph surrenders himself totally to her, looking up to her for some sort of protection: "Singh sees a great deal of yearning in her, but up till the time of their first meeting others have depended on Singh and looked to him for guidance; now Singh begins to depend on Sandra, he trusts to her luck" (Theroux, 1972:73-74).

The sexual affairs which Ralph experienced earlier with several girls now seem grotesque; he sees those affairs now "like an imperfect world, some grotesque tunnel of love" (*MM* 44). But it is altogether different with Sandra, as Ralph expects much from her and also finds the best friend in her: "She reflected my own mood exactly" (*MM* 46). Ralph discovers in her a mirror image of his own isolation: "She had no community, no group, and had rejected her family. She saw herself alone in the world and was determined to fight her way up" (*MM* 44).

Ralph becomes attired up by her spirit and when she asks him to propose formally, Ralph responds immediately. Ralph and Sandra get married at the Willesden Marriage Registry Office, with two fellow-students as their witnesses. A marriage usually promises assimilation, but in this 'mixed' marriage, involving a groom of Indian origin and a bride of English origin, marital loyalty is not normally expected. Two different worldviews with a polar gap cannot coalesce harmoniously. In the Willesden Marriage Registry Office, the registrar, quite intelligently sensing the failure of such a marriage offers Sandra some advice and gives her the address of an Association concerned with the protection of British women overseas. Even during the marriage ceremony, Ralph feels like getting away "at once, to reflect, to be alone again" (*MM* 49).

Ralph does not inform his mother of his marriage with Sandra. Naturally, when he leaves for Isabella with a lot of expectations and self-assurance, to set right the ruined pieces of his life with his newly-wed wife, a conflict is expected. And the problem arises, when his mother and Sandra meet at the dock side. In this situation, Ralph's assessment of his own people as "a melodramatic race" (*MM* 52) is significant. Ralph's mother, a widow and Hindu by religion, finds this marriage as a blow both to her Hindu spirit and identity, and to her own plan about her son's marriage. In establishing such a bond, she feels that Ralph has obliquely denied his own identity as a Hindu, because choosing a non-Hindu bride for marriage is not only immoral to Hindu people, but also irreligious. Ralph's religious identity is now at stake. Ralph with his new multiculturalism had dreamt of an acceptance in the same house and hoped that the addition of Sandra from a different community would only serve to strengthen their 'house'. But his mother disapproves this marriage and rejects the possibility of Sandra's accommodation in her house. The newly-wed couple, being deprived of a home, stays in a hotel. Possibly, Ralph never thought of staying in a hotel in Isabella, which was his homeland, where he was born and brought up. This is the first hotel he boards in his life. The negative attitude of his family represented by his mother towards Ralph is due to his establishment of an 'irreligious' marital relationship with an English girl. Home also stands for family life. When the newly-wed couple is seen to be deprived of a home, staying in a hotel, the future of the family life seems to be uncertain and insecure.

Ralph now wants to dive into an utterly material world of name, fame and money, and so he attaches himself and Sandra to the neutral, fluid group of people comprising young and promising professionals, mainly Indian, with a few local whites and coloured, who "had all studied abroad" (*MM* 55). Ambition to go up in society is often a motive that lurks behind such marriages. The narrator-protagonist significantly comments on the common connecting bond of these people: "...on Isabella they were linked less by their background and professional standing than by their expatriate and fantastically cosmopolitan wives or girl friends" (*MM* 55). The dazzling glamour of this emergent moneyed society, with all its freedom and cosmopolitanism is something artificial and showy, as

Singh now realizes: "There were no complicating loyalties or depths; for everyone the past had been cut away" (*MM* 55). Naipaul shows Singh's gradual detachment from his ancestral background: "...the initial seeming warmth, acceptance and approval gradually disappeared in course of time for Isabella is an unstable, shallow, mixed and chaotic society" (Theroux 1972: 73). The house where Singh was born and brought up is now of no use to him. It disappears and all its bonding is now insignificant to Singh. The newly-built society of the rich people appears to be harmonious and comfortable, but in reality, it lacks warmth of human relationship. This dichotomy between appearance and reality is an important issue associated with the hollow societies that Naipaul depicts in many of his novels.

With a peculiar sort of placidity Ralph begins his "new life of activity" (*MM* 57). At this stage he can well detect a change in himself, which is 'involuntary' but "something personal and ordained": "Within me, with that very placidity, with that departure from London, and that total acceptance of a new, readymade way of life, I felt that I had changed" (*MM* 57).

London was his 'second' home, though it was just a boarding house where he stayed. The influence of London is so much on him that now he cannot adjust himself to his old home, his native country Isabella. Actually, Singh is suffering from the dilemmas and sense of insecurity of an immigrant in both the places and consequently he feels not at home in any of these two homes. Singh realizes his situation and hence desperately grabs a new, ready-made way of life by simply pushing himself into the moneyed social whirl. Now he needs money and consequently Ralph looks forward to his inheritance—the Bella-Bella resources, a 120 acres block of wasteland into plots for homesteads. The site promises a good currency-value for easy availability of water and electricity and its proximity to the city. Ralph gives the name 'Kripalville' to the development project, which becomes 'Crippleville' in the mouth of the local residents. This change of name and its grotesque shift of meaning beautifully suggest the rapid transformation of a culture with Indian roots into something other which is Anglicized, and sounding a little funny. What is surprising, Ralph, the older-narrator-hero of the novel also uses the changed and corrupted name 'Crippleville' to denote his own project in the later part of the novel. However, Singh's scheme of selling the plots becomes successful, for he handles it with "method, precision and time" (*MM* 59). Success leads to success and money returns money. Ralph starts buying more land, divides it into plots, sells and brings for him and his wife status and recognition in the aristocratic social circle.

But things are not so easy in his domestic front. Boundless ambition and unlimited money gradually bring fatigue and crack their marital life. Sandra starts speaking increasingly of her childhood, schooldays and her former environment—things she has already left. She suffers from an expatriate's dilemma, insecurity and anxiety and also from a dull monotonous marital life. She drifts away from Ralph and confines herself in a separate room as she begins to feel that friends, theatres, galleries and all other sides of the island-life are meaningless. Even the enthusiasm, with which they had started to build their dreamland—the Roman House, vanishes. After the chaotic house-warming ceremony is over, Singh flees from the Roman House to an old slave plantation due to sheer irritation. The house that they had both dreamt of and built with a lot of expectation becomes a source of irritation and frustration for both. And Sandra, who is just on her way to leave this peripheral island society, takes her exit from Ralph's life.

The decision she makes now is entirely hers, as it was during their marriage—"And in fact, marriage was her idea" (*MM* 41). Earlier Lieni was found exercising her influence over Ralph; he followed her decisions. Now up to this point of the narrative Ralph still remains the same on whom others' decisions and ideas work. While writing his autobiography he realizes how ill-directed and mistaken he had been in deciding that Sandra's luck and efficiency would compensate for his own incompetence and fear of life. At the time of leaving Singh for a better life, Sandra also leaves a note which contains a shocking racist message: "The Niger is a tributary of that Seine" (*MM* 80). To overcome this present trauma and to get a temporary refuge, now he looks back to his Aryan ancestral root but visualizes an empty world: "...in the middle of an assessment of my situation that is so practical and realistic, I am like that child outside a hut at dusk, to whom the world is so big and unknown and time so limitless; and I have visions of Central Asian horsemen, among whom I am one, riding below a sky threatening snow to the very end of an empty world" (*MM* 82).

Singh compares himself with a 'child' and therefore shows his identity as a rather helpless being. The phrase 'outside the hut' implies that he has lost connection with his ancestral background, as 'hut' itself stands for house in the simple life style of his Aryan ancestors. He also finds himself as one of the 'Central Asian horsemen' in his vision, who came to look for a home in India, but this identity is of no use now, for he has lost his roots in Aryan ancestry and culture. This multicultural society, where he lives now, seems to him to be an 'empty world'. So, he does not belong anywhere.

Thus, the marriage of two cultures which once held so many bright prospects and promises, ends in emptiness and suggests the failure of an attempt to unify two radically different world views of Ralph and Sandra. Naipaul portrays Singh as a typical expatriate, who lives always n constant fear of change, insignificance and alienation. The anxiety of being marginalized always pains Singh and consequently he attempts to escape into an ideal vision of the self, to deny the continuity of life around him. Bruce F. MacDonald proposes: "The individual chooses the act which best symbolizes the needs of his particular condition… (and) expresses a dissatisfaction with the present and an attempt to see oneself as part of an ideal reality or 'god'" (MacDonald, 1979: 254). The final responsibility for order lies with the individual who has to face the reality of his own situation without any intention to escape. Singh write his 'auto-critique' precisely to face his own situation and dilemma, to overcome his fear of a peripheral existence, to make a sense of his exile, and above all to achieve an identity.

However, Ralph Singh now looks back to his boyhood experiences and the period of his schooling in Part Two and therefore, examines the possibility of finding a meaning out of these experiences. He attempts to diagnose how he became a 'mimic' man in this 'half-made' society of Isabella. Mimicry is a common natural habit of children, but in an embryonic form, Naipaul's prose projects a picture of the maladies and evil tendencies associated with children's mimicry. He satirizes their eagerness to escape from the reality of their situation in a post-colonial setting, and their ridiculous attempt to conceal original names given by their parents. These people intend to depart from their past, poverty and powerlessness, but their inability to reach their desired destination, draws them to disappointment and frustration.

In a 'once-upon-a-time' pattern the narrator-protagonist begins with 'On Isabella…', and he makes a remarkable comment about the situation in Isabella in the very first page of Part Two: "It was my ambiguous New World background, no doubt" (*MM* 83). Then he starts delineating his 'ambiguous' situation with reference to his own father first, who "was a schoolteacher and poor" (*MM* 83). Next he quite shamelessly confesses that the identity of such a low-profile father and the other connection on his side were then a matter of humiliation to him—"as a boy I did what I could to suppress the connection" (*MM* 83). Soon he admits that he has exploited this connection on his father's side that he was the son of a spiritual mentor to achieve a political identity later in his life: "it was through my father that I was later to be dragged into public life" (*MM* 83). His father, first for being a Brahmin and then a teacher, shows Ralph's connection with the Hindu world view, which is expressed in his vision of the Aryan ancestors and his rationalization of life's different phases in terms of the four 'asramas'. In the same paragraph, Singh introduces his mother's family, which belongs to a "small group known as Isabella millionaires" (*MM* 83) and also shows his likeness to lay claim to this family—"I preferred to lay claim to my mother's family" (*MM* 83). His mother's family owns the Bella-Bella Bottling works and they are the local bottlers of Coca-Cola. In age of brand-names, materialism and Americanization, Ralph fails to deny the 'colonial' temptation to attach his identity to the dominant capitalist group and to mimic the behavior of its members.

Though as a boy, Ralph senses a sort of security in his much preferred relationship with his mother's family, his father shows a sharp hatred for them. The narrator Singh illustrates it intelligently: "On another day, when my father heard that I was going on a tour of the Bella-Bella works, he went to the mousetrap and brought out a dead mouse and with a worrying smile whispered into my ear, 'I bet you six cents, a shilling, you wouldn't drop this in the vat or whatever it is they use. I bet you wouldn't'" (*MM* 84).

This metaphoric representation of the dead mouse and the deadly mousetrap uniquely warns Ralph of the consequences of blind mimicry. Ralph's father shows his violent reluctance to accept the dazzling conglomeration of Western brands and consumerism in his act of breaking as many as ninety six bottles of Coca-Cola at a stretch in one day. The vision of a society which consumes what it cannot produce itself, haunts Naipaul and makes several pockets in his narrative to store the futility, rage and sometimes somber pathos due to a sense of impotence. Singh does not conceal his disappointment: "We, here on our island, handling books printed in this world, and using its goods, had been abandoned and forgotten" (*MM* 146).

The pathos lies in the basic ignorance of the fact that mere possession of some European goods does not lead to mastery. Behind the mask of this cargo-cult, the face of an independent society is lost, and the ultimate achievement is identity crisis, disappearance of a national identity.

However, Singh's father also possessed an Austin, in which he made family-trips to far-off places, which suddenly came to an end with a chaotic Sunday lunch. Though he often created sensation in the island behaving like an eccentric, the missionary people liked him. A missionary lady had even recorded the early life of Ralph's father in her diary. In it there was a description and a faded photograph of Singh's father. To Singh it projected a picture of 'shipwreck'. One day, suddenly, Ralph's father resigned from his job in the Education Department, left his home and family, and went to the hills as a preacher and mentor to a group of frenzied disciples including the dock-workers, the slaves and some 'volunteers'. He wore the Hindu mendicant's robe, became a Gurudeva and initiated a religious movement: "...for all the emblems and phrases of Christianity that he used, it was a type of Hinduism that he expounded, a mixture of acceptance and revolt, despair and action, a mixture of the mad and the logical. ... His movement spread like fire" (*MM* 128-29).

The island people, mainly the lower-class, got excited by this movement which soon turned into a rebellion. Singh's family won popular respect and therefore, easy recognition, which Singh later exploited to build his own political career.

But the Gurudeva who usually liked to offer "disorder and drama" (*MM* 129) can never be a remote personality. Singh comments significantly—"Disorder was drama, and drama was discovered to be a necessary human nutriment" (*MM* 127) in the island society. To the island society, which was by nature chaotic and full of tensions, Gurudeva again offered drama by killing the race-horse of Deschampsneufs's family—Tamango, with the help of some followers in an obscene manner to make a ritual: "Asvamedha: to myself alone I spoke the word.... An ancient sacrifice...now rendered obscene" (*MM* 140). This incident which strikes the sensitive Singh intensely becomes not more than an event in course of time and is estimated as "expected and dramatically right" in "the regional history books" (*MM* 141). But to Singh the situation brings disillusionment; he now seems to be no more interested in finding his own root in Aryan ancestry. The obscene killing unnerves him and the total situation proves to be burdensome. He simply wants "to fly, to begin afresh, lucidly" (*MM* 142).

Singh, presently exiled and agonized, and conscious of his displacement, writes more of his childhood experiences on the island of Isabella, which stands for his real 'home'. He introduces us to his black ally Browne who insists on his racial past and injuries. Naipaul here does not miss his scope to uphold a subtle comparison between the two uprooted displaced boys with two different senses of cultural and racial history—Singh and Browne, as both of them are products of colonialism and ashamed of their families and origin. Bruce King makes an apt equation: "Browne is his double, his opposite, his friend and eventually his enemy" (King 1993: 77). Not only in Trinidad, but in every 'mixed' society, the Indians and the blacks usually lead separate social and cultural lives, and naturally there remains an ideological gap, however small it is, between the two views of life. When Browne attempts to impose on Ralph an awareness of racial distress, the latter shows his intention to withdraw: "Withdrawal: it became urgent now for me. Before it had been part of fantasy, part of the urge to escape shipwreck, and to return to lands I had fashioned in my imagination, lands of horsemen, high plains, mountains and snow.... Now I felt the need only to get away, to a place unknown, among people whose lives and even language I need never enter" (*MM* 145).

Ralph Singh plans to get rid of this obscure peripheral scene and thinks of some other place usually regarded as the center—"the true, pure world" (*MM* 146). His adolescent fantasies and restlessness are redirected, through reading, to idealized lands and landscapes elsewhere. It is at school where Singh learns of the Laurentians, Liege and "la circulation, not circulation, but traffic" (*MM* 146). What the children like Singh learned at school, they thought it to be real as their own situation, though reality was quite different. Singh acknowledges it in an unashamed way: "We pretended to be real, to be learning, to be preparing ourselves for life, we mimic men of the New World, one unknown corner of it, with all its reminders of the corruption that came so quickly to the new" (*MM* 146).

The phrase 'pretended to be real, to be learning' hints that they were not learning actually, and just making a show or gesture of learning. These 'mimic men' who lack originality, who are not 'real', were merely imitating the westernized people. As they lacked originality and did not learn really, they were compelled to live in 'one unknown corner', in anonymity. These 'mimic men' of the 'margin' realized that "the first requisite for happiness was to be born in a famous city" (*MM* 118), and refused to find themselves in such a world that lack power. In this connection Bruce King makes a memorable comment: "If the first exile is from the mother's breast, and progressively from the father and family, the second exile is brought about through education and reading" (King 1993: 78).

Naipaul shows the terrible influence of blind mimicry and race-consciousness in the world of the adolescent school boys by referring to two incidents in the second part—the change of the protagonist's name and in Hok's denial to recognize his own mother. As a student, Singh feels a fascination for a long name, like the French names, broken to parts. Though his attempt of self-baptism seems comic, at a deeper level it shows a child's struggle to eradicate his past, to change his destiny as well as identity. He expresses his disapproval of a low background without the least sense of shame: "To be descended from generations of idlers and failures, an unbroken line of the unimaginative, unenterprising and oppressed, had always seemed to me to be a cause for deep, silent shame" (*MM* 83).

Ralph's friend Hok, who is of mixed Chinese and Negro descent, nourishes the same sort of idea which gets exposed in his denial to recognize his mother on the street outside home. Hok ignores his mother only because she is a Negro, whereas he, being of mixed descent, does not look like a Negro. Naipaul has drawn our attention to the wounds of racial strife in the Caribbean society in this scene of rejection:

> One boy said, 'Sir, Hok went past his mother just now and he didn't say anything at all to her.'
>
> The teacher revealing unexpected depths, was appalled. 'Is this true, Hok? Your mother, boy?'...
>
> Hok looked down at the pavement and went purple, rubbing his hands together. We looked for the mother, the hidden creature whom Hok saw everyday, had said goodbye to that morning and was to see again in two hours or so at lunchtime. (*MM* 96)

Virtually, Hok and Ralph belong to the same tier of social existence and feel quite the same sort of anxiety and insecurity. Singh remembers "the class had decided that we were both 'nervous'" (*MM* 95). The knowledge of powerlessness and impotence of their independence must have come to the children intuitively and just for that reason they let so many fantasies and secrets to grow.

This terrifying anomaly of the situation can be explained as resulting from dependence and impotence imposed by the center on the margins of empire. It has been already pointed out that *The Mimic Men* "incorporates an extreme version of the opposition between center and margin" (Ashcroft et al. 1989: 88-89). The novel "contrasts the metropolitan center, which is the location not only of the power which comes from the control of language but also of order itself, with the periphery of colonial world in which only the illusion of power exists and in which disorder always predominates" (*ibid.* 89). The polarity between the ordered existence of the center (i.e. London) and the disordered existence of the periphery (i.e. Isabella) is repeatedly shown in the novel.

However, for the young Singh, the opportunity to leave Isabella comes ultimately, when he secures a seat in a London school. On the eve of his journey to London, he visits his father, the 'Gurudeva'. He is informed by a woman with whom his father had been living then, that the Gurudeva "has given up the world. He has become a true Sanyasi!" (*MM* 177). Then he meets his father, who is then living, as it is said by that woman, the last phase of the Aryan life-cycle, the last of the four 'asramas'. His father meets him and embraces him, but in silence. Then his father enters the inner room of the hut again. He has chosen his space in the house of life and retires there. He discovers his identity in the life of a recluse. On the other hand, Ralph gives the woman one hundred and thirty dollars intending "to repay a debt" (*MM* 177), and then feels free and relieved. He is now ready to face the world awaiting him. The second part comes to an end with Singh's receiving the news of his father's death from his sister. Last but not the least, the third part of the novel portrays Singh's political existence in the hollow, disordered society of Isabella and his ultimate victimization.

As the dark romance of a mixed marriage at last meets its logical end, Browne replaces Sandra's place in Singh's life. He introduces Singh to the island politics and soon the Roman

House becomes a center of political activity. The roman House which was Singh's personal space remains no more personal. After associating himself with Browne, Singh starts writing for a political pamphlet named *The Socialist*. Singh, who starts thinking about politics as an antidote to a broken marriage, suddenly "finds himself in politics as a matter of chance rather than choice" (Kamra 1990: 75). Ralph's identity as a businessman is replaced by a new identity, that of a left-wing politician. He does not begin his political life in the conventional way, by competing with the established political persons. Rather, by simply ignoring them he attempts to "put an end to the old order" (*MM* 190). Together with Browne, Singh devotes himself to hectic political activities and public meetings at street-corners. As Singh's father started a movement with some frenzied disciples, they also initiate a movement. But "the chaos lies within" (*MM* 192). They profess to destroy the feudalistic pattern of society and to give it a socialist structure. But they have no set political philosophy or plan, the lack of which ultimately leads them to 'confusion':

> Confusion: in the end it possessed us all…we never defined our purpose. And it has happened in twenty countries: this realization of the concept of the people, the politician's humanity, this bewildering proof of the politician's truth.
>
> What did we talk about? We were, of course, of the left. We were socialist. We stood for the dignity of distress. We stood for the dignity of our island, the dignity of our indignity. Borrowed phrases! Left-wing, right-wing: did it matter? Did we believe in the abolition of private property? (*MM* 198)

These political people who are identified her as 'socialists', use 'Borrowed phrases' to escape the real situation. Some members of the party promise to root out poverty just in twelve months, to abolish bicycle licenses, to discipline the police, and even to "nationalize every foreign-owned estate" (*MM* 299). These rhetorical palliatives and ideological panaceas comfort the public and consequently success comes in the form of victory in election.

After coming to power Singh realizes that they have drawn their strength from a mob which is both unskilled and unproductive. There is no binding force of nationalism and the people in Isabella only stand on the frenzy of violence: "...the vision of the world going up in flames" (*MM* 203). Ralph also learns about the interrelationship between power and poverty and their dictatorial pressure in a post-colonial society, about the hollowness of his island's independence. He acknowledges the helplessness of politicians to ameliorate the situation: "We learned about power. We learned about our poverty. The two went together, but it was our poverty which made the understanding of power more urgent.... The situation was squalid.... We were trapped in our situation" (*MM* 204-05).

The word 'trapped' suggest the condition of the politicians almost imprisoned within the limited space of a newly-freed country. One thinks of the mousetrap shown to ralph by his father in this connection.

It is not only about the corrupted island politicians that Singh enlightens us but also about the predicament of a sincere politician in a newly independent ex-colony. Singh feels like a fish out of water in his own native place. He can hardly adjust himself to his present surrounding. At the center of *The Mimic Men*, suggested through the Caribbean landscape and natural imagery, is the search for wholeness and a complete identity. About his new realization, Singh comments: "On power and the consolidation of passing power we wasted our energies, until the bigger truth came: that in a society, like ours, fragmented, inorganic, no link between man and the landscape, a society not held together by common interest, there was no true internal source of power, and that no power was real which did not come from outside" (*MM* 206).

The novel thus conveys a sense of despair, stemming from the belief, that it is impossible to reverse the consequences of history, because the organic link between man and landscape has been irrevocably sundered. Singh's sense of taint derives from his view of the Caribbean situation as an instance of the unnatural bringing together of people, who could achieve fulfillment only within the security of their own societies.

However, it takes four more years for Ralph Singh to complete the process of education in the school of politics and power-game, and also to get disillusioned. He is made the scapegoat in several affairs of the government and consequently disgraced. After the failure of a delegation led by Singh, the situation becomes worse. As the news of his arrival to Isabella from Britain spreads, public feeling towards him turns hostile. Several events of his private life—his scheming way of making money, his 'mixed' marriage and its failure, his relationship with Wendy, and his escapades with Stella—are used by his opponents to damage to damage his public image. People, distraught with anger and outrage, consider themselves betrayed by Singh, and asses him as a cunning and deceitful figure. His image of a 'sincere' politician shatters down. None hears his explanation and he experiences a strong humiliation. Finally, he leaves his 'homeland', without the least possibility to return. He returns to London, with sixty-six pounds of luggage and fifty thousand Isabellan dollars; starts leading a life of a resigned recluse, writing his memories. It is this act of writing, which for him "has turned out to be the most fruitful" (*MM* 248) pursuit. It is through writing his 'auto-critique' that he rediscovers himself, reviews his own idea of life and reconstructs the meaning of his life: "So writing, for all its initial distortion, clarifies, and even becomes a process of life" (*MM* 251).

At the age of forty, Ralph Ranjit Kripal Singh's relation with his society and his active life comes to an abrupt end. William Walsh comments that this final phase of his career is "one of withdrawal into privacy and anonymity" (Walsh 1970: 82). Ralph becomes totally disinterested in his West-Indian society, and realizes the seventy of oppression and powerlessness. Very much earlier, nearly at the beginning of the novel we notice Singh's confessional apology: "I no longer seek to find beauty in the lives of the mean and the oppressed. Hate oppression; fear the oppressed" (*MM* 11). Ralph has lived out different roles in different worlds, with the desire to impose order on his life and to extract meaning out of it. The roles vary from that of the Aryan horseman of his adolescent fantasies, the playboy of London life, the childless husband depending heavily on his wife, the successful estate-businessman, the politician to that of the recluse in a London suburban hotel. All these roles of Singh, very much like the different facets of a jewel, work to constitute a pattern of life.

At the end of the novel, Singh is seen staying at a hotel—a homeless refugee after all. Singh acknowledges that his last identity of a homeless recluse suits him better than any other role he plays in the entire narrative: "So this present residence in London, which I suppose can be called exile, has turned out to be the most fruitful" (*MM* 248). The condition of being a deracine and self-exile driven out of his homeland seems 'most fruitful' to Ralph. We are reminded of his father leading a 'rich' life of a recluse. However, the impact of the past on Singh is noteworthy as it has brought him to this present state. From this novel onward, Naipaul's theme changes from the protagonist's search for a home to his failure in establishing a home due to the disturbed social condition.

The Mimic Men deals substantially with the contemporary world of the West-Indian independence, its 'new' politics, power game and the subsequent problems and conflicts. Whatever is the form and the colour of politics, the permanent characteristics of the Caribbean society dominating their politics (i.e. power-game and poverty) remain the same. Most of the population consists of immigrants, slaves, freed slaves; none is native in any admissible sense. The languages and the life-style are European, even if imitative or superficial. Naipaul's fictional portrayal of this socio-political malaise in *The Mimic Men* provides us with a much deeper philosophical perspective: lack of interrelation between the different segments of community leads to a denial of one's environment. The individual is left with hardly any choice and loses himself in fantasy and escapism. Ralph Singh, one of the 'mimic men' of the New World, has been thrown up by a process of colonial partisan politics of Black appeasement in the new political hierarchy. Singh's vision of banishment, loss and alienation, his impression of belonging to the fringe of all societies, his identity as a homeless recluse, his escapism, his writing of an 'apology'—all these, as found in the narrative, represent his sense of failure to find out a meaning of life and man's whole existence. Ralph Singh in *The Mimic Men* paves the way for Naipaul's future protagonists, who being chained to their bleak surroundings are completely exhausted.

Works Cited

Ashcroft, Bill, Gareth Griffiths and Helen Tiffin. *The Empire Writes Backs: Theory and Practice in Post-Colonial Literature*. London: Routledge, 1989.

Dascalu, Cristina Emanuela. *Imaginary Homelands of Writers in Exile: Salman Rushdie, Bharati Mukherjee and V.S. Naipaul*. New York: Cambria Press, 2007.

Deena, Seodial Frank H. *Situating Caribbean Literature and Criticism in Multicultural and Postcolonial Studies*. New York: Peter Lang, 2009.

Dooley, Gillian. *V.S. Naipaul: Man and Writer*. Columbia: University of South Carolina Press, 2006.

Kamra, Shashi. *The Novels of V.S. Naipaul*. New Delhi: Prestige, 1990.

King, Bruce. *V.S. Naipaul*. London: Macmillan, 1993.

MacDonald, Bruce F. "Symbolic Action in Three of V.S. Naipaul's Novels." *Critical Perspectives on V.S. Naipaul*. Ed. Robert D. Hamner. London: Heinemann, 1979. 242-54.

Mason, Nandita. *The Fiction of V.S. Naipaul*. Calcutta: World Press, 1986.

Mustafa, Fawzia. *V.S. Naipaul*. Cambridge/New York: Cambridge University Press, 1995.

Naipaul, V.S. *A House for Mr Biswas* (1961). New Delhi: Penguin India, 1992.

——. *The Mimic Men* (1967). Harmondsworth: Penguin, 1969.

Ramraj, Victor. "The All-Embracing Christlike Vision: Tone and Attitude in The Mimic Men." *Critical Perspectives on V.S. Naipaul*. Ed. Robert D. Hamner. London: Heinemann, 1979. 127-36.

Rao, K.I. Madhusudana. *Contrary Awareness: A Critical Study of V.S. Naipaul's Novels*. Guntur: Sarathi, 1982.

Theroux, Paul. *V.S. Naipaul: An Introduction to His Work*. London: Andre Deutsch, 1972.

Walsh, William. (Ed.) *A Manifold Voice: Studies in Commonwealth Literature*, London: Chatto & Windus, 1970.

——. *V.S. Naipaul*. Edinburgh: Oliver & Boyd, 1973.

Section B

V.S. Naipaul's Travel Narratives: A Post-colonial Passage to the Globe

9

Discourse on Travel Theory and Naipaul's Travelogue: *Among the Believers: An Islamic Journey*

Shashank Shekhar Sharma and *N.D.R. Chandra*

> Travellers move about under strong cultural, political, and economic compulsions.... These different circumstances are crucial determinations of the travel at issue—movements in specific colonial, neo-colonial, and postcolonial circuits, different diasporas, borderlands, exiles, detours and returns. (Clifford 108)

Introduction

Travel theory is one of the major terms appearing from Contemporary Criticism. Travel has recently emerged as a key theme for the humanities and social sciences, and the amount of scholarly work on travel writing has reached unprecedented levels. Very early in the contemporary resurgence of interest in travel writing, relations with the analysis of ethnography, thus with the history and function of anthropology in the West, and with postcolonial theory generally, became vital and generative. Literary critical work on travel writing, or relevant to the reading of it, has continued along with and sometimes between the same covers as the work of historical and cultural revision. As a kind of writing, 'travel writing' provokes certain kinds of essentially literary questions and formulations. Most interesting here are works of literary criticism that find themselves directly facing issues of power, knowledge and identity as a consequence of the very nature of the formal matters raised (1983: 192).

Exponents of Travel Theory

Major theorists of travel theory include Sara Mills, James Clifford, Anne Mc Clintock, Mary Louise Pratt, Homi Bhabba, Edward Said, Paul Fussell, Steven Clark, Inderpal Grewal, Guy Debord, Umberto Eco, Caren Kaplan, Dean Mc Cannell, James Urry, Jean Baudrillard, David Spurr and others.

Travel writing has taken a mixed and middlebrow form throughout its history, and this gives the genre a peculiar recalcitrance. Anyone can have a go, and usually does. The travel book is unabashedly commercial: it commands large advances, wide distribution and substantial returns. The profit motive is as apparent in the auctioning of Elizabethan logs as in the posthumous proliferation of Chatwin's notebooks; Samuel Johnson paid for his mother's funeral by writing the Abyssinian fable *Rasselas*. Although there has been no shortage of first rate writers choosing to operate within the form, its force is collective and incremental rather than singular and aesthetic. The tactic of singling out texts such as Kinglake's *Eothen* or Byron's *The Road to Oxiana* as isolated masterpiece simply devalues the vast majority of these narratives.

Arguments for the expiry of the travel book in the post-war period ['travel is now impossible and tourism is all we have left' (1980: 41)] have been notably ill-founded. As a popular genre, it has proved strikingly resilient; and in the hands of its most recent exponents, provides a niche for a distinctive kind of postmodern literacy. As Raban notes, travel writing 'accommodates the private diary, the essay, the short story, the prose poem, the rough note and published table talk with indiscriminate hospitality' (1987: 253); its perennially marginal position both grants a license for idiosyncratic formal innovation, and allows the production of a self in the course of writing by means of perpetual detours into communal utterance, public codes.

Basic Tenets of Travel Theory

Travel theory examines travel writing and process of travel itself. Even so, that definition falls short in the same way defining autobiographical theory as 'the study of life writing' would also reduce its complexity. Like autobiography, still categorized as a sort of illegitimate and lesser offshoot of biography, travel writing—associated with guidebooks and other tourist apparatuses—struggles for its place as a distinct (and respected) genre, and the study of travel writing suffer a similar fate and confusion. The shift in focus from biography to autobiography in the mind to late twentieth century occurred in tandem with growing skepticism about any clear divide between fact and fiction, debate on the existence of a knowable self, and controversy on the way subjectivity is inflected by circumstances, gender, and race. Similarly, interest in travel and travel writing emerged as the result of an intellectual climate that is interrogating imperialism, colonialism/postcolonialism, multiculturalism, ethnography, Diaspora, visual culture, and spectacle (2002: 1).

One way to gauge whether a discipline is 'taking hold' would be to note whether it has developed its own vocabulary. Those studying travel writing often use words from other disciplines, but give these terms a different 'spin'. Further, in theorizing travel, scholars have created their own set of terms and expressions, instantly recognizable to others investigating travel writing. Travel theory's lexicon includes words such as transculturation, metropolitan center, imperial eyes, contact zones, border crossing, tourist/traveller, imperial frontier, diaspora, road narrative, mapping, expatriation, repatriation, cosmopolitanism/localism, hybridity, margin, exoticism, pilgrim/pilgrimage, displacement, migration, exile, nationalism, home/abroad, arrival/return, to name just a few (2002: 2).

By necessity, travel writing treats both spectacle and culture. Travel may occur, in the specific sense that James Clifford uses the term as the 'volunteerist' practice of leaving one's home to visit another 'place', or, more urgently, as the involuntary practices that occur, for example, when people flee to save their lives and seek asylum elsewhere. Travel, then whether undertaken voluntarily or involuntarily—generally entails going to another culture, and travel writing is—in large measure—the record of what one sees on that journey.

Travelogue

A travelogue is usually a single person's account of a trip, journey or otherwise. We have numerous famous travelogues written by some of the European explorers. Marco Polo's work stands as a good example of his journey to and his subsequent experience of China during the Mongol Ascendancy. Naturally, the early travelogue would have been handwritten on either paper or in blank books to chronicle the adventures of the traveller. Such writing is highly individualized, and is an experience of a journey seen through the eyes of the traveller. It can include virtually anything encountered on a trip: what a person ate, what a person saw, conversations, or notable features of a culture. A personal travelogue is most frequently written in first person.

It is not a bad idea to keep a travelogue, since it can later help one to remember significant details of a trip. His personal impressions might be for his eyes alone, but the trend in chronicling a trip is now toward sharing this information via book publication, or more commonly on travel shows or the Internet. Some people keep a video journal instead of writing down their thoughts in a book. Others use laptops and cameras to record interesting aspects of a vacation or journey. They may then publish information about a trip in a travel blog on the Internet, or use their writings to review some of the places they have seen and make recommendations to others who might visit the same places.

***Among the Believers: An Islamic Journey* as a Travelogue**

V.S. Naipaul's account of his travels in the four Islamic countries as recorded in his *Among the Believers* with a sub-title *An Islamic Journey* published in 1981 was immediately acclaimed as one of the finest travel records by an artist who has been recognised as a 'modern master'. Commenting on the great achievement of Naipaul, Martin Amis in *The Observer* thus records: "...he remains our most exhilarating explorer, with a corpus of travel writing which now surpasses that D.H. Lawrence or Graham Greene" (1981: 5).

Naipaul's main aims and objectives in trying to penetrate into the Islamic world and present the same to his Islamic readers is that he undertook this journey to the Islamic world because, "I want to see Islam in action" (1982: 15). Therefore, he was not very much, in Mr. Sherwani's explanation, aware of the true Muslims who were very few or that "Islam was a complete way of life and for that reason was too hard for most people" (1982: 27). Actually, Naipaul wanted to know and understand, perhaps, the essence of Islamic faith and it is for this reason that he made friends with Ahmed and came close to him: "My search for Islamic institutions and experiments—the search that had brought me to Ahmed—was still going on; and Ahmed was the rational man to whom I returned after venturing into other man's Islam" (1982: 34).

Similarly, when he was brought to Mr. Mirza, who was represented to him as one of the most distinguished men of Pakistan, he turned to him with utmost hope that this man would tell him, all that he wanted to know about the Islamization of institutions. Chiefly, because, as he explicitly expresses, "I had come to find out about this application of Islam to Institutions, to Government, to law" (1982: 102). This being his objective, to see Islam in action and to analyse the applications of faith to institutions, he works out a design for this book and, like the great satirist Swift in *Gulliver's Travels*, he too makes use of a very fine device in order to see Islam in action and analyse the Islamic faith. Therefore, he chooses four Islamic countries—Iran, Pakistan, Malaysia and Indonesia where he travels and establishes contacts in order to find out and see for himself the essence of Islam as practised by the Muslims in these countries.

Tourist/Traveller

According to *Oxford Advanced Learner's Dictionary of Current English*, the term 'tourist' means: a person who is travelling or visiting a place for pleasure and interest. And 'traveller' means: a person who is travelling or who is travelling or who often travels. Our cultural ambivalence toward tourism has engendered an ongoing battle between 'travellers' and 'tourists', a struggle for self-identification that ultimately exists only semantically. Among twentieth century cultural critics, Daniel Boorstin provides the most energetic and aggressive defence of the separation between traveller and tourist identity. By emphasising the historical connection between 'travel' and 'travail', he reminds us that in effect to travel is to work, thus making a crucial distinction: The traveller is active, and, by contrast, the tourist is forever passive. Travellers seek and earn experience, while tourists sign up for a program and sit back to wait for experiences to come to them. For travellers, there is work to be done; it will not be easy, but it promises rewards worth the discomfort.... For tourists, there is little work to be done; it will be easy, and it promises comfort (1985: 84-85). Using 'traveller' is only a problem, if one believes that doing so removes the respective traveller from a touristic context. But in reality, both these terms are interchangeable and any difference is arbitrary and misleading.

Thus, Naipaul sets out in his journey as a tourist or traveller, and the book opens when he is already in Tehran pushing a car with the effort to make a trip, with an interpreter named Sadeq to the holy city of Qom. He says:

> We went to look at the car. It was suspiciously well parked at the side of the road, and not far from the hotel gate. Sadeq sat in the driver's seat. He called out to a passing man, one of many idle workmen of Tehran, and the man and I began to push. A young man with a briefcase, possibly an office worker on his way to work, came and helped without being asked.... (1982: 4)

The revolution that overthrew the government of the Shah and installed the Ayatollah Khomeini as the chief of state has taken place; there has been a great deal of killing, and, in August, 1979, the killing is still going on, but the direction of the revolution remains unclear. We learn more, by flashback in a later chapter, about the trip to Iran and the narrator's activities in Tehran before going to Qom.

Naipaul travels during his stay in Iran to the holy city of Qom and to the far of Mashhad in the north eastern corner of the country near the Russian border, where the tribal life of central Asia can still be powerfully felt. In Qom he meets the Ayatollah Khalkhalli, the famous hanging judge of the revolution, and the Ayatollah Shirazi, reputed to be a learned holy man, and in Mashhad he visits another powerful religious leader, the Ayatollah Shariatmadari. He stays at hotels such as the Hyatt Ommar Khayyam. He traverses streets in Tehran, clogged with lethal traffic with names such as Revolution Avenue (formerly Shah Reza) where a hungry person in a hurry could buy a box of Our Fried Chicken (no longer from Kentucky). He could do so, that is, if he is a foreigner, or if night has fallen, for this is the month of fasting, Ramzan, and for a Muslim to be caught eating in public during the day, the punishment could be severe, a flogging at least.

Naipaul attends a political/religious meeting on the Muslim Sabbath at the university where women in chadors and men by the thousands flock to hear the call of the revolution mingled with the call to worship Allah. He visits a newspaper office where he is nearly offered a job. He is the ambiguous object of what appears to be a sort of slapstick black comedy when he involuntarily finds himself in the role of straight man—stooge for the short, round, buffoon like killer Khalkhalli. He says:

> A hanging judge, a figure of revolutionary terror, dealing out Islamic justice to young and old, men and women: but the bearded little fellow, about five feet tall, who, preceded by a reverential petitioner, presently came out of an inner room—and was the man himself—was plump and jolly, with eyes merry behind his glass. (1982: 53-54)

Turning from scene to scene and event to event, Naipaul, the traveller and Naipaul, the writer clings for meaning to people—real live people with names, hopes, fears, and confusions of their own—and, finally, his account is most memorable of its people. For example, Behzad, his guide in Iran, a student, a self-styled communist and a son of a communist, who concludes bitterly, when Naipaul returns six months after his initial visit, that "there will have to be another revolution.... We, too, have to do a lot of killing. A lot" (1982: 69). Or Mr. Jaffrey, a Shi'ite from India, who had started an English newspaper in Tehran with high hopes for the revolution but who is seen at the end of the book in his desolate office with only one employee, desperately concerned about finding the money to help his son studying in the United States and with getting a visa for the other son to the same place. Naipaul says during his stay in the Hyatt Omar Khayyam Hotel:

> But what was incongruous to me was less so to Behzad. In the restaurant he said, "Look at that family. The old woman is holy or religious. Nobody else. The old woman has come here for the Imam. The daughters and the sons-in-law have come for the hotel, to swim and to relax and to eat. They can eat during this Ramadan period because travellers can eat, and in Mashhad they are travellers." (1982: 66)

After Iran, Naipaul visits Pakistan, unique and reserved in non-Arabic Islam as the very centre of the resurgence—the first modern state to define itself, from its inception in 1947, as an Islamic state, or at any rate as a state dedicated to the ideal of achieving that perfect condition. He proclaims:

> Pakistan had a high reputation in the Muslim world. It was the twentieth-century Islamic pioneer, and for some time, there had been reports of its "experiments" with Islam. Pakistan, it was said, was experimenting with Islamic law, with a Koranic alms—levy that would eventually sustain an Islamic welfare state, and with a banking system that would do away with interest. (1982: 102)

Naipaul searches in vain for rational answers here, such as the administration of justice, the rules of land tenure, and solutions to problems of economic development in the 'Islamic state'. What he finds is public flogging (and a newspaper article criticizing the mass transit system for not having enough buses on the street to enable the people to attend the flogging), martial law, and an economy where the major industry is the export of people who go abroad to England, Canada, the United States, to wherever they can get in and get work and from where they can send money home, a 'remittance economy' as the author calls it.

But in Pakistan, again, he meets people, memorable people like his guide, Masood, with whom he visits the foothills of the Himalaya and sees the tribal life of the north going on in the unbroken rhythm of centuries, or the journalist Nusrat, who nearly put his newspaper out of business because he ran an article, reprinted from the Arabian *Arab News*, about a great Arab woman. The article had offended the Shia community and the newspaper had nearly been wrecked as well as shut down. The event occurred during the five months between Naipaul's first visit and his return, and in the interval, Nusrat, the busting, competent journalist and columnist whose dream was to publish a book of his columns, as Art Buchwald had done, had gone grey and had developed a perpetual, worried look.

According to Naipaul, Pakistan, or its central province of Sind, had become a part of Islam as a result of Arab conquest in the seventh and eighth centuries, a conquest whose original purpose had not been religion but was for the usual purpose of taking loot, slaves, and women. By contrast, Islam had arrived in Malaysia, Naipaul's next port of call, and Indonesia, his last, as an idea, carried by merchants and missionaries from the Indian subcontinent. There, the faith, at a double remove from its Arab roots, mingled with vestiges of a Hindu culture, still visible to this day in the shadow puppet plays and in the traditional court dances of the Malay people, as well as in the archaeological monuments of Bali and Java. It mingled also with the animism and country rituals of the simple village people for whom the countryside is populous with spirits. To this day, Malay construction workers will not work on a building where a worker has died until appropriate rites of exorcism have been performed by a village '*Bomoh*' or medicine man. But more—a new auditorium on the beautiful and ultramodern university campus is not properly dedicated until it has been ritually purified by a '*Bomoh*'.

Colonialism/Multiculturalism

The famous critic Jurgen Osterhammel has defined 'Colonialism' as a relationship between an indigenous (or forcibly imported) majority and a minority of foreign invaders. The fundamental decisions affecting the lives of the colonized people are made and implemented by the colonial rulers in pursuit of interests that are often defined in a distant metropolis.

Rejecting cultural compromises with the colonized population, the colonizers are convinced of their own superiority and their ordained mandate to rule (2005: 16). And *Oxford Advanced Learner's Dictionary* defines colonialism: the practice by which a powerful country controls another country or other countries.

Again, 'multiculturalism' connotes either some mode of transnational interrelationship between the cultures of two or more countries, or it suggests in a more circumscribed manner the broader dimensions of multiple cultural identities within the boundaries of a single nation. The word comprises different nationalities, ethnicity, races, cultures and genders, yet they are mixed, intermingled and hybridised. Multiculturalism, as a term, first came into vogue in the 1960s to counter "biculturalism," a term popularized by the Royal Commission on bilingualism and biculturalism. In short, "multiculturalism is a negotiation between two or more cultures within the country and beyond it" (2005: 471).

The implementation of the tenet colonialism is seen while Naipaul visits Malaysia. He says:

> And they also grow to understand that in the last hundred years, while they or their parents slept, their country—a new idea: a composite of kingdoms and sultanates—was colonially remade; that the rich Malaysia of today grows on colonial foundations and is a British-Chinese creation. The British developed the mines and the plantations. They brought in Chinese (the diligent, rootless peasants of a century back), and a lesser number of Indians, to do the work the Malays couldn't do. Now the British no longer rule. But the Malays are only half of the population. (1982: 227)

We follow Naipaul through the multicultural melange of Malaysia with its brilliant and colourful mix of Malay. Chinese, Indian, Occidental, Eurasian, Muslim, Hindu, Sikh and Christian, a country so repeatedly colonized culturally, religiously, economically, or politically for centuries are that the so-called *'bhumiputras'* or sons of the soil the indigenous Malays, feel like strangers in their own land, and we sense the rage of their desire not to be dispossessed like the 'red' Indians, the native Americans of North America. This rage mingles with the rage for 'purity' of the new Muslim movement and overflows in race riots like those in 1969, or in the more recent episodes of idol-smashing at Hindu temples.

Road Narratives

The road narrative is a combination of earlier genres, such as the travelogue and picaresque, that has evolved into a highly popular form of literature in America. A road trip is a fantasy that gives its readers and writers liberty to declare their desires. These trips encourage independence and strength of will, which make the road the perfect setting for a *Bildungsroman*, especially one that, embodies the transitioning world around the protagonist. In his book *Romance of the Road*, Ronald Primeau says that the genre of the road trip thrives because of a culture in which "writers and readers share clearly articulated literary techniques to question, reaffirm, and explore who they are and where they are going" (1996: 123). He further says "the American road genre expresses this kind of emergence, reflecting in the road hero evolving social and cultural values and beliefs" (1996: 124). In America, the road genre has evolved into a highly popular form of fiction. The idea of the open road, a fast car, and what might happen along the way has always fascinated Americans presumably because it brings with it a sense of adventure and freedom from ordinary life.

Naipaul has widely used the 'road narrative', one of the lexicons of travel theory to draw a realistic picture of the narrative. This is brilliantly expressed while he travels through Iran: We passed the pavement booksellers and print-sellers and at the end of the block, we turned off to the right, following the university rails. The side street, slopping up to North Tehran, was lined on both sides with plane trees and narrow water channels, flowing fast (1982: 62). Likewise, when he sets out his journey in Indonesia with his companion Prasojo, a nineteen-year old college student, he provides a beautiful pen-picture:

> The houses—as we saw later, driving inland from Surabaya—matched the rice strips. They were very

> narrow and went back a long way. The housed stood a little distance from the road, and the front yards were scraped clean, but shady. Banana trees grew out of the bare earth, and coconut trees, mango trees, sugar cane, and frangipani. The rice fields began directly at the back of the houses. During that drive we seemed to be going through one long village: Java here an unending smallness, hard to associate with famous old kingdoms and empires, a land that seemed only to be a land of people of petty diligence, the *wong chilik*, the little people, cursed by their own fertility, four million in Java at the beginning of the last century, eight million today. (1982: 318)

It is worth mentioning that Naipaul narrates the incidents beautifully. His pictorial description of the roads, groves, trees and rice fields, etc. are stunning and fascinating. In a way, he proves himself as one of the pioneers to portray the panoramic beauty of nature and people.

Telescoping Historical Events

Naipaul has such tremendous power of telescoping historical events as to throw open a big span of time through a very limited use of words as may be seen in the following passage in which he sums up the changes that have occurred within six months in the world:

> Karachi, Pakistan six months later. Many things had happened in those six months; the Muslim world had been on the boil. The American embassy in Teheran had been seized by Iranian students and more than fifty embassy staff held as hostages. There had been a siege and gun battle in the mosque at Mecca, hinting at underground movements in the Kingdom of Saudi Arabia. The Russians had invaded Afghanistan. (1982: 364)

In this connection it may be noted that Naipaul almost makes a resurrection of history in his *India: A Million Mutinies Now* (1990), when he connects two different events in different parts of the world to focus a similar situation as a result of which he appears to add some veracity to what may be called myth and legend in history: "In the Sikh catalogue of the torments and martyrdoms of its founding Gurus, the bricking up alive of the two sons of the 10th Guru has a special place. The story with its echoes of King John and Richard III—has some of the quality of myth" (1991: 539). Similar analogical inference is found in the same travelogue, where he telescopes the Golden Temple of Amritsar. He says:

> To be baptized was to take nectar, amrit. The Golden Temple was at Amritsar, the pool of nectar. It was said that there had been a pool here known to the first Guru. Sacred sites usually have history: it was also said that the place was mentioned in a version of the Ramayana, and that 2000 years and more before Guru Nanak, the Buddha had recognized the special atmosphere of the Golden Temple site. (1991: 519)

In the same, Naipaul has beautifully narrated the martyrdom Sikh Gurus: "The 10th Guru gave amrit, baptized the first Sikhs, and established the Sikh martial order, in 1699, in the town of Anandpur. Two years later he was besieged in the town by the Mogul forces. The siege lasted for three years. The Guru escaped with two of his sons; but the Guru's mother and his two other sons were captured" (1991: 539).

Pilgrim/Pilgrimage

The term 'pilgrim' originated from the Latin word *peregrines*, which means a traveller (literally one who has come from afar) who is on a journey to holy places. Typically, this is a physical journey (often on foot) to some place of special significance to the adherent of a particular religious belief system. In the spiritual literature of Christianity, the concept of pilgrim and pilgrimage may refer to the experience of life in the world (considered as a period of exile) or to the inner path of the spiritual aspirant from a state of wretchedness to a state of beatitude. Similarly, a 'pilgrimage' is a journey or search of moral or spiritual significance. Typically, it is a journey to a shrine or other location of importance to a person's beliefs and faith, although sometimes it can be a metaphorical journey into someone's own beliefs. Many religions attach spiritual importance to particular places: the place of birth or death of founders or saints, or to the place of their "calling" or spiritual awakening, or of their connection (visual or verbal) with the divine, or to locations where miracles were performed or witnessed, or locations where a deity is said to live or be "housed," or any site that is seen to have special spiritual powers. Such sites may be commemorated with shrines or temples that devotees are encouraged to visit for their own spiritual benefit: to be healed or have questions answered or to achieve some other spiritual benefit. A person who makes such a journey is called a pilgrim. In America, the term pilgrim is typically associated with an early colonial Protestant sect known for their strict rules of discipline. There is a Chapter entitled 'Pilgrimage' in his *An Area of Darkness* (1964), where Naipaul delineates the tenet 'pilgrimage' very minutely:

> How had the cave been discovered? How had its mystery been established? The land was bare; it offered no fuel or food. The Himalayan summer was short, its weather treacherous. Every exploration, like every pilgrimage even today, had to be swift.... Beyond the Amarnath Cave was the mountain of Kailas and beyond that the lake of Manasarovar. And legends attached to every stage of the Amarnath Pilgrimage. (2010: 165)

There is also the use of these two tenets in the travelogue *Among the Believers: An Islamic Journey*. During his visit to Pakistan, Naipaul meets Mr. Sherwani and Mr. Deen, and they are talking about: Pilgrims, they decided. In the morning, another pilgrim ship was going to cover the event, and I could go with them. Mr. Sherwani thought it a very good idea: unless I saw and talked to the pilgrims going to Mecca, I wouldn't understand the depth of their faith... (1982: 104). Naipaul appears extremely critical when he talks of the message of Islam that the trainees from the Islamic school in Indonesia will take to the world. Here he appears to talk with his tongue under his cheek when he observes: "It seemed to me that the deductions might work against them, because the message they were going to take to the world was extraordinary; a divinely inspired Prophet, arbitrary rules, a pilgrimage to a certain stone, a month of fasting" (1982: 225).

Islamic Fundamentalism

Islamic fundamentalism (Arabic: *usul*, the "fundamentals") is the group of religious ideologies seen as advocating a return to the "fundamentals" of Islam: the Quran and the Sunnah. American historian Ira Lapidus calls Islamic fundamentalism "an umbrella designation for a very wide variety of movements, some intolerant and exclusivist, some pluralistic; some favourable to science, some anti-scientific; some primarily devotional and some primarily political; some democratic; some authoritarian; some pacific; some violent. He distinguishes between mainstream Islamists and Fundamentalists, saying a fundamentalist is "a political individual" in search of a "more original Islam," while the Islamist is pursuing a political agenda (1990: 823).

Of course, now and then Naipaul makes certain valid points regarding the drawbacks among the Muslims. In his criticism about the failings of Islamic fundamentalism, he makes rather correct assessment of the erratic judgement. He specifically criticizes the fundamentalist's rigidity and vagueness and further comments that in their infusion of history and ideology, they have no idea of reform or any ameliorative process. Commenting on fundamentalism in Pakistan he further observes:

> The fundamentalist, insecure, with their un-historical view, feared alien contamination. But fundamentalism offered nothing. It pushed men to an unappeasable faith; it offered a political desert. It violated the 'basics'; it could never wall out the rest of the world. And I thought it was possible, looking not many steps ahead, to see how in Pakistan, by the very excesses of fundamentalism, Islam might be preparing its own transformation. (1982: 111)

In the beginning of the book, Naipaul makes another startling comment with a tone of irony while talking of the *purdah* for women and the dignity given to women in Islam. Here he seems to ridicule the very idea as he observes:

> Another evening, on another programme, an Iranian woman came on with her head covered to tell us that Islam protected women and gave them dignity. Fourteen hundred years ago in Arabia, she said, girl children were

> buried alive; it was Islam that put a stop to that. Well, we didn't all live in Arabia (not even the woman with the covered head), and many things had happened since the seventh century. Did woman–especially someone as fierce as the woman addressing us—still need the special protection that Islam gave them? Did they need the veil? Did they need to be banned from public life and from appearing on television? (1982: 12)

In this passage Naipaul seems to challenge the claim of the Iranian woman regarding the protection given to women in Islam. Secondly, he questions the importance and the necessity of *purdah* in Islam and third he wonders as to why the Muslim woman should be banned from public life and from appearing on television.

As Paul Theroux writes in *Fresh Air Friend* (2002), the "unique function" of a "travel book" is to express "the dissonance as well as the melodies, the contradictions..., in short, and the messiness of life" (2002: 53). Naipaul's *Among the Believers: An Islamic Journey* rightly fulfils it. Apart from the perceptions and impressions of Naipaul's experiences during his travels and sojourns in these countries, it is the novel mode of the narrative technique, which makes his non-fiction novels most popular and absorbing. As we have found out the above mentioned tenets and lexicons of travel theory in *Among the Believers: An Islamic Journey*, we can conclude by saying that this is a lively travelogue, full of quick vignettes, word sketches and pieces of conversation. Naipaul has got amazing style of narration, and his technique of writing made him worth to be Nobel Laureate.

Works Cited

Amis, Martin. "Review of Naipaul's *Among the Believer's: An Islamic Journey*." *The Observer*. 29 June, 1981. 23-24.

Boorstin, Daniel. *The Image: A Guide to Pseudo-Events in America*. New York: Atheneum, 1985.

Buckeye, Robert. "Form as the Extension of Content: 'their existence in my eyes'." *Review of Contemporary Fiction* 3.1. 1983. 192-95.

Chandra, N.D.R. "Canon, Multiculturalism & *The God of Small Things*." *Contemporary Literary Criticism: Theory and Practice*. New Delhi: Authors Press, 2005. 471-81.

Clifford, James. *Routes: Travel and Translation in the Late Twentieth Century*. Cambridge: Harvard University Press, 1997.

Fussell, Paul. *Abroad: British Literary Travelling Between the Wars*. Oxford: Oxford University Press, 1980.

Grewal, Inderpal. *Home and Harem: Nation, Gender, Empire, and the Cultures of Travel*. Durham and London: Duke University Press, 1996.

Hornby, A.S. *Oxford Advanced Learners Dictionary of Current English*. Oxford: Oxford University Press, 2000.

Jurgen, Osterhammel. *Colonialism: A Theoretical Overview*. Princeton: N.J.: Markus Wiener Publishers, 2005.

Lapidus, Ira. *Islam, Politics and Social Movements*. California: University of California Press, 1990.

Naipaul, V.S. *Among the Believers: An Islamic Journey*. New York: Vintage, 1982.

——. *An Area of Darkness: His Discovery of India*. Picador: London, 2010.

——. *India: A Million Mutinies Now*. Vintage: London, 1991.

Raban, Jonathan. *Coasting*. London: Picador, 1987.

Siegel, Kristi. *Issues in Travel Writing*. London: Peter Lang, 2002.

Theroux, Paul. *Fresh Air Friend: Travel Writings 1985-2000*. Boston: Houghton Mifflin, 2002.

10

V.S. Naipaul: A Pioneer in Non-fiction Writing

Amod Kumar Rai

Twentieth-century literature has been a kaleidoscope of ever-changing forms and genres. Interdisciplinary bond of literature, philosophy, art, science and other disciplines have been strengthened. Initially, critics and eminent literati have normally evaded the necessary and critical distinctions between literary genres. Nevertheless, twentieth-century literary authorities have evinced predilections for independent literary genres and wouldn't allow useful and critical distinctions going un-emphasised. For more than a century, novel has been the most popularized, most promoted and most awarded art form. But in the last few decades, non-fiction is dislodging novel from its supreme position if not in to, then slightly: "We can't fail to see how uneasy the novel is with the narrative mode, which once made its vital principle, and how its practitioners seek by one device or another to evade or obscure or palliate the act of telling" (Trilling 37).

This non-fictional writing has emerged strongly and prominently in the sixties as the most widely read and influential of books. Now in order to decipher clearly what a non-fictional writing is it is indispensible to have a lucid apprehension of what a fiction is. In an inclusive sense, fiction is any literary narrative either in prose or in verse dependent much on "imaginative excursions" (Morison 93) rather than about real events. In a narrower sense, however, fiction denotes only narratives that are written in prose and sometimes is used simply as a synonym for novel. By systematic contrast, non-fiction is directly concerned with the rendition of actual events, real people and presently existing places.

The *New Encyclopedia Britannica* defines non-fiction as a "story of actual people, actual events, told with the dramatic techniques of the novel" (567). From the same source, we come to know that Truman Capote is the founder of this recent offshoot and the book which procures him this critical acclaim in his *In Cold Blood* (1965). In its next phase of evolution, Norman Mailer's *The Executioner's Song* (1979) takes this newly born babe, non-fiction a step further. This non-fiction novel involves uses of a variety of novelistic techniques to give a graphic rendition of recent characters and happenings and is based not only on historical records but often on personal records and interviews with the chief agents. But neither the Encyclopedia nor any Glossary to literary terms include or even refer to V.S. Naipaul among the practitioners of non-fiction writing. A simple reason for this is that Naipaul's works are strictly non-fiction and not non-fictional novel.

Now, the word non-fiction has been subjected to a promiscuous use by the scholars and critics, for reportage, critical writings, diaries, travelogues and journalistic writings and so on. We have to explore threadbare the differences in between and then only a possibility of a clear-cut meaning of non-fiction, as for as Naipaul's works are concerned, will emerge.

Academically, these two aforementioned definitions of the Encyclopedia and Glossary have been consented upon by all and sundry in the intellectual field. But the problem that may baffle one is how far and where to this non-fiction writing differs from early practices from reportage, critical writings, diaries, travelogues, biographical and journalistic writings, etc. Since these are concerned only with an individual personality or personalities. It more or less focuses on surroundings but the principal aim is to highlight the character and life of man.

Eighteenth century witnessed a spurt in biographical writings with Dr. Samuel Johnson's *Lives of the Poets* (1779-81) and the most phenomenal James Boswell's *The Life of Samuel Johnson* (1791). Travelogues are unswervingly concerned with the experiences, feelings and adventures of custom, culture, heritage and living style of the people of travelled areas. Naipaul himself writes about certain travel books—"No travel book could be only about the roads and hotels. Such a book can be written about certain countries in Africa" (7).

Right from the Renaissance period, travel writing had been so. Richard Hakluyt may be the father of travelogue writings, collected the testimonies and celebrated the exploits of contemporary sailors, traders, adventurers and explorers in *Principal Navigations, Voyages and Discoveries of the English Nations.*

A little later came the tide of diary writing. It too was not exactly non-fiction in its complete projection. The diary served as an indispensible historical resource with the vivid account of courts and parliamentary intrigues and misfortunes, viz. the plague of 1666, the great fire of London 1666-67. Samuel Pepys and John Evelyn will always be standing at the head of this kind of writing. But the problem with Diarists is that they cannot remain disinterested and allow much of their personal whims and fascinations to be inserted in their writings. Moreover, diaries can include only a particular span of time in the history of a country or person whereas non-fiction will render the total impact of History on the present of a particular phenomenon. Likewise journalistic writings are to be tied up with newspapers and magazines as they are of tiny statures whereas non-fiction is bulky and organic structure dealing not with a single episode but with the entire body of a culture, civilization, nation and society. Defoe's *Journal of the Plague Year* (1722) is a commendable attempt at reportage writing and journalistic writing and while it remains a non-fiction piece of writing, technically it is still far from being non-fiction in the sense in which Naipaul and others have handled it.

Having discriminated non-fiction with other similar varieties of literature we will now investigate first what non-fiction in the post fifties stands for and then how Naipaul has tackled this form for his purposes. Non-fictions in the postcolonial era mean a form of writing where:

> Writer may use the fiction writer's techniques of plotting, suspense, dramatic technique of conflict, character development but he may not go beyond the facts he is able to dig out. This story must present a conclusion, a point of view, that conclusion must be reached, as in the scientific method, only after all available evidences have been weighed and after as much biases and prejudices as possible has been ruled out. Thus the ideal of journalistic objective is part of and vital to the process. (Andre Fountain 3)

Clay Felker and Tom Wolfe, editor of the *New York* magazine consider it as the "new journalism." However, in an article in *The Bulletin,* Tom Wolfe says that the non-fiction was pioneered by *Esquire*, under Editor Hayes and Felker in the early 1960s. Proceeding further in the analysis of salient characteristics of this non-fiction Wolfe considers it as "saturation reporting's", here reporter spends weeks, months, years with the subject of his story so that he can observe first-hand action which reveals motivation (86). Moreover, it is equally grounded in journalistic writing or what the English academicians call creative writing. From journalism it takes the reporter's aggressive and constant search for facts, his accuracy and sensitive trained eyes, his skepticism and adeptness of checking and cross checking the things he is told against documents, other spokesmen and original sources.

From creative or fiction writer, it takes imagination, skill at plotting and portraying character, the techniques of building a dramatic story for evoking the reader's emotions and most importantly the impositions of writer's individual judgment on the story. In his book *On Creative Writing*, Paul Engel says that creative writing means "quite simply writing to which something new has been added" (26-27). Now the simple question that arises is how that novelty can be created? Professor Cathy Covert of Syracuse University is aptly quoted here who says: "Creativity is taking a bit of knowledge from this discipline, an insight from another, an experience one has lived, assimilating them into one's mind, going through a process of complete chaos and ultimately coming up with something quite new" (86).

This is more or less a ricochet, a resonance of illustrious Eliotian doctrine of objective poetry which he expounds through a scientific analogy. Poet's experience of a particular phenomenon and his emotions (insight) about it that merges in the presence of a catalyst (i.e. his own mind) and produces a new thing or idea which has not even the least trace of the catalyst. It is exactly so in this newly born non-fiction, the non-fiction artist goes beyond the facts to get the truth. He spends a long span of time about his subject. He makes himself an expert, a savant by reading and interviewing the experts. He relates what he learns from the problems, worries, interests and yearnings of the people. A perfect non-fiction artist must know to whom he intends to write. He must go for the idea that would affect the largest number of readers. In this respect, an interesting remark, made by Summer Blossom, the editor of American magazine is worth quoting, "I'd rather have a story on noses than on red hair. Because more people have noses than red hair" (7).

The difference between amateur and professional writers is that the amateur writes for himself and the later writes for his readers. It is only for the lurid taste of his readers that he adds the spices of crime, sex, sports, society, culture, customs and manners in harmonious proportion. One may not suspect the assimilation of sex and crime in non-fiction writing. The writer sharply observes the sexual habits and belief of a particular culture or region and then passes his judgment on it. People are primarily and instinctively interested in themselves: their problems, the things they do everyday, their hobbies, their relations with other people. A non-fiction artist realizes it well and gives what men and women naturally hunt for. Research, therefore, has been a great succor for non-fiction writing. It has been termed by Andre Fountain as "legwork" and it consists of going where something has happened, looking acutely, listening accurately, questioning participants and ultimately giving a coherent and organic garb. In their book *The Reporter's Trade* Washington columnists Joseph and Stewart Alsop remark: "If you get out and see for yourself what is going on and talk to a great many people who are responsible and involved in what is going on, you can hardly help in doing a good job of reporting" (132).

Nonfiction equally depends on interviewing. The art of interviewing breaks down into two parts—how do you get to see the man? And how do you get them to tell the things making your story pertinent, lively, and readable? For being an interviewer par excellence, one must make his art lively and challenging. Having done all this work nonfiction artist goes for the evaluation of his raw material. He summons his mind, his huge mass of facts, figures, statistics, expert opinions, conflicting viewpoints, anecdotes, tangential information, the motives and emotions of the characters and tries to make a judgment about where the truth lies. The evaluation also helps the writer in organizing his work. The art of organization process is first to refine out the single idea or theme that the facts indicate. Everything in the piece, viz. anecdotes, interviews, reporting, and individual judgment should support the author's point of view.

Naipaulian Innovation in Nonfiction

More or less of what has been enumerated in the earlier pages can be applied to the nonfictional writings of Sir V.S. Naipaul too. But he seems to assert a certain distinction by having some special features distinguishing sufficiently his nonfiction from those of his contemporaries and predecessors. This may be, directly or indirectly, because of the lurking fear of each original and creative writer as propounded by Harold Bloom in his *The Anxiety of Influence* (1973). It is the same anxiety and fear of influence which weaned away Keats from completing his *Hyperion*. Naipaul's non-fictions undergo several phases of research, interviewing and evaluation—evaluation not only of the facts he recollects but also of the preconceived notions and judgments about a particular phenomenon. For instance, in the very beginning of his *An Area of Darkness* (1964), he talks about one of the mega-hits of Indian Cinema, without referring to name, but the indication is direct enough to the blockbuster

Dosti (1964): "a funeral dirge or a blind man's lament could become a hit. They delighted in decay" (8).

Whether Indians' only source of delight is decay or something else is a matter of long debate and could be made somewhere else, but here the remarkable thing is Naipaul's inadequate judgment about a film, which was largely celebrated by Indians. Naipaul's nonfiction starts with the inception and shaping of the idea for the story, it takes the reader through research process, the evaluation of evidences, the organization and the method of presentation, etc. This shows us clearly a beautiful fusion of fictional and nonfictional techniques in his writing. Firstly, facts and evidences are presented to readers followed by his individual judgment imbued with impeccable dramaturgy. In other words, first the factual property of nonfiction artist and then a judgment or view of the novelist comes. But while giving judgment the artist shouldn't go too far and allow his bias to override the facts. Naipaul as an artist has a noble purpose that is his "commitment to deliver the truth." He has achieved it dexterously in the big corpus of his nonfiction. Naipaul uses specific details while portraying his concerns. He has learned it instinctively. What makes a story new and colorful are the details. He hardly forgets to leave even the least particle of any construction.

A nonfiction artist should be precise and with Naipaul the art of precision reaches its apogee. Seldom does the reader fail in getting the intended idea or figure of something depicted. This precision is often altered with his uses of connotations. Even the simplest word triggers different pictures of figures in the mind of different people. Psychologists who give different word association tests see this everyday. This is the dimension of writer's work; he must use these connotations to get his meaning implanted in the reader's mind. In her book, Freya Stark says:

> Words dress our thoughts and should fit; and fit not only in their utterances, but in their implications their sequences and silences just as in architecture the empty spaces are as important as those that are filled. The problem of all writing is the same as that presented by the compositions

> of the telegram, one has to convey a meaning with the use of a few and always inadequate words.... The whole generalship of writing is in the summoning and marshalling of these unseen auxiliaries. (106-07)

It is the exuberant use of connotations that make his nonfiction having two levels. He tells one story but tell it in such a way that it seems to be telling another. One is manipulated and second is tacit.

Ultimately, but not least crucial Naipaulian nonfiction writings are teeming with his adept dramatic skills. Naipaul has had the realization that totally objective, factual and uninvolved representation will leave the reader the same way, not stirred, and not moved. Such writings will be purely a reporter's news. Dramatic writing is crucial for keeping nonfiction vital and interesting. Even being dramatic, it remains objective because the writer takes no position, pleads no cause and it is factual only the way of presentation is changed. Flashback technique is his frequently used device in making his writing dramatic. Everybody knows the essence of dramatic writing is conflict. The deep ancient conflicts are few and simple: "man against nature, man against man, man against himself" (Andre Fontain 36).

The adept writer, like Naipaul always tries to evoke either primordial fear or joy—lurking in their 'collective unconscious.' The first type of conflict yielding fear is missing in Naipaul's writing. The conflict of man against man lies behind many stories—social, political, economical sport, etc. in which man battle other man for power and position. This conflict is recurrently present in Naipaul's writing.

Naipaul's nonfiction is beautifully intervened with historical, political and geographical matrix without inclining to anyone in particular. He explores history for tracing the root of a particular phenomenon, at times for substantiating his judgment and for showing the contradiction between past and present. He includes all the topographical, regional and geographical aspects of a particular nation. Politics naturally mix place for itself in nonfiction since much of the life is determined and directed by the political authorities of the country.

Naipaul's nonfiction largely varies from History but the chord connecting these two disciplines is also perceptible. It is possible because consciously or unconsciously Naipaul's nonfiction adumbrates the same philosophy and doctrine as propagated by icons of history. History, like nonfiction, encompasses human races, culture, society, economics, politics, religion, custom and assumptions, etc. thereby the question which springs how far this nonfiction differs from History must be entertained. History not only provides men with an insight to understand their evolution but also explains their present existence and supplies prolepses for their tomorrow. To take note to Collingwood in his *The Idea of History* (1981) seems to be reasonable: "The past which a historian studies is not the dead past but a past which in some sense is still living in the present" (23).

Without having a historical cognizance is living like a child. But to study History simply as a dead past is another wretchedness. It equates present, past and future for the maximum benefit of the posterity. Art on the other hand is full of descriptions of feasibility and probability. Artists have a special vision and render nature in accordance to their vision. Unlike History Naipaul's nonfiction scrutinizes the family history of even ordinary individuals who are none other than his interviewee. It is substantiated by Naipaul himself in his *A Turn in the South*:

> There must always be certain things that drop out of History. Only the broadest theme and movement can be recorded. All the multifarious chopping and changing, all the individual hazards and venturesomeness and failures can't be recorded. History is full of mysteries, even as family history is full of gaps and embellishments. Certain things are lost, the way for me, the grandson of immigrants from India to Trinidad, ancestors as close as grandparents are mysterious and some unknown, making it impossible to give answer after just a hundred years to a question like: where did your people come from? (87-88)

This is truly a problem with History that in its endeavor of seizing broadest movement it segregates the entire individual 'hazards and veuturesomeness.' It never attempts to emphasize the ordinary folk things which may be proved crucial later. The author beautifully gives his own example. Naipaul, the Nobel Laureate, is not confidant about his own real native land because such things are lost in History. After a generation or two when the posterity would be keen to know Naipaul's ancestry, History would be disappointing them by giving them insufficient and inadequate information. It is what has happened with History. We don't know anything definite about Kalidas's parents, about Banbhatt's family, even about the ancestry of first great Indian King Chandragupta Maurya. History teems with such examples.

Giving family history in his nonfiction in full detail is Naipaul's forte. Persons and facts which are unknown to History, which have given crucial succor to phenomenal incidents recorded in History, are mentioned frequently and mentioned with their useful contribution in Naipaul's nonfiction. The contribution which is almost absent in History, is constantly present in his nonfiction. Naipaul, for instance, emphasizes the varied incongruity between the Black communities whereas History takes it as a whole. He tells us in *A Turn in the South* (1989):

> What is not easily called to mind now is how close, in the slave days, the slave territories of the Caribbean and the south was. When the French planters of the West Indies were negotiating terms with the Spanish authorities for setting in Trinidad, one of the pressures they applied was a threat to take their slaves to American south. That would be better for them as planters, they said especially since after the war-since the war of independence...and how rich and tempting that flat well-watered lowlands of the Caroline coast must have appeared to people who knew only the islands!
>
> And how strange to reflect that the black people of Trinidad, I grew up among other with another twist, have been born in Carolines and might have had an entirely different history. The chief difference lies in the distance of two societies from slavery. Slavery was abolished in British colonies in 1834 and with the Caribbean colonies were

> thereafter neglected...American slavery ended with the civil war. But it might be said that freedom came to them only in 1954. So American blacks have reached where they have reached just in thirty years. In those thirty years American blacks have grown to see opportunity, while the larger independent territories of the British Caribbean—Trinidad, Jamaica, Guyana—has in their various ways been plundered and undone. (123-24)

Where does History comprehend this disparity within the slave community? History never has had any scope and provision for prologue. It just acquaints the reader with what happened and how it happened. It doesn't indulge in enunciating the aftermath. It is exactly what Nirad C. Chaudhury propounds as precepts for a historian in his *The Autobiography of an Unknown Indian* (1951):

> The historian must be content to state facts as they happened or to use a modern phrase, to show a development without intruding us opinions and predilections into narratives. His position is not among his fellowmen of whom he is writing. He doesn't share their joy or passions nor single in their affairs. His position is that of a spectator who stands on a balcony and watches a crowd under him. (111-12)

Naipaul is never gratified as being merely a spectator. He in one of his interview given to press during NRI's celebration affirms that the errors of History must be reformed. He can't allow the stupendous mistakes to persist continually. He pokes History with his personal judgments and while doing so he does not leave any prospect for arguments. His nonfiction is inextricably preceded by a prologue. It is through this prologue Naipaul focuses the origin of work and gives an impression of place, person and palaver obliging him to write. The prologue also makes the readers ready for knowing the same old things but with new meanings. *An Area of Darkness* (1964) is a corollary of just a prohibition of carrying liquor, the prologue does tell this and marvels the readers by positing the entire country as a land of myths, simply as an 'area of darkness.' Prologue of *A Turn in the South* tells us that a single sentence, uttered by

Howard—"I would go home to my Mumma"—stirs the writer to write a book about the south with the Home that Howard had.

Notwithstanding its differences from History, it is its similarities with History which is quite wonderful to know. Naipaul believes, or it is the circumstances which make him believe so, E.H. Carr's philosophy of History, i.e. "History is a continuous process of interaction between Historians and his facts an unending dialogue between present and past" (37-38).

The past does leave an ineffaceable impact on the present and the present palaver has its root in the abyss of the past. This is what Carr means by "unending dialogue" between the present and the past and vice versa. Despite rigorous endeavors made by government and non-government Casteism and hypocrisy are still persisting in India just because it is strong in our past. Naipaul gives another instance of this incessant interaction between past and present:

> Foresyth country was forty miles or so to North of Atlanta. In that country in 1912 a young white girl was raped and beaten so badly that she died a few days later. A number of blacks were implicated. One was lynched; two others were tried and hanged. All the blacks of foresyth were chased out of the country; and since then no Blacks had been allowed to live in the country. (121)

A single event occurred almost a period of hundred years ago, has its indelible impact on present. Naipaul uses common assumptions and belief of common people to make History moving even further and seldom does he try to give any independent and personal judgment in such cases. He'll just expose all the facts of a phenomenon and leave his readers quibbling for the most authentic and right one. Historians can't dare to do so. He ought to reach some reasonable conclusion.

History is rarely completed without geography, sociology, politics, economics, religion, etc. so does Naipaulian nonfiction also. It traces not only the history but also the geographical, social, political and religious position of the concerned areas and its nearness and distances from other localities. This helps readers in deriving clear and unending picture of the particular region. It also helps them to know the validity, utility and scientific base of their culture and tradition in comparisons of others.

As it is with Naipaul's vision of History where he intends to frame his own Historiography, he brings forth some surprising shifts in the entire discourse of our national leaders and sages. He conceived History not as a record of linear progression of established truths but simply as a discourse which is constructed with mutual consents, now reliable and then unreliable. Thus, there is always a possibility of recreating History. As only this recreated History could support his verdicts. Naipaul's own conviction regarding this History is apt to be quoted here, "History is interplay of various people and it has gone on forever. I can think of no culture that has been left to it" (32). This absolutely matches with Naipaul's practiced strategy in his nonfiction. History is created largely through the individuals whose roles Naipaul reconstructs from letters and documents they produced or appeared in the theme that emerges from this material is the disparity between the heroic images History has imposed on the protagonists, or they themselves conceived, and the greed and lust for fame and power, especially the illusions, the evasions and deceits their ambitions entailed. There are innumerable instances of it throughout his oeuvre, e.g. the image of Gandhiji, Vinoba Bhave, Columbus, and Sir Walter Raleigh, etc.

Thus, we see that Sir V.S. Naipaul has innovated the genre of nonfiction and it is his novelty that counts for his immense popularity. Without the aforementioned new features, he would not have been able to hold his readers for such a long series of nonfictional works. Where other writers of his age struggle for one or two piece of writing, Naipaul has handed over more than twenty-one works of nonfiction and the journey is still on.

Works Cited

Abrams, M.H. *Glossary of Literary Terms*. Bangalore: Prism Pvt. Ltd., 2009.

Alsop, Stuart and Joseph. *The Reporter's Trade*. New York: OUP, 1958.

Bloom, Harold. *The Anxiety of Influence*. New York: OUP, 1973.

Blossom, Summer. Ed. *The American Magazine*. Vol. II. December. California: California University Press, 1992.

Chaudhury, Nirad C. *The Autobiography of an Unknown Indian*. California: University of California Press, 1969.

Carr, E.H. *What is History*? New Delhi: OUP, 1972.

Collingwood, J. *The Idea of History*. Cambridge: Cambridge University Press, 1981.

Engel, Paul. *On Creative Writing*. New York: Andre Fontain, 1985.

Felker, Clay. Ed. *New York*. New York: Creative Press, 1980.

Fontaine, Andre. *The Preface of the Art of Writing Nonfiction*. New York: Andre Deutch, 1968.

Khan, Md. J. Akhtar. *V.S. Naipaul: A Critical Study*. New Delhi: Creative Books, 2004.

Morrison, Tony. "Novel as a Discovery" in *New York*. London: Vintage, 1989.

Naipaul, V.S. *A Turn in the South*. London: Andre Deutsch, 1989.

——. *An Area of Darkness*. London: Andre Deutsch, 1969.

——. *India: A Million Mutinies Now*. London: Viking, 1990.

Stark, Freya. *Saying What One Means*. New York: OUP, 1967.

The New Encyclopaedia Britanica. Cambridge: Cambridge University Press, 1998.

Trilling, Lionel. *The Changing American Literary Scene*. Ed. Joseph Epestein. London: Andre Deutsch, 1974.

11

V.S. Naipaul's Reflections on India: A Critical Examination

Aju Mukhopadhyay

Renowned Nobel Laureate of Indian origin, V.S. Naipaul, whose forefathers settled in Trinidad as part of Indian Diaspora, finally settled in the Great Britain after some studies as a professional writer for the rest of his life. But he feels nowhere at home. However, much he has been honored by England he cannot feel it his own country, having come out of Trinidad where his forefathers settled as bonded labours he does not feel to have any more connection with it but a memoir only. To India he owes his birth and being though not physically, he realizes. So he has travelled India many a time and has written three important books on India's past and present, commented on its civilization, religion and political growth. India forever remains in his consciousness, modifies his thoughts and ideas, helps him achieve as an Indian, though not officially. Though British, he may be considered an Indian English writer as Salman Rushdie is, as writers of Indian origin.

Though Naipaul is an accomplished novelist, he is more known throughout the world for his travel books containing his views on race and religion, country and civilization whether acceptable or controvertible. Born in Trinidad in 1932, he grew up with further education at Oxford, England, settling there since 1950. Eventually, he became a writer by profession trying his hands in no other profession or job. He began visiting India from time to time beginning in 1962. He is by birth Hindu

Brahmin so it never leaves his consciousness, though he has said that he has apathy towards religion in general and rituals in particular:

> I really miraculously had no faith at all, was born without faith and have continued to be without faith. My father was much more philosophical, and he despised, angered by the expression of ritual, and I suppose I have allowed myself to be influenced by that, but I think it was also my nature. I have no religious faith. (Kohn)

Naipaul travelled through West Indies, South America, Africa and other countries, recording his ideas about such countries and races. Due perhaps to a clash of Islamic civilization with the Hindu and Christian civilizations for centuries, he was equally or more interested about the Islamic countries; their expansion and plan of conversion. Consequently, he travelled to such countries in 1979 and published *Among the Believers: An Islamic Journey* (1981). In 1995, he returned to Indonesia, Iran, Pakistan and Malaysia and published *Beyond Belief: Islamic Excursions among the Converted Peoples* in 1998. In the chapters beginning his prologue in his *Beyond Belief* (1998), he wrote,

> This book is a follow-up to a book I published seventeen years ago, *Among the Believers*, about a journey to the same four countries. When I started on that journey in 1979 I knew almost nothing about Islam—it is the best way to start on a venture—and that first book was an exploration of the details of the faith and what looked like its capacity for revolution. The theme of conversion was always there but, I didn't see it as clearly as I saw it on this second journey. (1)

I do not find any sense of communalism in these studies. Awards are given by all established institutions on the basis of some choice; may be political, national, racial or even otherwise but for that, I feel that the writer cannot be branded as communal even if some political group has loved his choice. And is not religion, either for adoring or rejecting it, the cause of fame to writers like Rushdie which is applicable behind the fame of Taslima Nasrin also? Is it not a fact that writers have censored other religions also without any apparent reaction on the part of the establishments or people who tolerate? It seems that Naipaul has some prejudice against Islam as compared to other religions, for which he has assigned reasons through his narratives.

Another severe charge against the writer is his tilt towards some high caste in Hindu religion. A few words about Indian Caste system which has been variously and acrimoniously attacked by the intellectuals and some leftist ideologues may be relevant here. At the beginning when such caste system was introduced it was on the basis of human qualities and tendencies of nature, as were evident in groups and individuals. Higher or lower were the ideas of the society. Brahmins were not the richest people nor were they the kings usually. It is on record that movement of individuals from one caste to another could be made on shift of attitude or progress in certain quality achieved for example the case of *Rishi* Vishwamitra or Jabala Satyakama as in the *Upanishad*. It was not a rigid system. It helped the division of labour and smooth functioning of the society comprising different wings of human activities. Degradation of the system in later years are regrettable facts, they have been amended by various processes from time to time. It is amply palpable that divisions among the aristocrats and plebeians, among the ranks and files, divisions between the rich and poor, among the comrades, existed and exist in innumerable forms in different societies throughout the countries. In no civilized society all humans are treated as equal. The system of untouchable, low-caste barrier and various religious discriminations in Hindu society were deviations, a product of the Dark Age. They have been officially done away with in modern India. On the other hand, extreme system of reservation in favour of certain castes and tribes has created a reversed position for those who it was thought to be privileged. Humans are born neither equal in quality nor equal by opportunity; any argument against it is fallacious, decries reality. What is ideal is that everyone should have equal opportunity of growth with all other human rights of a modern society.

V.S. Naipaul has not entered into such disputes. What he has done is, discussions and dialogues between him and the persons who accompanied him at different places in India, interviews with individuals of different segments of society, placed as narratives as in novels making them interesting. Now his selection of his guide or companion, revealing the facts of a society or place at a given point of time and his idiosyncrasies to react to such situations may be questioned. One may question his judgment about many social or historical positions but they are as they are, as in a novel or a travelogue. They stand on their ground. On many such findings he has discussed histories and has pointedly shown his preferences and ideas. On the whole, these are words of wisdom and judgment from a writer's point of view, as he is. I find that series of travels undertaken by him have been successful as in tune with his mission though his view points may always be contradicted or challenged, which has happened. His Indian trilogy consists of *An Area of Darkness* (1964), *India: A Wounded Civilization* (1977) and *India: A Million Mutinies Now* (1990). My discussions are based mainly on the last book comprising the trilogy. Below are some excerpts from some such documents which carry lively discussions spiced by my viewpoint somewhere.

Let us come to his statement identifying India as his identity, which supports and sustains his being:

> It was also the India of great civilization and the great classical past. It was the India by which, in all the difficulties of our circumstances, we felt supported. It was an aspect of our identity, the community identity we had developed, which, in multi-racial Trinidad, had become more like a racial identity. (*Mutinies* 8)

But coming to India for the first time in 1962, he found it to be much vaster than his imagination, with innumerable communities. So his imaginative identity of an Indian community was lost. It was many identities: "The poverty of the Indian streets and the country side was an affront and a threat, a scratching at my old neurosis. Two generations separated me from that kind of poverty, but I felt closer to it than most of the Indians I met" (*Mutinies* 8). How nostalgic he becomes while visiting India as a tourist, reminding us of an Indian's foreign identity!

It was in Bombay of those days which he visited first to which the roads belonged, as mentioned. He later mentioned similar roads at Bangalore and elsewhere. Now while going to meet a local politician in Bombay, in keeping with an appointment he observes,

> Without Charu I don't think I would have made it even to the internal staircase of the place—I was so demoralized, so choked, driven so near to a stomach-heave, by the smell at the entrance, with wet mangled garbage and scavenging cats and kittens in a little patio, and then, in the suddenly dark passage, by the thick warm smell, catching at my throat, of blocked drains. It was Charu, with his brahmin's sense of duty...like a father leading his child, led me on and on...giving glimpses of family and living spaces. (*Mutinies* 61)

He met a script writer for film in Bombay who was telling him his experience with an actor-cum-owner, responsible for production of a film: "For three hours he told me a story.... It was a horrifying experience.... And.... It flashed through my head: If I tell him it's a very good story, I've got a job" (*Mutinies* 88). So he said and was instantly accepted on payment of 5001 rupees. "It's an Indian custom, that extra one rupee.... It's for good luck" (*Mutinies* 88).

Then he had a long meeting with the Dalit Panther leader, Namdeo, to whom poetry and political movement streamed out from the same source. He, once from the underground world, was a very strong man, became a leader of the downtrodden. In answer to what Ambedkar meant to a Dalit, Namdeo said, "There was a time when we were treated like animals. Now we live like human beings. It's all because of Ambedkar" (*Mutinies* 119).

In this exchange between them, the reader comes to know of the life of Dalits even before 1955, quite after the independence. But the cloud was getting cleared gradually. At the end of the chapter Naipaul added few words to focus the position of such people, as a witness, making it clear that he understood it,

> ...a greater understanding became possible of the long, patient line of dark men and women on one side of the road on the morning I had arrived: not just the poor of India, but an expression of the old internal cruelty of that poverty; people at the bottom, full of emotion, with no politics at that moment, just rejecting rejection. (*Mutinies* 119)

I may add that it was not only the cruelty of poverty but cruelty of the degenerated, superstitious social system of caste. Naipaul is not caste supporter here.

He then moved among the dangerous underground dons of Bombay and described their cruel *modus operandi*, unfailing revenge and group cult, which is very difficult for an ordinary man to comprehend. He has further depicted in detail their way of living in space extremely narrow and crowded but exactly fitting in their lives, a depiction of famous slum life of Bombay. In between his narratives he discusses history and gives his considered opinion, sometimes positive, sometimes negative.

From Bombay, he travelled to Goa and then entered Karnataka, mostly living in Bangalore. Speaking about Goa he said:

> Portugal had arrived in 1498 and triumphed in 1509-10. Just over half a century later the great Hindu empire of the South, the empire of Vijaynagar, was defeated and physically laid waste by a combination of Muslim rulers; almost at the same time, in the North, the Mogul power was entering its time of glory. It might have seemed then that Hindu India, without the new learning and new tools of Europe...without the political ideas...was on the verge of extinction, something to be divided between Christian Europe and the Muslim world, and all its religious symbols and difficult theology rendered as meaningless as the Aztec gods in Mexico, or the symbolism of Hindu Angkor. (*Mutinies* 143)

People of Hindu majority, as it should be as they were the people without a tag of Hindu religion in the past, inhabiting India from ancient time with a cultural unity throughout history, presently cohabit in a politically secular India with mixed population from all other religious denominations, live here as after multiple colonization.

While in Bangalore, speaking of woman's freedom, he mentioned someone named Kala with whom he had discourses that, "She wasn't allowed to go and visit her people when she wanted to. She could make no decision as to what she would like to do with her own life. Somebody always decided for her..." (*Mutinies* 178).

From the paths of Bangalore, he moved away to further down, in Madras city, as it was then called. Here he found,

> The restaurants and hotels that were vegetarians were clean.... The cleanliness and vegetarianism were connected; they were both contained in the southern idea of Brahmanism...[The] vegetarian food of the South—which drew the crowds to the Woodlands—was too subtle, too light; it made no impression on my stomach; it never left me fed. (*Mutinies* 208)

Here he comments on caste and compares it to degree. Here he learnt the difference between foods of North and South but it seems that he did not partake plenty of rice with *Sambhar* which is the main staple food of the South, supplemented by *Dosa* and *idly* in the morning. Coming to Madras, he stumbled upon a name called Periyar which he heard but not as the name of a person. Coming to know of him he painted a biographical picture of Periyar:

> He was an atheist and a rationalist.... He ridiculed the Hindu gods. He cruelly mocked caste Hindus; comparing the poverty of their scientific achievements with the achievements of Europe.... Periyar's grave was in a corner of the plot. All around the grave were polished grey granite slabs engraved with some of Periyar's sayings. One of the sayings, virtually an incantation, was very famous: *There is no God. There is no God. There is no God at all. He who invented God is a fool. He who propagates God is a scoundrel. He who worships God is a barbarian.* This was how Periyar began all his discourses. (*Mutinies* 218)

The writer concluded his discourse on Periyar with,

> Periyar was a local figure; he never outgrew his cause. Without Gandhi and the Congress and the independence movement his cause wouldn't have had the power it had; he was riding on the back of something very big. That might have been why I hadn't heard of him. (*Mutinies* 222)

Without commenting much on the writer's observations on Periyar, this seems right that he was a local figure only, really ignorant of the Indian heritage. The writer later met Veeramani, a follower of Periyar who was for forty years engaged in a local revolution like a little war, a Dravidian movement. He met Manyammai, the widow of Periyar, with Veeramani. From their conversation with the writer we come to know that Periyar was very frugal, "He was custodian not only of human rights, but of the party property rights. He multiplied those rights by investing in Mills and Banks" (*Mutinies* 272).

The writer further tells that Dravidian movement always represented the middle castes, that Periyar belonged to a *bania* or trading caste that their movement never bothered about the class. He mentioned the rebel atheist poet Bharathidasam was a part of the movement. Then he stated the Maoist rebellion by the lower castes which raged the North of Tamil Nadu for some seven or eight years, which was subdued. The writer beamed about the aboriginals or tribal people who were exploited by the *Zamindars*; they are known as Adi-Dravidas. He met Lakusthan, the Maoist rebel. He mentions about the Brahmins who too took lessons from the struggle and amended their ways of life and livelihood though they were cornered by all means. It continues. Towards the end of the Madras chapter, the writer met some leaders who waged class war at their place as true comrades, and while coming out visited their bathroom out of need:

> Opening carefully the closed bathroom door, I found the toilet bowel unflushed, and the seat and floor pissed over. Was it social experience alone? Or was there also—in this man who fought the class war—some very deep caste

> feelings about the uncleanliness of the latrines: places so unclean they were beneath one's notice, places for other people to notice, other people to clean? (*Mutinies* 278)

From Madras, the writer moved to Calcutta which he first visited in 1962 and then around 1989, before publication of this book. Before going into Calcutta affair, let us move to Lucknow, the citadel of the Muslim culture as the writer thought, while moving with Rashid. Naipaul along with the local person, Rashid moves to the historical monuments of Lucknow and studies the history of Indian independence which started with the Mutiny in 1857. Naipaul, as a historian, observes the facts of corpus of the Mutiny in the following words. The words are purely without flagrance,

> The Indian independence movement didn't grow out of the Mutiny.... In colonial time and for a period afterwards, this was called by some the first War of Indian Independence. But this was a 20th century view...a seeking to give India something of the socialist dynamism the Russians found in their own history. The Mutiny was the last flare-up of Muslim energy in India until the agitation, 80 years or so later, for a separate Muslim state of Pakistan. (*Mutinies* 351)

During his narration in the Lucknow chapter he took time to mention,

> The Indo Pakistan war of 1971 was a watershed not only in Muslim lives, but also in Hindu-Muslim relationships. The myth of Muslim superiority was ill-fashioned. Here was India playing a decisive role in the subcontinent. Every Muslim had a soft corner in his heart for Pakistan, and everyone was sad that the experience had failed after less than 25 years. The dream had died. Then the Pakistani soldiers were prisoners of war for two years. That was a constant reminder. (*Mutinies* 370)

Here it may be said that the writer might have been exalted at their defeat but it has not been anything decisive except in the history of Bangladesh. Neither it has been merged with India nor has Pakistan ceased to exist. The war-results of 1965 were more real show of Indian might than this time, had it been pursued to the end. Here the cause was help to another country so India had little gain than receiving further refugees then and thereafter mainly into the heart of Bengal, Calcutta. The great thing was that Bangladesh was helped on humanitarian ground. And this India did even defying some superpowers trying to play their silly game.

While going through the history of Sikhs during his next visit to Punjab the subject of Mutiny was once again broached. The writer's guide was a scion of the erstwhile kingdom of Patiala. About the Sepoy Mutiny he said, referring to the archive maintained in the palace,

> The mutineers pressed Bahadur Shah into being their titular ruler, and he wrote letters to all the Indian States asking for their support. But at that time his domain wasn't even Delhi. His domain was literally only the Red Fort.... In June 1858, when the Mutiny had been more or less suppressed; William Howard Russell went 'with a party' to look at the defeated emperor.... The emperor was squatting on his haunches in an empty passage off a small roof patio. He was a small withered man of eighty-two, barefooted, in a dirty muslin tunic and thin cambric skullcap. (*Mutinies* 467)

While referring to William Howard Russell's visit to Lucknow from Calcutta as in his *My Diary in India in the Year 1858-59*, Naipaul wrote that while Rashid grieved for the lost glory of Lucknow as before partition, he had no such glory but he remembered his homeland, "There was no such glory in my past. Russell's journey from Calcutta to Lucknow lay in part through the districts from which, about 20 or 25 years later, my ancestors migrated to Trinidad, to work on the plantations there" (*Mutinies* 392). This was somewhere in the Eastern part of Uttar Pradesh. It seems that Sir Naipaul spent a few years of his childhood in a village named Chaguanas which was where his mother's family lived but his father's family lived in the Brahmin village of Dubes. So, he is considered to have had such an ancestral Brahmin title. This is just for finding out his ancestral root to which much attention has been paid, much research made. So it seems that he has a birth-sentiment towards Brahmanism.

While ruminating over Punjab he delved deep into the history of the Sikhs which have been disputed by some critics. He narrated how Moghuls persecuted the Sikhs who sometimes had differences with the Hindus and definitely the British played against them very badly on many occasions. Here Naipaul is worthy to be referred,

> The British, at the height of their empire, had a general disregard for all Indians. Even in 1858, while the Mutiny was going on, Russell noted this slighting British attitude towards the Sikh soldiers who were fighting on the British side. But by being incorporated into British India the Sikhs were immeasurably the gainers. (*Mutinies* 422)

Behind the feelings of Naipaul against the Muslims and the mixed feeling about India, he took pride in India's past glory. I think there is a "wounded" feeling of an unknown Indian whose forefathers left the land, most probably under compulsion. It reminds us of Nirad C. Chaudhuri's *The Autobiography of an Unknown Indian.* Another wounded feeling was that of an Indian, variously subjugated and converted by the Mughals in the past. His observations on many occasions seem to be made alright. But he seems to forget British attitude, does he feel a pride in it?

Coming to Calcutta and its hinterland, the countryside of Bengal:

> When I had first come to Calcutta, in 1962, I had, after the early days of strain, settled into the big-city life of the place; had had the feeling of being in a true metropolis, with the social and cultural stimulation of such a place.... The British were in Calcutta for a long time. It might be said that the Anglo-Bengali culture—out of which modern Indian grew—is as old as the United States. Raja Ram Mohan Roy, the first exponent of the culture, was born in 1772, four years before the declaration of independence. (*Mutinies* 346-49)

Talking about Calcutta's past, he takes us to the time of Sir William Jones who came to India as a Puisne judge of the Supreme Court but was a great scholar and in tune with his nature discovered the hidden treasure of ancient India. He wrote on classical Indian literature, translated from Sanskrit and founded the great Asiatic Society of India in 1784 which became the harbinger of Indian Renaissance. We know him as a great scholar and keep inside us deep respect for him as for Sir John Woodruff, Max Muller, William Cary and such others who helped us know our glorious past. What we did not know of him has been brought out by our writer, that he wrote a letter in 1786 from Calcutta to an American friend at Virginia,

> But your observation on the Hindu is too just: they are incapable of civil liberty; few of them have an idea of it; and those, who have, do not wish it...they must be ruled by an absolute power; and I feel my pain much alleviated by knowing the natives themselves.... Are happier under us than they were or could have been under the Sultans of Delhi or petty Rajas.... In the cultural ruins of much-conquered India he saw himself like a man of the Renaissance in the ruins of the classical world...I have never read the *Shakuntala*, and never shall. I do not learn the language of the gods to amuse myself with trifles.... (*Mutinies* 396-98)

Here I feel distress for the writer did not know properly with what vigour a greater scholar than Williams Jones, Sri Aurobindo, presented the Indian past glory to the Indians, sometimes helped by such nationalists like Balgangadhar Tilak and some others. The Europeans who revived Indian classical literature were amply helped by Indian pundits in Sanskrit. Vidyasagar was a teacher of the English in Fort Williams before becoming the head of Sanskrit college who was a great educationist. Vivekananda was a greater cause than Jones towards "Indian Renaissance." The fall of India in the middle ages (all were not petty *Rajas* before that, read history please) and recoveries with English touch from the time of Raja Ram Mohan Roy has been discussed many a time. We now know the real desire and feelings of many Indologists. They worked more to realise their own dreams than helping the Indian people.

Excuse me! Such resilience of Europe must be as Sir Naipaul was there exactly from the beginning of the second half of the century. We do not know whether he is aware of the plight and predicament of Europe now within the framework of European Union. In recent past, people from Greece were fleeing to safer areas. The crisis in civilization continues with continuous interference by the mightier nations in the affairs of weaker nations, wreaking havoc in the life of the people, for which assistance is sometimes readily available from European countries. I am sorry to say that Tagore never used the words, "in this poverty-shamed hovel which is India," for he was not an outsider seeking fame by criticising India, for he was himself India. He was not nearing eighty; it was his birthday completing eighty. Let us see the original work, read by Kshiti Mohan Sen in his presence:

> Today I complete eighty years of my life. As I look back... I am struck by the change that has taken place...a change that carries within it a cause of profound tragedy. Our direct contact with the larger world of men was linked up with the contemporary history of the English people whom we came to know in those earlier days.... As I look around I see the crumbling ruins of a proud civilization strewn like a vast heap of futility.... And yet I shall not commit the grievous sin of losing faith in Man. "By unrighteousness man prospers, gains what appears desirable, conquers enemies, but perishes at the root." (Tagore quoted in Sisir K. Das 722-26)

Please try to revere your root, Sir Naipaul, remembering that Tagore long back threw that knighthood upon the faces of those unrighteous men who conferred him that title. Remember that Tagore with his Himalayan wisdom could easily foresee the departure of the English more than six years before their compulsory exit. It is evident from a tiny part of his speech presented above that he not only saw what the colonizers were leaving behind but also what was at hand, that at hand was the great famine of Bengal in 1942-43 artificially created by creating food scarcity by the colonizers who were afraid of the entry of Japan with Subhash Chandra Bose during the Second

World War as a war preparation reserving food for the soldiers. They played a guerrilla tactics of creating famished Bengal and Calcutta lest they would venture to help the incoming force of Subhash Chandra Bose. Calcutta received the hungry population in thousands dying in its footpaths, man made to a great extent. The Hindu-Muslim strife as was always rife under the reactionary provincial government helped by the foreign rulers was not only foreseen by Tagore but foretasted three months before he left the world as in the speech above.

If the writer has honestly felt pride at the capacity and resilience of Europe, he should realize that Calcutta, flooded with people from the neighbouring and other provinces for hundreds of years for business and various occupations, accepting all, flooded with refugees for the deliberate partition of the country by the leaders whom it did not affect directly, from time to time and ever since, tortured for becoming the first revolutionaries against the colonial rulers and with many day-to-day calamities including the death-romance of communist adventurism, has still been living with ever more population, crossing 120 crore, consisting of more people from other states than from Bengal, at least in core Calcutta, with improved metro rail system, with its hinterland expanded to accommodate additional people in different areas adjacent, including the Salt Lake, as it was growing when the writer was noting these in his diary. We wonder how the writer forgot to mention the great names of the city that struggled and became martyrs, working during the period mentioned, time, of Shyama Prasad Mookerjee and Subhash Chandra Bose? Satyajit Ray was an artist and film director of great caliber whom he has mentioned but there were more of his genre.

Though the communist extravagances and idleness and condition of the roads are rightly mentioned, he should also note that the Naxalite struggle in the seventies of the last century was a real struggle against the capitalists, which resulted in the brutal killings of young revolutionaries, very aptly shown by Mahasweta Devi in her novels. Almost half of the book covers the story of Calcutta which the writer has mentioned frequently as beginning to die or a dead city already. Though Calcutta is always in the struggle, too much politicized, and its average people cannot be said to be very ideal and the health of Calcutta is strained, we strongly believe that it will very well survive which the writer may verify again and again till he lives.

We wonder how he never visited New Delhi, India's capital, at least not mentioned significantly in his book, when he wrote such a serious book on India. He mainly visited the cities and towns mentioned but not the country side or villages to feel the country's pulse. We remind him that the secret ideas and agenda of scholar Max Muller, feelings of Macaulay, and desires of Mortimer Wheeler have been known to us through research scholars, like the one of William Jones as the writer has presented. They were, after all, foreigners with ideas foreign to us. What the writer did not comprehend adequately is that India is plagued by corruption and that patriots have been replaced by mere politicians.

Though we appreciate the keen observation of the well-known writer and his grasp over the history and civilization, we must say that his viewpoints are true to his personal reactions to the past happenings tinged by his personal experiences, peculiar to his enviable position in life which he achieved and wishes to retain. Certainly, he is not impartial in his views and comments. Let us hope with Tagore that "Perhaps that dawn will come when unvanquished Man will retrace his path of conquest, despite all barriers, to win back his lost human heritage" (Tagore qtd in Das 72).

Works Cited

Das, Dr. Sisir Kumar. *The English Writings of Rabindranath Tagore: A Miscellany*. New Delhi: Sahitya Akademy, 1994.

Kohn, Rachael. "India through V.S. Naipaul's Eyes". Web. 07 June 2013.

Naipaul, V.S. *India: A Million Mutinies Now*. USA: Penguin Books, 1992.

——. *Beyond Belief: Islamic Excursions among the Converted Peoples*. New Delhi: Penguin Books, 1998.

12

Naipaul's *The Masque of Africa*: Exploring History, Culture and Civilization

Bishun Kumar

Sir Vidiadhar Surajprasad Naipaul, an extrovert in expression, always brooding upon the Third World affairs and showers the statements of controversies on the silent surface of ocean of critics, often raising a buzz of conflicting, colliding and fusing ideas and thoughts, is an epitome of creative genius. V.S. Naipaul, a widely travelled man is undoubtedly filled with the experiences of history, culture and variety of civilizations of both the First and the Third Worlds. His special focus is to spot and crush the hypocrisy and irrationality of religion, be it Hindu, Islam or Christian—that brings him in the line of social critics like Tagore, Munshi Premchand, Charles Dickens, Mark Twain and Mulk Raj Anand who found religion entrapping the entire humanity. Naipaul's first novel *The Mystic Masseur* (1957) comments on the fake practices of Hindu religion; the second *A House for Mr Biswas* (1961) also is an attack on the religious conviction, third, his travelogue on India, *An Area of Darkness* (1964) took a harsher view of Hinduism and the caste system. Similarly, *Among the Believers* (1981), *Beyond Belief* (1998) and *The Masque of Africa* (2010) are critique of African belief and Islamic religion with the reflection of colonial gaze of The Jesus Christ, the Christian religion.

The Masque of Africa: Glimpses of African Belief, Naipaul's the last travel narrative perchance, is a blend of History and narratology, fusion of satire and humour, subtleties of culture and civilization and a textuality of African history without deviating himself from the anticipated theme of the book *African Belief*. The book is objectively divided in six chapters: the first chapter, "The Tomb at Kasubi" deals with the ancestral history of African rulers and colonial interruption in the affairs of the states; the second chapter "Sacred Places" deals with the religion and mythical belief in Africa; third chapter "Men Possessed" deals with how men are under the possession of irrational customs, tradition, myths and more especially witchcrafts, and with impact of colonial intervention; fourth chapter "The Forest King" deals with governance of King Houphouet, pigmies and pagan religion of the forest, fifth chapter "Children of the Old Forest" deals with the postcolonial and postmodern generation that evidences cultural change in the ancient tradition and sixth, the last chapter "Private Monuments, Private Wastelands" deals with the destructive side of technological and industrial development of Africa. Thus, the travelogue is an architectural devise of History, Culture and Civilization with Chaucerian narrative style, characterization and a record of cultural crisis from Middle Age (Dark Age) of irrationality to modern and post-modern age of enlightenment and of ontological and epistemological thinking.

The Masque of Africa deals neither with Arnoldian aspect of culture nor with the aspect of *Primitive Culture* (1871) of Edward B. Tylor but with the anthropological view of culture that deals with "a whole way of life". For Arnold, in his *Culture and Anarchy* (1869), defines culture in idealist terms 'something to strive for', that which continues to influence thinking about the value of the humanities in higher education. Moreover, culture of a time, place or country is never immobile. It is always dynamic and is in state of flux. As Arnold claims, culture is a process, 'not having and resting, but a growing and becoming' and so one is never completely free nor successful in acquiring culture but rather always unfinished, to one degree or another, and thus still enmeshed in the social, still to some extent a 'slave of thought' (94).

The other feature of culture is that it camouflages as per the expectation of the throne and variation in the sects of the throne and its welcoming nature of the outsiders becomes the real cause of the dynamics of culture. Since people of a country are senseless machines which are used as per the needs and ambitions of their sensible leaders and rulers. Naipaul has portrayed both how and why the non-African religions have been welcomed. But his major focus is to comment on the hypocrisy rather to attack on the falsehood and irrationality of African religion.

The first chapter of the book begins with the author's own historical overview of travel in Africa. He tells that in 1996 he stayed for approximately nine months in East Africa, one month in Tanzania, six weeks in Kenya highlands and rest of time in Uganda and that eluded him to write the book about "African belief". He himself averred: "I was hoping to get started there on this book about the nature of African belief, and I thought it would be better to ease myself into my subject in a country I knew or half knew. But I found the place eluding" (*Africa* 1).

The historical inferences in the book should not be confused with the entire history of Africa, rather "glimpses" that means, undoubtedly, the portion that eluded Naipaul for the construction of creative critical zeal. His admittance "I knew" or "half knew" defends him from the attacks of critics. First of all Naipaul visits the Makerere University located in Kampala, the capital city of Uganda where he meets Susan Nalugwa Kiguli, a melting pot of experiences and an anti-colonial in outlook. Finding himself tired of his books, he drives to Entebbe, an airport on the edge of Lake Victoria 15 miles from Kampala, one of the British colonial towns. He discloses the division in African society between capitalist and the poor for the upper class there was money and cars to travel but for the poor, there were 'boda-bodas', the bicycles and motorbikes that for a small sum offered them a fast pillion ride while in colonial period this pillion-ride was taken as illegal.

The glimpses of history that Naipaul unravels are either reported by his hosts such as Prince Kassim, Luke-Naipaul's guide, Pa-Boh, Richmond, Rossatanga, Fatima and Claudine or by a historian John Henning Speke. The history begins with the colonial figure Idi Amin who was said to have killed a hundred and fifty thousand people while Milton Obote who liked hair to slope up high from the parting known as English style became the cause of the displacement of a million and a half people to the north and many died of an epidemic that proves to be the dark phase in African history. The author moves analeptically to the period of 1840, describes the causes of colonial encounters of Arabs and the English.

The reported history of Africa in Naipaul's *The Masque of Africa* is much like the political History of India drawing parallels with the history of foreign invasion and colonial encounters of the world. The common circumstances are segmentation of the empire, autocracy of governance, the conflict between the ruler and the ruled, king's preference of physical and material pleasures, false traditions, and lack of proper education, rational thinking, prudence, proper planning, management, and social networking and finally lack of good governance. However, writer's intention is not to historicize his writing but to choose character types from history to provide real evidences to the readers. Thus, every figure portrayed in the book whether historical or social is a type. For instance, the reign of Kabaka Sunna is the major drawback in the history of colonial Africa. He reports, "The Kabaka Sunna, known for his great cruelty, had welcomed the Arabs. He liked their toys. He especially liked the mirror" (*Africa* 5). According to the history of Africa, an Arab slave Ibrahim Battuta challenged Sunna's brutality to his subjects reminding him of the life after death and accountability. Prince Kassim too says, "Well there is so much to feel sorry for. In 1966 the Kabaka went into exile. It was and is now, a period of moral degeneration and a period of anarchy" (*Ibid.* 39).

Though colonial reign is a blot on the ethnicity of a country but it developed the sense of reasoning and enlightened the people of the subject country. Visionary explorations of John Henning Speke transformed Mutesa, the son of Sunna almost as cruel as his father. Mutesa turns a Victorian Christian and becomes philosophical and religious. It is reported that, "Mutesa turned against Islam, which he had partly adopted. He said that

Arabs were liars". And after thirteen years he meets the explorer H.M. Stanley and asked his help in getting English missionaries to come to Uganda and here begins the history of colonization of Africa.

The book deals with the four phases of African history first is the reign of kings of African states like Kabaka Sunna, Mutesa and Prince Kassim, second is the reign of Arabs with different sects like Ahmadia, Ghadafi of Libya, etc., third the reign of English missionaries and the fourth finally comes back to the postcolonial era of African democracy with the collision of the prevailing features of enlightenment and the fading impacts of Arabs and missionaries. Indubitably, when colonial masters or foreign traders or invaders came to exercise their powers, however, never through coercion which is a crime, they, before colonizing the land, colonized the mind through their ideology and civilizing mission cobwebbed with culture. They first fascinated the natives with their good governance, their administration, art, craft, literature, architecture, law, judiciary, town planning, management skills, flexibility in religion, their pretty attractive dressing sense, their sincerity, co-operation, education, preference to reasoning rather than to blind belief, scientific enquiry to every problem and especially their humanist attitude, the un-ignorable quality which guaranteed beautiful life and made a man civilized. Naipaul's book clearly marks the difference between pre-colonial ancient and post-colonial modern Africa.

Every comment on the colonial impact is made by the real or fictitious figures in the text but through the course of analysis of pros and cons of colonialism, Naipaul, overtly or covertly favours colonialism and finds that post-colonialism, an age of post-enlightenment is an over ripe fruit of colonial governance. The colonial subjects have taken back their states, the power from British Government but they have not given back the enlightenment received from them. What they got is the charge of spoiling African culture, civilization, and belief. Richmond comments on colonial powers; "The colonial masters came here for business. Slave trade was business. May be bad, but, to was purely business. They took, but they gave us the church. That was a death Knell to traditional religion.... The Church came and overturned this. They brought in Jesus" (*Africa* 175).

The book reports so many clashing ideas but the author finds it "a past dying, a new way coming" (176). In other statement, Richmond praises the policy of the English and the reason why the Christian church had caught on: "It was new. It has a policy of assimilation, like the French in the Ivory Coast, but the English did it in indirect way. They offered a faith that also brought education. It weakened the traditional religion; in that way it was like Islam. The only thing that has remained intact is the chieftaincy" (178).

The political history of Africa is presented through the politician like Flight Lieutenant Jerry Rawlings who earned as much greatness of his name that he became a mythic figure. He, who has been elected twice as a president, became a legendary hero just like Subhash Chandra Bose of Calcutta in India, a nationalist leader, earned a mythic figure after his death. Rawlings was born of mixed ancestry in 1947, the year India got freedom, of Ghanaian mother and Scottish father. But the colonial figures not only deprived the African heroes, the retainer of African myths but also colonized them linguistically too. It brought crisis for ethnic language that has a special quality of retaining ancestral and historical elements.

History of African traditions reminds us of the tradition of India too. In Africa before 18th century, the colonial encounters, inhuman and shocking traditions of Africa were prevalent on the name of loyalty. Richmond tells us that the servants of Houphouet were so loyal that they sacrificed themselves assuming death as their final service when their kings died. With the passage of time this tradition took a very cruel turn. The servants, whether wished or not, were buried forcibly with the burial of their kings. This nerve deluding custom became worse than *sati-pratha* in India. But the death of Houphouet resulted the death of inhuman customs and the beginning of colonial empire. But the private life of the ruler, the king was always a mystery. In the Ivory Coast, there were French people who helped Houphouet's show to keep on the road. They were welcomed as investors and they were glad to come since they could repatriate ninety per cent of their profits, at the time they did not affect the political situation of Ivory Coast but surely prepared the ground for 'a many-sided' civil war;

> People of the country against black immigrants from the neighbouring poorer countries, a tribal with the French on one side, with the French then retaliating against hostile Africans, and finally Africans against the French, so that yet another aspect of Houphouet's legacy vanished. The day came in 2004 when gangs of black men roamed the streets of Abidjan looking for white people to kill. (*Africa* 207)

India too has played a significant role in the African history of democracy. Gandhi, who was sent by a wealthy businessman in relation to a legal dispute, was treated very badly in South Africa where race was as prevalent as religion in part of Africa. Initially nervous, Gandhi took it as a challenge and united Indians in South Africa to demand his rights that turns Africa into an apartheid democrat.

Forest in the chapter "The Forest King" symbolizes the land, the kingdom of the irrational civilization, over powering cruelty, the rule of power and crucifixion of democracy and humanism as well. The word "Kingship" relegates disparity among the people, the citizens of Africa. The tenants of the king have to sacrifice their lives for the king. But in Africa it was found a different story. There was no tyranny but the belief "the belief in African traditions" or the religion of oral traditions. The forest king discloses the history of colonial happenstances in Africa. Houphouet-Boigny, the President of Ivory Coast was loved by the French; his people called him a king. Africans believed in orature rather than in literature and the mythic history survived from generation to generation through told tales by persons like priests, spiritual guides, family heads, and initiations. Richmond is one of such story tellers who tell about highness of Houphouet. He was equipped with supernatural powers that turned him into a snake after having been cut into small pieces and cooked in a cooking pot, the unbelievable truth for author and for us as well. There are no anti-religious or anti-colonial struggles but surely the conflicts between the ethnic and the colonial have affected the existing culture and civilization of the country.

The African society looked the criss-cross of several religions, like Christian, Islam and witchcraft and the traditional myths of Africa. Every religion has its own claims for "There was a mosque or church on every hill and major ecclesiastical building everywhere else" (*Africa* 4) which claimed, "as though religion here was like a business that met a desperate consumer need at all levels. There were competing masques of various sorts, Sunni, Shia, Ismaili, and Ahmadia" (*Ibid.*).

Here, Naipaul himself makes no comment on the "belief" especially, of religious, but his Chaucerian style of narration discloses the competitive segmentation of the Almighty into several sects. The entire society of Africa, like that of any other country except the England, was divided in hierarchical classes and subdivision within the divisions. Ismaili was considered at the top, the powerful in East Africa while school of Ahmadiya sect honoured a nineteenth century Indian-born prophet of Islam therefore, was not accepted by all Muslims even Ghaddafi too was anxious to open a very big Libyan mosque on a prominent hill site in old Kanpala, the rising market of religion. The colonial masters promised not only to provide good governance and development of country but also good religion, as compared to African's ethnic religion and culture. Mutesa, the head strong follower of the Kabaka tradition went against Islam, finds Arabs to be liars. While his successor prince Kassim sided Islam, the family was torn into two halves for both of them had their own promises as compared to African religion; "Both Christian and Islam would have been attractive to Africans for a simple reason. They both offered an afterlife, gave people a vision of themselves living on after death. African religion, on the other hand, was more airy, offering only the world of spirits and the ancestors" (*Ibid.* 7).

Kassim's this statement is an evidence of "African belief", "belief only", belief in ancestors but without logic, belief in spirits but without rational thinking, belief in false traditions without human concerns, finally one can say that they believed in the religion that has no God, no spiritual education, perhaps no existence either abstract or concrete but "belief" and "belief only". The African religion survived through the told tales of family heads rather than having any written history of religion or God as is in Christian, Hindu and Islam. Burial process in Kasubi is very surprising and striking. It is an evidence of a culture that has no culture. The burial process is as, "The corpse of the king would have been dried over a slow fire for three months. Then Jawbones would have been detached and worked over with beads or cowries; this together with the umbilical cord, also worked with beads, and the penis and testicles, in a pouch of animal skin, was what would have been buried" (*Africa* 12).

Let us not be bothered about what Africans do with the dead. Moreover, it would not question humanity. With the living being, it is quite shocking and a blot on humanity but in Africa "human sacrifice was a common practice when they put up the pillars or laid the foundations of a tomb". The writer suspected even the strangely uneven floor of Kasubi, covered by ruffian mats. It was not only Kabaka Sunna's family that believed in this airy religion but Kojo in Ghana who was even brought up as Christian. In this part of West Africa, this usually means a background, or indeed a foreground, of traditional African belief. But Kojo loved the "Ashanti spirits" and believed that Christianity had made it mellower and less warlike. Such as "The Ashanti have ancestral gods, as figures of healing. Certain rites have to be sperformed at times of death, birth, and puberty which passed on generation to generation through elders of family" (*Ibid.* 156).

The logic of belief in the spirits, as Pa-Boh explains, bridges the great distance between African people and the Supreme Being who is like Jehovah. These spirits, the lesser deities and the gods have physical representations; they can be tress, stumps, stools, carved idols, rivers and books, and every community has its own set of deities of this sort who protect, heal and solve the difficult matters arising in communities. If high priest and the prophetesses take up an issue, they go into frenzy, tear their clothes off, and bare their breasts and starts talking in unknown language.

This drama of priests and prophetesses reminds us of rituals taking place in some sects of India too. Low class uneducated people in India even today get their problems solved by these deities. *Natbir baba*, Bhagwati, and Bhawani are some deities that need sacrifice if not of men, certainly of some animals like goats, calves and sheep especially at the time birth of first child, marriage, etc. The altar service to some gods and goddesses in both India and Africa are illogical and irrational acts of men that make the country a "dark continent". But colonial education, despite its dark desire to colonize the land and exercise its power, has enlightened the people, taught education of one God, the Almighty and imparted the lesson that sacrifice whether of man or animal is an inhuman and cruel act of man. Human disputes could be solved by humans only through logical and humanist thinking. Problems like diseases can never be treated by witch doctors but by proper diagnosis and required therapy and medicines.

Naipaul has picked up such episodes, events, customs, rites and traditions that portray the condition of ancient Africa, which, here, seems worse than of India. Hence, historical facts need to be textualized. They are no more history but at least twice removed from reality; first on the perspective of the historian or the reporter and second on the perspective of the writer choosing things which he found suitable for the theme and mission of his book. However, the author seems, here, neutral to any matter. He acts only as a facilitator of the information he experienced during his travel but his significant role in his selection and collection of information is un-ignorable.

In his book, Naipaul has portrayed the major causes of communal riots in Africa. An innocent lady who was of mixed origin escaped only because she looked like Moroccan and she herself claimed that she is not a white but Moroccan searching for the white that gave her, "severe palpitation". The most hurting thing about African belief is that there is no chapter of humanism and sincerity to life. Neither of human nor of animal sacrifices there is any provision for legal prevention. Instead of protection of wild life, elephants are killed just for fun and feast. The wretchedness of developers and Abidjan encroachers is well evidenced in Binger's house in the Bingerville which was named after French Governor of the Ivory Coast. Despite scores of private and public buildings there, "Binger's house is now, more appropriately, an orphanage: Africa drowning in the fecundity of its people", tells Richmond regretfully (*Africa* 211).

Developer's encroachments in Africa are a universal problem. Developers are the another name for neo-colonialist, the harbinger of internal colonization, are in process to make their country worse than hell and destructing the human civilization many more times than the external colonization. British colonialism, though, exercised power but their process maintained balance between nature and scientific development, harmony in modern society and ancient culture, and rationalism and religion. They built churches, botanical gardens and schools for the purpose. But botanical garden came to a tragic end during wars broke out by the French who were welcomed by Houphouet while practicing magic for himself. He wasted the country like Shelley's *Ozymandias*. Richmond admits that the land is full of cruelty which is hard for the visitors to bear. Trucks of cattle are sent to be slaughtered. People ate cats, elephants, calves and even bats too. However, bats brought destruction of mankind transferring the Ebola virus in man (*Africa* 215).

The device of narration of history and belief of Africa is an evidence of author's expertise in his art and intelligence. V.S. Naipaul, here, says nothing, makes no comment either in favour of African belief or against it to escape the risk of being blamed by critics of having no experience or less experience of African life. Every bit and piece of information has been reported by the responsible and well experienced persons of Africa itself. Though, from time to time, situation to situation, anti-colonial voices have been raised in the text but the sum total, the overall effect of the British colonization receives favours of the responsible thinkers of Africa. Guy Rossatanga-Rignault, a lawyer and an academic, a former Dean of the University of Gabon, said, "The new religions, Islam and Christianity, are just on the top. Inside us is the forest" (*Africa* 217). The statement is evidence that colonialism has affected the political economy of Africa and the world as well. It gave us education, and unfailing means of enlightenment that taught us oneness of the God, oneness of human race, respect for other's cultures and language. The effect was construction of a ground for multicultural, cross cultural and multilingual society bringing men out of the incarceration of national, religious and cultural precincts.

The chapter titled "Children of the Old Forest" denotes a symbolic significance. It suggests that children, an image of new generation that has killed the forest within them which was prevalent in old generation. The impact of colonial education has filled them up with the spiritual awakening that enhanced in them the value of life and a visionary aspect of human existence. The children of mixed ancestry have affected the African belief and culture and enhanced the cross-culture effects. Rossatanga, like Mouphouet, is of hybrid ancestry, of French father and African mother from Ivory Coast, Gabon. These children reflected both the welcoming of rational Christian education and the fading belief of African old forest that prepared a ground for hybridity, and multiculturalism. They praised the ancient African myths but failed to be the active part of that. They glorified and tried to rationalize the irrational customs and traditions as these succeeded generation to generation. Rossatanga is not cruel like typical Africans. He has soft heart even for the trees, realizes life in them; even cutting of trees, he takes as murder, and the logs as the dead bodies of the trees. But he at the same time glorifies the Gobon (African) traditions, the supernatural powers of spirits and jinns. Rossatanga shares his first experience of super natural linked to the overwhelmingness of the forest when he was at five and going for his circumcision rite, a rite of passage to manhood as they believed, "Everyone in Gabon believes in the forest and in the principle of energy that the forest exemplifies" (*Africa* 222). Rossatanga said, "Every living thing is energy. Every one of us is like a battery. In our version of the world even the animals are batteries..." (*Ibid.*).

Belief in supernatural powers is not only of African origin, it is universal found in almost every religion be it Hindu, Christian or Islam. Only their appearances or physical figures are different. The existence of jinn, the giant supernatural power is one of the African beliefs. A jinn living in the river side did not allow the

Dutch to build a bridge. At first the engineers laughed at him but later, one by one, all were killed. Ultimately, the jinn were pleased by a priest.

Rossatanga believes in organic world and finds Elizabethan chain of being in not only living creatures but also in non-living things in nature. Naipaul's this travel book focuses more on the merits of British colonialism rather than its own demerits. He says that in forest we must believe in Pyramidal organic world. He says, "The first level is the minerals and ore; the second level is the trees and flora, and the third level is the animals. The fourth level is the human beings" (*Africa* 225).

It seems, if not the colonial religion, certainly its education and trade are the boon for the development of human society that have been accessed to the underdeveloped countries. They have brought people from their seclusion to open space. Rossatanga believes in Wordswothian philosophy that "Children are spiritually stronger than the middle aged who useless and wind" (*Ibid.*). He equates children to the elderly for one recently comes from the world of God and the other approaches to go there.

In spite of unexpected educational and technological development, modern generation is caught between both the rational enquiry into the matter and the age-long ancestral customs. Though the situation is universal and common to all countries and all religions but in Africa it is still dominant. The reasons behind this problem are many but initiation rite, the first religion of the forest is binding, therefore, is most effective. When the head, the retainer of African legacy of beliefs, becomes old, an initiation rite is organized to transfer and train the new head of the family to practice all the traditions and customs. The circumcision rite reminds us of Freudian phallic symbols. After circumcision of a boy's penis, a banana is planted and the length of banana is compared with the rising length of boy's penis.

In Gabon, women are very powerful; for society is matrilineal but they cannot exercise it, they have to give it to their sons. In many of ritual sacrifices, eyes are removed and ears are torn out of a living victim. These rituals are common in rural India too which, it seems, might have come from Africa. Light skinned people are prized for sacrificial offerings. It is, therefore, Rossatanga does not let his white skinned children out in the evening. In the forest, people are forest mind.

Eboga is the significant plant of the forest. Professor Gassiti tells of the value of this Gabonese plant. The professor studied in university and was a pharmacist in his own right. He too, was a part of Gabonese traditions, known as an expert on local medicine and traditional ways of healing—the healing ironically showed the other world, the other side of reality. The medicinal use of eboga plant was no less than Indian Ayurveda. The history of use of eboga is explained by Gassiti to author as "...the first tribe to know of the eboga were pigmies.... They were the true masters and now an American has a patent and is making millions from it" (*Africa* 230). However, Claudine calls it "the mystical world"—that stands for anything beyond rationality. The pigmies were considered subhuman—is like our memories of the past. They hold the knowledge of that world. The surprising thing about them was that they too were fascinated by modern ways of life. It is for this reason; the masters of pigmies gave their daughters to the educated and rich customers asking them to teach them so that pigmy race also could bridge the gap between the traditional world and the new world. The master said, "Take my young daughter home with you. Adopt her and educate her in modern ways" (*Ibid.* 239). Pigmies adopted the Bantu style so that the two cultures Bantu and Pigmy had come together.

Buitee is yet another ritual comes after initiation. Buitee enabled the person to communicate with his ancestors who come at three in the morning. The ritual is only for men. But reality of the forest rituals of the pigmies is well reflected with the ironical tone of Claudine and other narrators of the African belief. Pigmies' belief in nature is shown in their dealing with dead bodies. When a master dies, they wrap him in a mat and put him under a big tree to rot and get decomposed, at last put the bones in grave. But there was voice of resistance against the centralization of power to Jesus only, "They fail to see why Jesus should have all the power. For them power has to be distributed among many chiefs" (*Ibid.* 242).

In the north of Nigeria, in dealing with the African belief, Naipaul vigilantly finds out the false practices. He is shocked by the traditional Koranic system that made people literate in Arabic and sent them into the 'Informal Network'. It sent them out to shine shoes, do drive okada motorcycles, the hawk things in the street and generally to do 'low' work which kept them at a subsistence level. In Kano, the great city of the North, men in blue or white Muslim gowns, were working garb for them, standing in a semicircle well away from the passengers, some of them were selling prayer beads and white Muslim prayer caps, "The town is seen to be a town of dust and dirt" (*Ibid.* 140).

The condition of children at Kano is a comparative presentation of the cultural fracture between north—a place of Muslims where Christian missionaries had not been allowed and south—where the missionaries were prevalent. The difference is not merely in education and work culture. One of the reasons of degradation was polygamy. The author finds, "children innumerable, thin-limbed, in dusty little gowns, the unfailing product of multiple marriages and many concubines" (*Africa* 141). One can guess the condition of Africa knowing that, Habib, a Ugandan Muslim businessman, now of great wealth, had fostered the Libyan connection. His grandfather, being a preacher for Islam, "took three more wives while preaching at Rwanda, one Hutu and two Tutsis. He had twenty one Children" (*Africa* 41). As a Muslim child he was trained to have nothing to do with African religion.

Another heart distorting tradition of Africa is the enthroning ceremony. Mutesa's mother had to burn her sons one by one to death consulting Mutesa who to burn next for there could be no clubbing, slashing that drops blood. The culture of Africa was discriminatory with women that made their doom and degradation everlasting. The following traditions raise serious and sensitive issues of feminism.

In African culture, women are in the worst condition, however, the situation was same in almost all the countries but improved earlier as compared to Africa. Women had no identity of their own, assumed as a commodity for sexual pleasure.

Naipaul's book is not simply a travelogue but an attack on Islam where polygamy, the way of life of the harem, had its own rules. Women were separated from their children. They could meet only at the time of breast feeding but with their covered face so that child could create no disturbance with its fostered mother.

Polygamy, as the sound Islamic way had its well-educated champions and theoreticians. A Muslim could have four wives while a ruler any number of concubines. The rulers had a harem—full of concubines (many of them gifts of the African rulers, discarded older wives, slaves and eunuchs). The ideology of enslaving the women worked through Islamic religion and its culture on such traditions. Laila, an educated, romantic and of rich upbringing, who had dreamt of love, the true love, becomes the victim of polygamy. Her husband forced her to agree with his next marriage which he told was necessary to be a royal ruler. Finding no escape, she determined to spare her daughter Mona. Having fascination for love, romance, education, she gets attracted towards a doctor from Dubai but later she comes to know that the doctor was interested in her daughter Mona rather than in her. Laila, believing it to be God's will, gifted Mona to the doctor without having any idea what life in Dubai could be like for Mona.

Sometimes, polygamy in Africa brought men in state of ambivalence. The pleasures with their wives often raised a problem for the husband how to control them. There was a tradition of Mumbo-Jumbo to treat women. It was much like a celebration of a festival of cruelty. When Mumbo-Jumbo was called upon either by husband himself or by his trustee, the villagers gathered there, no married women could stay away; even if it was for her only; "There is singing and dancing; it continues till midnight; and the Mumbo-Jumbo declares who the offending woman is. She is seized, stripped naked, tied to a post and flogged until dawn by the Mumbo-Jumbo with his stick. The villagers shout with pleasure; they mock the woman and show her no mercy" (*Africa* 89).

The author uncovers the reality of African belief through discussion of his problem to Jujuman, the witch-doctor and

Babalawo, the soothsayer who carried their rational business in their modern garb. Though the author had no daughter, he asked Babalawo, "Will my daughter get married?" (*Africa* 122). He, after processing, came to respond that, "The girl is not going to get married. You have many enemies" (*Africa* 122), and to break their spells cost money.

Naipaul's travelogue reveals comparative view of colonial and African standards of administration that affected culture and civilization. The arrival of Arabs enriched Africa with Masques of every top of hill and brought Islamic culture to transform people like Kabaka Sunna and Mutesa and reduced cruelty. Colonial governance built so many churches at almost every hill giving message of peace and humanity to the Africans while Buganda people have their own civilization. They have their social organization, their military discipline, and their elaborate court rituals evolved over some centuries. They built their roads as straight as was built by Romans. They had a high idea of sanitation; they had a fleet on the Lake Victoria with an admiral and naval techniques of their own spears and knives. They knew how to make bark clothes and were beautiful builders of grass houses with roof as neatly trimmed as though by a London tailor. This was on effect of colonial governance and education that brought this change in Buganda civilization.

Civilization is a stationary and concrete representation of culture itself. Ancient Africa had nothing but the tombs of the legendary rulers (though supposed sacred places) but Arabic colonialism gave numerous masques different than Tombs and British colonials introduced not only Churches but botanical gardens, and universities to provide true education to Africans. In Africa, the white people built themselves a moon-base for their civilization. French colonials also affected the ethnic civilization of Africa. What is significant is that the inescapable force of colonial encounters that enhanced trade, business and travel. As a consequence, roads, rails and airports added a new chapter in the history of African civilization. Kano, an ancient trading centre famous for trans-Sahara trade, had gone down for its conservative nature but the education gave new challenge to the trade of Kano. The change in African civilization can well be observed, "One man, a former Fulbright scholar, taught literature at the university. A man in a red fez did media, and worked for the government. A third man, modest and attractive, it was said he was a tiny writer in English" (*Africa* 142).

Historical monuments of the time are the concrete evidence of the then civilization of the place. Portrait of Mutesa watching Kampala was everywhere throughout the 'Dark Continent' visibly expressing that he was a dictator. A beautiful white mosque in the North African style and a cathedral in its design paid homage to St. Peter's cathedral even higher than St. Peter's itself were mighty emblem of the imported faiths. This was more than a cross-cultural building. Kasubi and Lope, a place in the 'Old Forest' have become UNESCO heritage sites with its own office there.

A curious reversal in the structure of the palace on the royal hill in Toro is a brilliant example of anti-colonial resistance in African civilization. Being ashamed of their in circular huts in Uganda, Africans imitated the rectangular structure of the British but realizing the colonial ideology they made the new palace circular "like a rejection of old colonial idea of modernity" (*Africa* 75).

Dynamics of culture-changed Africans clothing styles and tastes of games too. A football match has to be played in Abidjan stadium. People gathered outside the stadium looked picturesque something for a painter of crowds, an African Canaletto: a stippling of black faces, jeans, and tee-shirts orange, white or red, perfectly product of an urban city. Houphouet, to promote his town of Yamoussoukro, had built an auto route to it from Abidjan. Even Ivory Coast has become most fascinating place for the migrants. It is said of it, "From the days of Houphouet and the French there is a myth of blessedness of bush Ivory Coast where no one need starve" (*Ibid.* 210).

In South Africa at Johannesburg, the industrial and commercial nexus presented the new typical civilization. "The straight lines of the industrial buildings on the way to the great city belonged to a 'culture of science and money', the style of another continent, another civilization" (*Ibid.* 279). Like any other metropolitan city of the world, Johannesburg also could not escape the slums and slum-dwellers the counter-parts of the capitalists. The government of free South Africa, in a fit of Africanness had thrown open its borders to these people. The sturdy old warehouse had been given over to new merchandise for *muti* goods a parody of capitalists' industries. The hawker sitting on a stool was setting *muti* goods, the animal body parts—a jaw, a rib, three horse heads with furs was a pride of muti-market supported by municipal. But perhaps these goods were not as expensive as a white woman's breasts for offering as *muti*. The *muti* market adorned the beauty of modern wasteland.

No writer writes anything without a pre-conceived purpose. It is this fresh insight of Naipaul that forces him to pen down. Therefore, his travelogue is not merely a travel history but also a humorous attack on 'Islam' and 'African belief' and promoting Christianity for its enlightening feature. Textual interpretation of African history, culture, and civilization raises palimpsest themes and issues such as colonial conflicts, decolonizing voices, staunch feminism, postmodernism and multiculturalism that compelled Naipaul to shape the travelogue. Author's journey from Trinidad to Africa concludes with three other journeys: the first political journey of Africa from rule of autocracy to democracy, the second cultural journey from African rites and belief to enlightenment and humanism and the third civilizational journey from the Tombs (of Kasubi) to the skyscrapers, churches and private monuments making African cities modern "wasteland/s".

Works Cited

Arnold, Mathew. *Culture and Anarchy*. USA: Oxford University Press, 2009.

Beauvoir, Simone de. *The Second Sex* (1949). London: Four Squire Books, 1961.

Eliot, T.S. *The Wasteland Prufrock and Other Poems*. London: Waking Lion Press, 2008.

McLeod, John. *Beginning Post-colonialism*. Manchester: Manchester University Press, 2010.

Naipaul, V.S. *The Masque of Africa: Glimpses of African Belief.* London: Picador, 2010.

Nayar, Pramod K. *Post-colonial Literature: An Introduction.* India: Dorling Kindersley Pvt. Ltd., 2011.

Thiong'O, Ngugi Wa. *Decolonizing the Mind.* Delhi and Kolkata: Worldview Publications, 2007.

Section C

Identity, Home, Marital and Gender Discourse through Text/s: Critical Essays on V.S. Naipaul's *A House for Mr Biswas*

13

V.S. Naipaul's *A House for Mr Biswas*: An Incessant Quest for Identity and Independence

Madhu Sharma

The concepts of rootlessness, identity and independence have pre-eminently captured the interest of post-colonial writers of the age as they hail from erstwhile colonized nations. V.S. Naipaul too, one of the eminent post-colonial writers, has grabbed the immediacy of expressing his awful experience of being born in the once colonized society. He delineates his desperate search of an identity in the backdrop of his Caribbean post-colonial legacy by vehemently condemning and discarding the foreign traditions imposed on the erstwhile colonies by the dehumanizing colonial forces and recreates for him an independent identity. Through his sterling work of fiction *A House for Mr Biswas*, Naipaul effectively resurrects and preserves the cultural uniqueness of the Trinidadian Indian emigrant diaspora. In this context, my paper tries to show the significance of owning a house of one's own to establish a sense of belonging, self-esteem and a sense of freedom in the post-colonial society.

The early masterpiece of V.S. Naipaul's brilliant career, *A House for Mr Biswas* (1961) is an unforgettable story inspired by Naipaul's father that has been hailed as one of the twentieth century's finest novels. The novel takes its subject matter from the peoples who have lost their identities and recognition and have been alienated from societies to which they originally belong thus making their constant search of an identity quite ardent. A person with no home of his own does not have the feeling of belonging to a single place since he finds himself stuck in a mental turmoil which generally results in some psychological trouble and a traumatic experience of cultural displacement. In this context, possessing no home of one's own does not indicate being homeless. To be unhomed, as Lois Tyson states in *Critical Theory Today* (2006), "is to feel not at home even in one's own home because you are not at home in yourself: your cultural identity crisis has made you a psychological refugee..." (421). In this regard, anyone who carefully goes through Naipaul's works of both fiction and non-fiction can realize that Naipaul himself has a strong feeling of being homeless, although he has a home in Wiltshire, England.

In his writings, Naipaul truly delineates the lives of West Indian people who suffered from the immense pain of their loss of identity and at the same time he portrays the harsh reality of descendants of indentured servants by presenting the bitter experiences of his own family in miniature which virtually bring out the larger truths about the general colonial predicament in Trinidad in those times. In his book, *Reading and Writing* (2001), he says that he began to see what his material might be: "the city street from whose mixed life they had held aloof, and the country life before that, with the ways and manners of a remembered India" (Naipaul in Schmitt, 1998: 132).

In Naipaul's *A House for Mr Biswas*, the protagonist, Mr. Biswas is born into a post-colonial world providing him with no opportunity of self-realization and growth at all wherein he feels himself virtually suffocated and demeaned; a person who is only dependent on other people's lives for his livelihood thus making him strongly desirous of securing a place for himself, a home, where he can be his man and the leading actor of his own life. The house in Naipaul's *A House for Mr Biswas*, of course, is not any ordinary house made up of brick and cement. It has assumed the stature of the protagonist's passionate urge for an independent identity in the background of crude suppressing post-colonial society. The search and endeavors of Mr. Biswas to own a house for himself prove to be an absolutely trying journey during which he refuses to accept the ready-made orthodox household imposed on him; rather he aspires more of possessing his own house, his own portion of earth in spite of all troubles and tribulations in the way. The house, therefore, in the title of the novel becomes all the more significant as it does not merely mean a material possession to provide shelter and security to its inhabitants but it also displays a big accomplishment on the protagonist's part. He does not accept whatever old or worn out is catered to him and seems nowhere in the mood of surrendering or compromising with the unchanging circumstances of his surroundings. Instead, he strives really hard to attain an independent house of his own so as to carve out a mark on history by getting an independent identity. In fact, this way he can successfully escape the emptiness of his heart and mind which he cannot handle otherwise and thus find a comfort zone of one's own for himself and his family.

Naipaul too, through his narrative, successfully attains his long-cherished goal of both—a house and a home, and still more important, a literary tradition to establish himself strongly that his exilic ancestry had so far deprived him from. Many critics and scholars of the field also admit the fact that Naipaul has rightly grabbed the nerves of the readers by displaying his acute sense of concern for the key problems of displacement, identity and independence arising in the post-colonial scenario in his writings. Speaking in an interview, he himself confirms the above idea saying "When I speak about being an exile or a refugee, I am not just using a metaphor, I am speaking literally" (Naipaul 62). It is clear that even after having lived in England for many years, he, still, has not had the sense of belonging, as he says: "I still had that nervousness in a new place, that rawness of response, still felt myself to be in the other man's country, felt my strangeness, my solitude" (*EOA* 7). "He is", as Mohit K. Ray articulates, "an Indian in the West Indies, a West Indian in England, and a nomadic intellectual in a postcolonial world" (208).

Naipaul's masterpiece, *A House for Mr Biswas*, truly deals with complete characteristics of authentic West Indian life; how it feels to be a victim of bitter experiences of post-colonialism and even he transcends the provincial boundaries in order to suggest concepts which carry a universal appeal in their human implications. Moreover, the story is told from the point of view of an omniscient third party narrator who is well acquainted with the feelings and thoughts of many characters. Naipaul has based this novel in the backdrop of deprivation, crowding and insecurity which make the attainment of a private dwelling the supreme goal for an inhabitant of Trinidad. Mr. Biswas too, an Indo-Trinidadian, is a stranger bereft of any roots in his own land. Naive, irresolute, timid, and baffled by life, yet at the same time sharp, opinionated, temperamental, and derisively witty, Mr. Biswas spends most of his life under the thumb of his despised, domineering in-laws, who provide him with both a job and a roof over his head. He longs for a house of his own; and it is this longing that, in the end, defines his life.

He is depicted as a completely insignificant person with almost no power or influence on anyone around him but still he constantly mobilizes all his efforts in a single direction just to find his own shelter in the limited world of Trinidad. Throughout his life, he strives for success and is least successful. During the tiresome journey of his life—he is expelled from his ancestral house and for the next of his life, i.e. for thirty-five long years he is knocked by destiny from one house to another as an unwelcome guest or a lonely inhabitant but he remains unflinching throughout and eventually gets rid of his dark 'void' and steps into a well-organized universe symbolized by his very own house. Thus, Mr Biswas has been described as 'Everyman' but in a modern sense because in his confrontation with the vicissitudes of life he expresses a keen awareness of the absurd. He conforms to Albert Camus's fundamental definition of the absurd as he feels within him a longing for happiness and for reason. That's why; throughout his life he undergoes many trials and tribulations to ultimately attain a portion of the earth before he dies.

In the novel *A House for Mr Biswas*, Mohun Biswas is born to a poor but high caste family with an agricultural background. Unfortunately, he is considered as a stranger even in his own family since he was born at midnight, an inauspicious hour, with six fingers and feet first, signs for bad luck. Being treated as an unlucky baby, he stays as an outsider, a lonely individual in his own family. When one reads *A House for Mr Biswas*, one can easily observe that the sense of alienation that the protagonist Mohun Biswas experiences in his fictional life is the very sense that Naipaul has experienced in his real life. The struggle for their individuality brings them a bitter realization that the entanglements they have stuck into stem from the immature (uncivilized) structure of their own community. For Mohun Biswas, the rigid Hindu folk of the Hanuman House represent this structure, as for Naipaul it is all communities that constitute the West Indies and the Third World. Having been alienated in the form of normlessness, both Mr. Biswas and Naipaul react quite strongly relying on their creativity. They do not remain inactive in the face of their encounter with familial or societal norms rather display their unflinching sense of self-actualization.

The family suffers an unexpected reversal when Mohun is around seven years old leaving all of them fully dependent on the generosity of their well-off acquaintances and relatives. He grows up as a mediocre type of person who is in no way a hero in the traditional sense of the word; still he displays a keen sense of self-respect and an uncompromising attitude to surrender his independence at any stage in the course of his whole life. He tries his hand at a number of jobs and experiences a series of setbacks too. There is much that is absurd and ridiculous about him. Nevertheless, he is also the rebellious man completely obsessed with his desire to understand life in all its hues and colors and to make complete sense of his social surroundings. He simultaneously embodies the alienated modern man and the sensitive though ineffectual reformer. His desperate bid for improvement seems to be a self-centered one; but his struggle against a harsh social system makes his rebellion a true confirmation of universal beliefs and values. Subsequently, his struggle becomes universal which seems to have been initiated on the behalf of the whole fraternity. Indeed, it is the rebellion of a weak, mediocre man which originates from the man's strong desire for independence and self-esteem.

In his forty-six short years, Mr. Mohun Biswas has been shown fighting against destiny to achieve some sign of independence only to face a lifetime of disasters. Moving from one residence to another after the drowning death of his father, for which he is unintentionally responsible, Mr. Biswas yearns for a place he can call home. When he marries into the Tulsi family on whom he indignantly becomes dependent, he realizes that the Tulsi family has an orthodox communal lifestyle at Hanuman House which is quite domineering and suffocating. The household includes many of the family's fourteen daughters, their husbands and children. Life centers on the two young Tulsi sons, who are pampered by their mother, Mrs. Tulsi.

During the whole course of the novel, he has lived at various lodging places with all their shortcomings and drawbacks. Hanuman House is authoritarian and oppressive in its organization; the houses at The Chase and Green Vale are unbearable burdens because of the uncertainties surrounding their construction; the Short Hills and Port of Spain buildings are dispiriting because of their rapid deterioration under the hands of the exploitative Tulsi family. Determined to make his own way in life, Mr. Biswas embarks on an arduous—and endless—struggle to weaken their hold over him and purchase a house of his own. Thus, these lodging places form a backdrop and at the same time they motivate Mr. Biswas towards his goal.

A heartrending, dark comedy of manners, *A House for Mr Biswas* skillfully evokes a man's quest for autonomy against an emblematic post-colonial canvas. It truly symbolizes the colonial world wherein Mr. Biswas's personal battle with the stronghold of the Tulsi household (the symbol of the colonial world) represents a quest for existential freedom and the struggle for self identity. As Singh underlines; "Mr. Biswas is the unaccommodated man representing the outcast's symbolic quest for a place in the hostile universe" (1998: 126). The Tulsis are running a sort of mimic world of colonialism and the important thing is that the Hanuman House too is run on the traditional Hindu familial lines and protocols. On the surface, the Tulsis have made an admirable reconstruction of the clan in strange and hostile conditions. It has its own schemes, leaders, duties, law and order, religious rituals and provides jobs and help to men of their community on merits. Mr. Biswas is repeatedly accused of not being grateful to the Tulsis despite the fact, as Mrs. Tulsi says, "Coming to us with no more clothes you could hang up on a nail" (557).

At Hanuman House, on being suggested to give up the profession of sign-painting and take up a job on the Tulsi estate, Mr. Biswas replies to Govind that by giving up his sign-painting he would be staking his independence which he is not at all prepared for. He believes in acting independently and deciding his own fate. According to him, the Tulsis are "bloodsuckers" and that he would rather catch crabs or sell coconuts than work for the pack of Tulsis. But the Tulsis remind Mr. Biswas's time and again that he had come to them with no material possessions and that all the garments he owned at the time of his coming to them could be hung on a single nail. Tulsidom depends for its existence on the psychological undermining of the men and on the maintenance of their sense of inferiority. Every effort is made by the Tulsis to force him to recognize his littleness and admit a sense of subordination to them.

At first glance, Mr. Biswas's rebellion may seem meaningless and unfair as the Tulsi family without fail provides shelter and job for Mr. Biswas whenever he is in dire need, but nevertheless, he ungratefully rejects their help and support proposing the idea that the Hanuman House is no less than a prison and under its rigid structure of organization, one can see that the Hanuman House is not a coherent or benevolent entity of the traditional Hindu joint family. It is more like a slave society where the matriarch head of the family Mrs. Tulsi and her brother-in-law Seth require workers to boost their deteriorating power and economy. They entrap and then exploit the homelessness and poverty of needy men like Biswas and others for their own vested interests and motives. Hence, the acceptance of Hanuman House with its doubtful claims is the submission of subservience and slavery.

By drawing such a picture of Hanuman House and Tulsidom, Naipaul realistically portrays that subjugation is not something associated with the West, or to the whites only. He satirizes the Indians' orthodox attitude of following their older caste system within themselves while they detest white colonialism. Naipaul's protagonist does not enjoy mingling with the Hindu community in Trinidad and fights out a personal battle for freedom and recognition against this hostile society. For him, to build a house of his own means freedom and recognition and fortunately by the end of the novel, in spite of all its defects and shortcomings, he manages to buy this house which eventually wins him his wife's respect and saves him from his sense of being rootless and alienated amongst his own people. Thus, he spares himself from the Tulsi's tyrant way of life which was consisted of the outworn traditions of the East India.

Thus, Naipaul personally felt that the feeling of deracination, displacement and lack of a national community in Trinidad are the real concerns in *A House for Mr Biswas*. Hence, both Mr. Biswas and Naipaul pursue a constant search of a home by which they will be able to establish their identities; a sense of belonging and self in erstwhile colonized community of Trinidad. Being an East Indian descendent in West Indies, a colony of England, Mr. Biswas physically in one place and culturally in another (East India) was refused his independent position among East Indians which he is not at all ready to accept. Analyzing the sense of alienation and the agony and trauma of exile experienced by the characters, *A House for Mr Biswas* delineates the problems of a distorted and troubled past and tries to find a purpose in life. Alienated from his folk, family and from the Tulsi's Hanuman House, for Mr. Biswas, a house of his own symbolizes freedom and a place to strike a root afresh. When he dies, Mr. Biswas owes $3,000 on his house. This is an incredibly large sum to him, an amount that he will never be able to repay.

Naipaul, thus, became a writer and Mr. Biswas attained a house struggling with the snags of their society. Hence, it is quiet explicitly shown that their alienation from their society leads them to a condition of existential standpoint. Existentialists, discarding all forms of authority, believe in the practice of self-authority and they tend to reject all forms of power as authoritarianism or power conflicts with their basic views of life.

They are staunch believers of one's own self-actualization and self-determination. According to the existentialists, a self-determined person possesses the unique capability of comprehending his/her problems without recourse to any religious or political practices and ideologies and then realistically getting rid of these problems by bringing about practical solutions that fully and effectively cater to their purposes. Moreover, they always rely on their own potential which unfailingly motivates them not to give up their struggle for an independent existence and identity. This undying spirit of not quitting eventually leads Naipaul to be an eminent writer and to attain the most cherished dream of a house in the case of Mr. Biswas which provide them a unique sense of authenticity and of course freedom. Hence, for those alienated and displaced souls in the colonized countries, Naipaul seems to suggest that searching for some creativity by relying on their own authenticity and at the same time not surrendering to anything adverse is one of the basic means to find their lost and alienated identity. Kumar Parag also underlines "a house is not just a matter of getting a shelter from heat, cold or rain. In fact, it is both—an imposition of order and a carving-out of authentic selfhood within the heterogeneous and fragmented society of Trinidad" (139). Naipaul thinks they will thus be able to plunge into an era of creativity which will consequently fetch them rightful and original identities of their own.

In this novel, Naipaul carves out the position of the colonial man in a stagnant society; the protagonist finds himself as a stranger without any roots in his own land. He is depicted as a marginalized individual who is constantly mobile in order to find his place in the limited world of Trinidad. In the course of the events, the protagonist assumes, almost, the stature of an 'Everyman' who journeys through the slush of life and faces the knocks of fate to attain a portion of the earth before he dies. Moreover, he is a man possessing plenty of self-respect and an unquenchable thirst for independence. He can be called a hero by virtues of these qualities. He does not want to merge his individuality with the Tulsi household. When, after getting married to Shama, he discovers that as a Tulsi son-in-law he would have to lead a life of servility to his mother-in-law and uncle-in-law, he rebels against the system prevailing at Hanuman House. The Tulsi family believes in suppressing the budding individualities of the residents of Hanuman House, but Mr. Biswas cannot tolerate the extinction or even the suppression of his individuality. It is this instinct for self-assertion and self-development which imparts him a heroic quality.

Moreover, his hero Mr. Biswas is infused with the ardent desire to finally belong to, possess, settle down and leave a mark on this foreign land of his birth with which he thoroughly enjoys a love-hate relationship. This is a strong urge which is quite integral to all individuals of a diaspora. Mr. Biswas also therefore is no different. His journey from one place to another ultimately culminates in his attaining a space, a vocation or a workplace for himself in the nascent nation of Trinidad. His desire to belong and be associated with this place will fetch him an identity and selfhood is crystal clear. He was no longer content to walk about the city as he wanted to be a part of it, he wished to feel and understand it, to be one of those who stood at black and yellow bus-stops in the morning, one of those he saw behind the windows of offices, one of those to whom the evenings and week-ends brought relaxation. In a sense, he wanted to enjoy the feeling of being free and self dependent without any outside authority or hostility.

Just as attainment of a house truly manifests the desire of gaining a strong position in the hostile world of Trinidad, so also the wish to infiltrate the workplace is actually the delineation of the latent desire to be incorporated in the still developing nation. Interestingly, *A House for Mr Biswas* enjoys great resemblance with such classics of literature as Patrick White's *Voss* and Chinua Achebe's *Thing's Fall Apart* (1958) wherein by depicting the struggle of an individual, the complexities and aspirations of a previously ignored colonized culture are expressed and given epic and mythic stature. In this regard, many critics have observed Naipaul also as someone who occupies a kind of no-man's land as he is not Indian, nor is he English and he himself felt he was not Trinidadian either (De: Sunday Times). Likewise, the protagonist Mr. Biswas too shares Naipaul's own sense of alienation, the sense of traveling everywhere but belonging to nowhere. It articulates the purpose of unfolding the quandary of souls which remain unanchored in the exhaustive search of anchorage, in search of a house in the difficult times of life.

The metaphor of the house here accumulates all the more significance as it gives the struggle of owning a house of one's own of an individual almost mythical heights. The image of a house bestows both value and purpose on the postcolonial subject in the search for dignity. Although at the end of the novel Mr. Biswas's achievement is not fully attained, it does not deprive him of the thorough efforts he makes in order to attain it. Throughout the novel in his struggles in strictly organized, ramshackle and lonely houses the vision of the 'house', his house, sustains Mr. Biswas as to him it is not merely a materialistic thing that will provide shelter and security to his family but also a symbol of achievement—a pleasant feeling of having done something worthwhile, a sense of leaving a mark on history, a means to avoid annihilation and escaping the void. For Mr. Biswas, as well as for the author, it is the only way of becoming more than the short-lived flying ants carried away as food by the fire ants—so graphically depicted in the scene at the half-built house in the Green Vale phase.

Further, the journey of Mr. Biswas's life is disturbed by his seamless temporary halt ages at houses where he lives without ever leaving any marks of his being or existence on them; nothing which might make his absence felt or presence valued. He records this poignant and painful fact in an amusing way: He had lived in many houses. And how easy it was to think of those houses without him!... In none of these places he was being missed because in none of these places had he ever been more than a visitor, an up setter of routine. Was Bipti thinking of him in the back trace? But she herself was a derelict. And, even more remote, that house of mud and grass in the swamplands: probably pulled down now and ploughed up. Beyond that a void there was nothing to speak of him (135). He ardently wishes 'to lay claim to one's portion of the earth': Leaving a Mark on History in *A House for Mr Biswas*.

The pain and darkness of these lines bring out the pathos of the protagonist, and of Naipaul too, as both feel themselves culturally displaced with the keen sense of not being able to fall back upon anything beyond a borrowed identity in a land to which his forefathers had once landed as laborers. Thus, the 'house' in *A House for Mr Biswas* symbolizes the disrupted, void of native-traditions, displaced postcolonial writer's deepest ambition to form an identity without his destitute past as well as an individual's unending efforts to establish harmony through a concrete structure of brick, stone and cement in the face of shapelessness by erecting a coherent structure out of the chaotic circumstances and attempting at building a residence to annihilation.

Moreover, for Mr. Biswas, the search for a house becomes a search for himself, a search for a definite purpose and what he really wants out of his life, a quest for individuality and a search for a place in the flow of seamless history. The overpowering nature of his need explicitly emerges early in the narrative when the ancestral house has to be sold after his father's death—the narrator says: "For the next thirty-five years he [Mr. Biswas] was to be a wanderer with no place he could call his own, with no family except that which he was to create out of the engulfing world of the Tulsis" (38).

Thus, he was placed with two options, either to make do with what came his way or to start afresh from scratch to create a world of his own out of nothingness, a kind of choice confronting the postcolonial subject. Mr. Biswas feels badly dominated and repressed in the face of the matriarchal rule of Mrs. Tulsi and his brother-in-law, Seth. His predicament in Hanuman House is the true example of a slave society in miniature. It has been suggested that:

> Mrs. Tulsi needs workers to build her empire. She, therefore, exploits the homeless and deprived fellow Hindus. She has grasped the psychology of the slave system. Like the Caribbean society, Tulsidom is constructed of a vast number of the disparate families, gratuitously brought together by the economic need of the high caste minority.

> To accept Hanuman House is to acquiesce to slavery. Mrs. Tulsi, the cunning colonizer, justified her exploitation with her foxy explanation that she is really doing her subjects well. Seth, in his big boots, is the slave master: a brutal and brutalizing symbol. (149)

He had never thought it would be so lonely like this when he found himself in an establishment of his own. At afternoon, Hanuman House would be warm and noisy with activity. Here he was afraid to disturb the silence (*Ibid.*). Even in the Greenvale episode, when he was alone with his son Anand facing a disastrous storm, he feels the awful need of protection and community against the hostile behaviour of the natural world. Mr. Biswas's predicament clearly depicts the plight of the postcolonial subject—rebelling against the oppression of the Colonizer, trying to escape but does not know where to escape—having no past to retrieve, a future indistinct—and he fears falling into a void.

The novel highlights the image of the house throughout and embodies the protagonist's ardent desire for a house of his own which actually articulates his unflinching efforts to acquire his unique social identity in an ever changing society. Mr. Biswas's quest for identity in *A House for Mr Biswas* actually brings out the predicament of the anchorless existence, uncertainty and futile struggle for protection and identity in a postcolonial society. In this scenario, to be a colonized subject is to be safe and protected by the decisions of the rulers and to be thrown into freedom involves using one's own mind and capacities to take care of one. The story of the novel is interrupted with Mr. Biswas's recurring bouts of elation at being free and his breakdowns and backsliding into the refuge of the Hanuman House.

However, Hanuman House is not an evolving society but a kind of temporary refuge for those who are unable to find a foothold in Trinidadian society which runs short of resources required for authentic independence. Mr. Biswas's rebellion against this security provided by Hanuman House is bound to fail again and again without money, power skills or available employment for his westernized sense of self and individuality. His search for his house is not a desire to discard community or do away with family ties but the desire to create a new society whose nucleus will be he himself, never again having to take orders from others and work for the benefit of any agency other than his own. The ambition of not being associated with the pack of the Tulsi family is a negative ambition but his struggles nevertheless attain heroism in a background which lacks in heroes or heroic deeds. These lines of the prologue highlight the protagonist's desire for a tidy way of life and an anchorage in the world of flux. Here the house attains the stature of self-identity, self-worth and his unique foot print on the flow of human history. Mr. Biswas's appeal and universality lies in the fact that he emerges triumphant after his repeated failures to escape from the clutches of repression of selfhood, to finally achieve the possession of his own house, flawed though it is in material terms. The house thus becomes a much sought after legacy which Mr. Biswas can bequeath to his family. Just like that, through his writing Naipaul too attempts to preserve his own family history and the history of the Trinidadian Indian community.

The novel seems to be tragi-comic, but at the same time Mr. Biswas does not show any sign of comic buffoonery in his overall personality. No doubt, he does not spare anyone in the Tulsi household untouched from his ridiculously severe criticism; still he maintains a boisterous personality throughout. Despite being roughed up by economic, social and cultural factors beyond his control and frequently making mistakes, Mr. Biswas ultimately emerges out as a man of sterling dignity who unfailingly meets the challenges and vicissitudes of his times with quite grace and elegance. Thus, the novel is comic and tragic both as life itself are made up of a great fusion of joy and sorrow. It presents the struggle for identity of an Indian in Trinidad whose agrarian values are challenged by Western cultural influences when he moves to the city. As a result, Mohun Biswas must establish a harmony between apparently conflicting values and traditions of East and West and create an authentic self in both his family and society. This quest is not a simple recognition of some intrinsic features or characteristics, but rather the gradual revelation of choices made within the context of new situations, restraints, and sources of fulfillment.

To conclude, it can be said that though Mr. Biswas's view of the world, as reflected in the way he has lived, is not up to the mark and short-sighted but his struggle is not without its touches of heroism. At times, he is petty, cowardly and contemptible too but Naipaul has been able to present a hero in all his littleness and absurdity; has thereby successfully preserved a sense of the man's inner dignity and integrity. His romantic, self-centered egotism has denied him the simple pleasure of sympathetic human companionship and understanding until almost it is too late; but then he is the one who has paid the price of loneliness that lies at the heart of the human condition. His most commendable quality, which compensates for all that is despicable in him, is the unfailing presence of his faith in the value of the attempt. It is this faith which keeps him going; it is this which makes him appear a rebel. He refuses to conform, to give up his identity, and to allow the sordidness of his life to crush him. His courageous struggle in the face of absurdity and the quality of faith which this struggle reveals makes him a hero. And he makes a final effort to create a new world out of nothingness, thereby leaving behind his footprint on history and escaping annihilation and attaining fulfillment.

Works Cited

De, Shobhaa. "Politically Incorrect". *Times of India*, 14 October, 2001. Web. 07 June 2013.

Naipaul, V.S. "A Transition Interview with Adrian Rowe Evans". Ed. Feroza F. Jussawala. *Conversations with V.S. Naipaul*. Mississippi: Mississippi University Press, 1997. 104-16.

——. *The Enigma of Arrival*. Harmondsworth: Penguin, 1987.

——. *Finding the Centre: Two Narratives*. London: Andre Deutsch, 1984.

——. *A House for Mr Biswas*. New York: Penguin Books, 1982.

——. *Letters between a Father and Son*. London: Little Brown and Company, 1999.

——. *Reading and Writing: A Personal Account*. London: New York Review Books, 2000.

Parag, Kumar. "Identity Crisis in V.S. Naipaul's *A House for Mr Biswas*." Ed. Kerstin W. Shands. *Neither East nor West: Postcolonial Essays on Literature, Culture and Religion*. Sweden: Södertörns högskola, 2008. 135-42.

Ray, Mohit K. *V.S. Naipaul: Critical Essays*. Vol. I. New Delhi: Atlantic Publishers & Distributors (P) Ltd., 2005.

Schmitt, Deborah A. Ed. *Contemporary Literary Criticism*. Detroit: Gale Group, 1998.

Singh, Manjit Inder. *The Poetics of Alienation and Identity: V.S. Naipaul and George Lamming*. India: Ajanta Books International, 1998.

Tyson, Lois. *Critical Theory Today: A User-Friendly Guide*. New York: Routledge, 2006.

14

Significance of "Home" in V.S. Naipaul's *A House for Mr Biswas*

Vineet Kashyap

Naipaul's novels give an insight into how colonized subjects develop a sense of cultural inferiority and/or a sense of unhomeliness. In this paper, Naipaul's later fictions are discussed particularly *A House for Mr Biswas* (1961) in which he views places as changing, notions of home and belonging as unstable and the geographical order—the difference between primitive and civilized societies—as a fabrication. Naipaul's postcolonial novels expose the formation of imperialist myths of places, challenge them and deconstruct them. Naipaul deploys place in a complex and multi-faceted way that explores how place is constructed, represented, perceived and lived through boundaries that are set by power. Avoiding the re-mytholisation of lands and societies, Naipaul re-imagines places as more dynamic and less fixed, and represents the boundaries that enclose and define places as subject to re-alignment. Naipaul's novels contribute to a move towards a decentralization and decolonization of geography. He shares the idea that geography should be re-imagined and represented from the consciousness of the displaced, the marginalized and the homeless and secondly, the distinct ways in which he negotiates territorial and spatial concepts such as home and land are directly related to the socio-cultural contexts in which he grew up.

The significance of home in Naipaul's novels is both personal and collective. His autobiographical accounts reflects that he has always been involved with searching for his roots and his place of belonging and his anxiety over homelessness also reflects the collective sense of displacement of the Caribbean nationals over their detachment from their ancestral homes in Africa and India and the difficulty of establishing nationhood due to the diversity of cultures. In an intertextual reading of Naipaul's *A House for Mr Biswas*, Naipaul initially viewed colonial societies metaphorically in the form of shaky and unstable houses against the grand house of historically grounded nations (like England). As it is manifested in *The Enigma of Arrival* (1989), *Half a Life* (2001) and *Magic Seeds* (2004), Naipaul self-reflexively questions his earlier idea that there are certain places that are homely in the sense that they provide security, stability and a sense of belonging for their inhabitants. Indeed, he acknowledges that the unhomeliness of the postcolonial world is a reality that renders the desire for an ideal place or a stable home untenable.

The above-mentioned novels of Naipaul explore the idea of home and homeliness in different contexts; second, bring forth Naipaul's changing attitude towards the idea of homeliness of certain places. While *A House for Mr Biswas* shows Naipaul's vision that colonial subjects are entrapped in an unstable colonial social context in which they cannot feel independent or secure at home, The *Enigma of Arrival* shows that unhomeliness is not just the attribute of the colonial societies, but it is also an attribute of the metropolitan centre. The last two novels, *Half a Life* and *Magic Seeds*, engage once again with the theme of quest for home, but this time from the perspective of a postcolonial migrant. These novels suggest that while the very essence of homeliness is lost in the era of postcolonialism and capitalism, the postcolonial migrant can consider new ways of belonging to their habitats. Naipaul's approach to place in his novels is read as validating Doreen Massey's argument that notions of place (particularly home) as a source of belonging and security are untenable (Massey 192).

In a series of satirical stories, Naipaul reflects social and cultural issues of his homeland, Trinidad. *Miguel Street* (1959), *The Mystic Masseur* (1957), *The Suffrage of Elvira* (1958) and finally *A House for Mr Biswas* project the way Naipaul views and analyses his place of birth. Later, he admitted that these works stem from a sense of insecurity about place, saying that "the early comedy was really hysteria; the hysteria of someone who was worried about his place as a writer and his place in the world" (Nasta 106). The sentiment exemplifies the extent to which Naipaul, early in his career, felt insecure and uncomfortable because of his colonial background. *A House for Mr Biswas* is discussed in this paper as manifesting the unhomeliness of the Caribbean nations because they appear to Naipaul lacking historical grounding, strength and stability that is necessary to establish a sense of homeliness. The homeless anti-hero of the novel, Mr. Biswas, attempts to establish and ground his identity through the quest for home. His quest is contextualized in Trinidad, whose socio-cultural constraints hinder Mr. Biswas's achievement of the security and independence he desires.

A House for Mr Biswas is written in the literary tradition of *Bildungsroman*, a novel of education and development. Through exploration of the psychology of Mr. Biswas, within a traditionally structured family of Indian descent, the novel enacts the relationship between the community and its individuals as creators of each other. Steven Connor, drawing on Franco Moretti's thesis on 'Bildungsroman', explains that "such a novel offers a reciprocal mirroring between the individual and society" (Conner 5). This reciprocal interaction suggests that as much as an individual's personality is formed within the society, he/she is also a constituent part of a force for social mobility and development. *A House for Mr Biswas* also embodies the reciprocal mirroring between a colonized subject and the colonial society in which he lives. Throughout his life, Mr. Biswas aspires to independence from his wife's family who deny him his individuality. He attempts to buy or build his own house, yet, due to lack of experience and a strong personality all his attempts fail dramatically. Even when he finally succeeds in buying his own house, the building turns out to be poorly constructed, over-priced and unhomely.

While analyzing *A House for Mr Biswas* as what Conner calls 'social possibilities' the reader finds that the novel portrays 'social impossibilities'? The novel attempts to project on the one hand, the constraints that a colonial socio-cultural structure imposes on its individuals which in effect limits their agency for action, and on the other hand, the impossibility of social mobility when the colonial subjects as makers of the society fail to aspire to self-decolonization. These two aspects manifest the reciprocal relationship between colonial subjectivity and the place in which the subjectivity of the colonized is developed. Naipaul's vision of a colonial subject, including himself, as always peripheral and insecure is reinforced in this novel by showing that individuals cannot simply break away from the conditions of their background. From this perspective, place is within and with respect to which subjectivity is founded (Malpas 102). What makes Naipaul's vision of place contested is that he goes far beyond acknowledging the idea that people are situated in places and that their identity is formed in certain social and cultural contexts. If he viewed place as a social construct, he could show that people are responsible for its construction and in effect, through social forces they could equally undo it. Instead, he suggests that colonial beings are entrapped in place and spatial relations rather than located in certain social forms.

This paper explores how the formation of the colonial identity of Mr. Biswas is shown through allusion to the story of Oedipus, in order to show that Biswas is suffering from the sense of displacement and insecurity which is the main reason for his identity crisis and psychological distress and the manner in which Mr. Biswas's search for home embodies his need for security and grounding.

Mohun Biswas is a West Indian born to a poor Indian family on a plantation estate located in the suburbs of Port of Spain. As a child he loses his father and is brought up by his mother. She sells the family house under its market value and is forced to send her children to stay with her relatives. Biswas stays with the family of his Aunt Tara and starts working as a sign-writer to pay for his living. One day while at work as a sign writer in the Tulsi shop, he falls in love with one of the daughters of the extended Tulsi family, Shama, and soon he finds himself pressed into marrying her and moving to the Tulsi's large household, Hanuman House. He takes up several jobs as a shopkeeper and as a sign writer but all fail to secure him independence from the Tulsi family. Finally, he is employed as a journalist and moves his four children and his wife to Port of Spain where they can live in relative comfort. Following his ambition, Mr. Biswas buys the modern looking house he longed for a few months before his death, but the house turns out to be ill-designed and unstable.

There are two sides to Biswas's character: he is ambitious and rebellious but he repeatedly fails to put into action his ambition. His limited agency in acting on his desire comes to light in the course of his quest for buying or building his own house. Mr. Biswas's achievement in finally buying a house should not be overestimated. Indeed, his several failures, his psychological distress, and the poor condition of his final house renders his achievement ambivalent, in the sense that his final purchase embodies simultaneously his failure and his success. Gordon Rohlehr emphasizes the significance of the rebellion of a mediocre man. He points out that Biswas's rebellion is against the social structure of Hanuman House and its leaders which according to him can be seen as a microcosm of a slave society which suppress its members' aspirations to independence. Despite the fact that the house Biswas buys in the end is mortgaged to his uncle and that Biswas fails to own it, according to Rohlehr, Biswas succeeds in "expressing [his] identity in the very act of searching for it" (Rohlehr 93). Rohlehr in support of Mr. Biswas's endeavours argues that his rebellion rose from his desire "to understand existence and make sense of his milieu" (84). In other words, Rohlehr relates Biswas's struggle within the family structure to the struggle of Trinidad as a nation still struggling with the legacy of its slave plantation history.

According to Warner-Lewis, the conflict between Biswas and Tulsis is a cultural clash between the traditional versus the Creole, the rural versus the urban and the traditionalism versus individualism. Warner-Lewis argues that Tulsidom, which might be defined as 'encapsulating an idea of India-in-the-Caribbean' has come to terms with change which is reflected in the behaviour and attitude of the younger generations who do not speak Hindi and aspire to go abroad (97). This change, as Warner-Lewis argues, was initiated by Biswas who fought for his independence despite the financial security and emotional support of the traditional culture of Tulsidom, a trajectory that would be followed by the next generation who experience the Western-oriented Creole culture of Trinidad (98). By focusing on the quest for home rather than Biswas's rebellion against the Tulsi family, Biswas's lack of cultural and psychological capacity to act on his will comes to light. Mr. Biswas is not looking for any house but he is looking for a homely one.

Mr. Biswas's birth and childhood resonates with the life of the classic character of Oedipus the king. Having being born with 'six fingers' and in 'a wrong way', Biswas is different and distinguished from other children (14). He was unwanted, unloved and viewed as the bearer of bad luck to his family, just as Oedipus was as a baby. Like Oedipus, quite accidentally and unintentionally Biswas causes his father's death when the father dives into a pond to save him from drowning. The incident vilifies Mr. Biswas and becomes a turning point as it starts the process of 'homelessness' that characterizes his life thereafter. He is sent to stay with his relatives and "[f]or the next thirty-five years he [is] to be a wanderer with no place to call his own" (38). Biswas is destined to share Oedipus's misery; the latter is blinded and banished and the former is left displaced and homeless.

Oedipus the king is a key text in Freudian psychoanalytic studies. Freud uses the classic story of Oedipus and particularly his relationship with his biological parents in order to explain the process of sexual-identity formation in a boy-child (Wright 8). The notion of the Oedipus complex refers to the male child's rivalry with the father over the nurturing mother, and of his fantasies of killing the father and possessing the mother. In the Freudian Paradigm identity is formed when the Oedipus complex is accompanied by the castration complex in a male child. The father is seen as the source of authority and power so the boy abandons his love for the mother and moves towards identification with his father in the hope that he too can occupy the position of power (Wright 13). In the case of Biswas, the absence of a father leaves Biswas with no role model to identify with and in effect the process of identity formation is left unaccomplished for him. Another possible reading is that Biswas as a child refuses to adopt his father's colonial identity. The child's symbolic unintentional father-killing can be interpreted as a positive gesture to dispense with the legacy of dependency and colonial identity. Naipaul uses this as an opportunity for the young Biswas to acquire a new independent and decolonized identity for himself and his descendents.

Thus, Biswas sets on self-education to develop his own identity and to find his selfhood. The first step for him is to start looking in foreign magazines and books for a model of an ideal life: "He read the novels of Hall Cain and Marie Corelli. They introduced him to intoxicating worlds.... They made him despair of finding romance in his own dull green land" (77). There is a gap between what these books and pictures offer as the ideal life and that of life in the small Indian community of Trinidad. Biswas is aware of the cultural distinctions between the two distinctive geographies—the west and his own small island—and continues to look for a lifestyle compatible with his milieu. The second step would be to look around himself, and his own community to find the meaning of life on the island. In Aunt Tara's house, he develops his sense of need for a stable family life and the home he has been deprived of. Biswas thinks he has to have this stability if he is to have his own family. Discovering his talent for drawing and his love of writing, he chooses sign writing for shops as his profession, but the job turns out to be unstable, as he is out of work for several weeks. Similarly, his marriage to Shama Tulsi, and his move to the Tulsi household, Hanuman House, does not bring him the homeliness he expects. Living in the authoritative organism of Hanuman House requires the individuals to give up their individual identity and adopt the collective identity of the Tulsi family. The members were expected to respect the already established power relations in order to maintain the authoritarian system. Despite the fact that Biswas needs the financial support of the Tulsis, due to his own career being unstable, he refuses to exchange his individuality for the security of living with the Tulsis.

Biswas views the idea of ownership of a house as a means through which he could assert his selfhood. To Mr. Biswas, his house would indeed embody his self-worth and his independence and a sense that he has not lived an 'unnecessary life' (8). The prelude to the novel makes it clear how Mr. Biswas feels towards his final achievement:

> How terrible it would have been, at this time, to be without it: to have died among the Tulsis, amid the squalor of that large, disintegrating and indifferent family; to have left Shama and the children among them, in one room; worse, to have lived without even attempting to lay claim to one's portion of the earth; to have lived and died as one had been born, unnecessary and unaccommodated. (8)

Apart from an assertion of individuality, owning a house would show Biswas's ability to provide security for his family. In fact, Mr. Biswas is determined to change the 'fate' he is born with. His grandfather's expression used to be "[f]ate. There is nothing we can do about it" (11). But Mr. Biswas is determined to rebel against the fate of displacement and to break the cycle of homelessness he inherited from his parents. Such determination is better revealed in his relationship with his son, Anand. He attempts to provide him with a good education and particularly with a grounded identity. His quest for a house is also to a large extent due to his concern for the children not to be as displaced as he is, a concern that he directly asserts when he says to Anand, "I don't want you to be like me" (253). Here, instead of an oedipal rivalry between the father and the son, they form a relationship in which they occupy each other's position: "Father and son, each saw the other as weak and vulnerable, and each felt the responsibility for the other, a responsibility which, in times of particular pain, was disguised by exaggerated authority on the one side, exaggerated respect on the other" (394).

Such a relationship is in contrast to the relationship between Biswas and his own father, whose identity he refused to adopt. Biswas has no established identity or individuality Anand can identify with, but as the father and the son are both vulnerable and insecure, they help each other in the creation of an established and grounded identity. Mr. Biswas's unconventional relationship with his son on the one hand, and his excessive ambition to own a house, on the other show the extent of the psychological pressure to ground himself and his family. Yet, Mr. Biswas's strong determination to have his own home signifies a deeper cultural homelessness rather than just a personal identity crisis. According to Homi K. Bhabha, the 'overdetermined' and 'unaccommodated postcolonial figure' of Mr. Biswas is not compatible with the Anglo-American tradition of novels of big houses, like that of Charles Dickens or Jane Austen that are founded on sovereignty of characters and individual freedom (446).

Biswas's derelict life before marriage and his loss of individuality amongst the Tulsis are the environmental factors imposed on him by the small society in which he lives. All these factors deprived him of what Bhabha calls 'individual freedom' and elevate his need for independence. Thus, a concrete identity like a house takes on an inflated significance in embodying an area of independence. Yet, the houses he attempts to build or buy fail to fulfill such a need for independence and homeliness. Mr. Biswas's idea of home is that of the traditional definition of home which regards home as the embodiment of a grounded (masculine) self-identity. But the satirical narrative of Naipaul attempts to show how elusive the promise for territorial satisfaction of home is for a colonized individual. A strong white concrete house is the ideal structure that preoccupies Mr. Biswas's mindset, but the houses of Mr. Biswas are in one way or another far from this ideal home. There are houses which become a source of inspiration like Hanuman house or the Doll's house, and those which Biswas builds or buys, like the half-built building in the Chase and Mr. Biswas's final house. But the fact that none of these houses provide him with the territorial satisfaction he looks for, is indicative of a deeper cultural displacement that cannot be homed. In fact, the major houses and buildings that Biswas is closely involved with fail to provide him with identity, security and stimulation in one way or another. The idea to own a house as a way of asserting his individuality comes to Biswas in Hanuman House, where he moves after marrying Shama.

Hanuman House is a grand family house which is known in the area as a traditional and religious household. The Tulsis, a traditional Hindu landowning family have preserved their traditional customs as well as traditional family structure by cutting themselves off from outsiders and running the household as a self-sufficient enclosed state within the Indian community. To Biswas, "Hanuman House was a world...everything beyond its gate was foreign and unimportant" (195). The appearance of the house from outside is like an 'alien, white fortress' which is suggestive of power and authority (*Ibid.*). The internal structure of the house, though, corresponds with the power relations established within the household. Hanuman House consists of two buildings, the main building is in concrete and it consists of the visitor's room, a large hall and the residence of those in authority in the family, Mrs. Tulsi, her two sons and Seth, (Mrs. Tulsi's brother-in-law). The rest of the family, that is the girls and their husbands who come second on the scale of power, live in an old wooden building called 'the old barracks' (196), a term which Naipaul knowingly deploys because of its association with the barrack-like structures in which indentured Indians were housed during the colonial era. The hierarchy of power which is minutely identified is to be preserved and respected: Chinta below Padma, Shama below Chinta, Savi below Shama and so on. All the members, including the sons-in-law, work under Seth's authoritative watch over the family businesses. Such a well-established structure suggests that Hanuman House is as Naipaul defines it, 'a microcosm of the authoritarian state' (cited in Nixon 85).

Mr. Biswas is impressed by the grandeur of the house at the beginning, but he soon becomes aware that he cannot enjoy the authority of the heads of the family and that his place is a small room in the worst part of the building. Mr. Biswas upset by the unequal power relations in the house and the privileged position of Seth, Mrs. Tulsi and her sons, rebels against them. He fights with some men of the family but he understands that the structure of Hanuman House would not be dismantled with such trivial gestures. Looking more deeply Biswas views the traditional household as "an organism that possessed a life, strength and power to comfort" (315), but the price for enjoying these qualities is to give up independence and individuality:

> Suppose, Mr. Biswas thought, in the long room, suppose that at one word I could just disappear from this room, what would remain to speak of me? A few clothes, a few books. The shouts and thumps in the hall would continue ...in the morning the Tulsi store would open its doors.
>
> He had lived in many houses. And how easy it was to think of those houses without him!... Even more remote, that house of mud and grass in the swamplands: probably pulled down now and ploughed up. Beyond that, a void. There was nothing to speak of him. (135)

Biswas cannot stand being nobody any longer. He expected Hanuman House to be more than a family house, to be a home where he could feel he belonged, but it failed to bring him the sense of homeliness. Thus, Mr. Biswas aspires to own a house which along with independence would give him the sense of homeliness which he craves. The traditional Tulsis observe such assertions of individualism with contempt, mocking Biswas for wanting 'to paddle his own canoe' (139). Aspiring to buy his own house, Mr. Biswas looks for a model and he finds it in the image of a doll's house as a Western model of an ideal house. He watches other people's houses and compares his desired house to the ones that he sees in different places. His mental engagement with doll's house imagery goes to the extent that he projects the fantasy image onto the real buildings around him: "he fixed his eyes on a house, as small and as neat as a doll's house" (324). Mr. Biswas's obsession with the doll's house shows that his criterion for an ideal house is limited to the outside appearance rather than the internal foundation of the building. He even decides to share his fantasy world with his family. At Christmas, Shama and the children stay in Hanuman House and Mr. Biswas, on his way to pay a visit to them, buys his daughter, Savi, a doll's house as a Christmas present, for which he pays more than a month's wages. This extravagance leaves him with no money to buy anything for Anand. But more than the disappointment to Anand, Savi's expensive and flashy present upsets the residents of Hanuman House, Mrs. Tulsi and her daughters. Mr. Biswas while ignoring the hostile reaction of Hanuman House to the doll's house enjoys Savi's sense of pride and authority over the other children, a sense he was denied in the household: "Mr. Biswas...was pleased when the children acknowledged Savi's ownership by asking her permission to open doors and touch beds. Even as she explored, Savi tried to give the impression that she was familiar with everything" (225).

Mr. Biswas's choice of present for Savi reveals first, his unconscious desire to buy a perfect neat-looking house for himself and his family, and second, to assert the child's individuality in a household where her presence is rarely recognised and make her distinguished from the other children. In Hanuman House, though, the action is regarded as crossing an implicit boundary and thus not tolerated. The next time Mr. Biswas visits Hanuman House, he faces Savi in tears and the doll's house shattered. Shama had shattered the toy house as the hostility of her sisters towards her. Mrs. Tulsi also sees Mr. Biswas's action which gives Savi some kind of privilege over the other children as a threat to the long-held power relations and hierarchy in the household: "I'm poor, but I give to all" (226). Any ambition to go beyond the established positions (Mrs. Tulsi as the Santa Claus, for example) and to break the equality of children in the organism of Hanuman House leads to exclusion. The power of such exclusion goes to the extent that Shama is forced to break the means of privilege and return to her own place. Mr. Biswas is angry at what has happened, yet, he does not react harshly to the incident as he usually does. It seems that he comes to accept that he has to direct his ambition in another way. Thus, while keeping in his mind the image of a neat house like a doll's house throughout the novel, he sets out to build his own real house.

Biswas's vulnerability and naivety and his lack of a clear perspective on his abilities are best presented by his attempt at building his own house on a piece of land owned by the Tulsis. The Green Vale House is Biswas's first attempt to test his ability to achieve homeliness and independence and he starts personalizing his ideal home in his imagination, while this imaginary house seems to be 'real': "He had thought deeply about this house, and knew exactly what he wanted. He wanted in the first place, a real house, made with real materials. He didn't want mud for the walls, earth for the floor, tea branches for rafters and grass for roof. He wanted wooden walls, all tongue-and-groove" (219).

But it turns out to be the embodiment of his incapacity to manage the construction project of a good and stable house. Given that he is inexperienced in house-building, he hires a builder. The black builder Maclean realizes within minutes of speaking with Biswas, that he is inexperienced and naïve, and plans to exploit him. Mr. Biswas is so inexperienced that when asked what he wants to build, he has no idea other than 'small thing. But neat" (249). It is Maclean who starts giving shape to Mr. Biswas's image of his house: "You want two bedrooms.... And a gallery" (250). Mr. Biswas's lack of a clear perspective on the project hints at a dramatic failure to come. Mr. Biswas and Maclean and have different ethnic origins. The troubled relationship and the lack of trust between them imply the lack of trusting communication between the Trinidadians of different origins. Such a lack of trust appears to be one of the many factors that contribute to the failing of the project of building a homely house for the Trinidadian nationals. Mr. Biswas's vulnerability lies in his inexperience in handling such a project, and Maclean who doubts Mr. Biswas's ability to manage the project, takes advantage of him. As the construction progresses the problems appear: "asphalt hanging from the roof, the smell of rust filing the room, and so on" (276). Mr. Biswas at this stage senses the problem, but he does not dare to face it. Instead of confronting the builder and handling the problem, Mr. Biswas becomes distressed: "And every day the rain fell, the sun blazed, the house became greyer, the sawdust once fresh and aromatic became part of the earth...and Mr. Biswas worked more and more elaborate messages of comfort for his walls with a steady, unthinking hand and a mind in turmoil" (*Ibid.*).

Biswas's anxiety heightens as the constant rainfall causes the deterioration of the unfinished house. He starts biting his nails, having nightmares and becoming paranoid. The deterioration of Mr. Biswas's state of mind can be explained in relation to his lack of agency to act upon his will. This paper explains the collapse of Mr. Biswas's mental order when the procedure of the house-building goes dramatically wrong. Mr. Biswas's assertion of his individuality depends on building a house of his own and his determination and willingness to act on his will. But Mr. Biswas's lack of experience in house-building, his financial strains and his lack of trust in the builder puts him in a vulnerable position. He senses that things are not as they are supposed to be, but he is incapable of setting things right. Mr. Biswas knows what he wants and carefully plans his house in his imagination, but when put into action, his limited agency and his limited capacity to act on his will is revealed. Mr. Biswas has a nervous breakdown when he happens to watch the unfinished building collapse before he is able to own it. In fact, as the ordering of the space goes wrong, Mr. Biswas's mental order collapses. Such a stressful experience makes him give up his ambition for quite some time. He is resigned to failure for a while before saving and borrowing to buy his long awaited house, though as it transpires even the final house is ill-designed, poorly constructed and far from his imaginary ideal home. The house is as much a failure as an achievement. The beautiful façade of the house indeed covers up its lack of solid foundation and a good design, but Mr. Biswas takes comfort in the idea that he is finally independent and a house owner regardless of the shortcomings or even dangers that might await the family within the house.

The modern concrete house of Mr. Biswas can be interpreted as embodying the ungrounded and unstable independence of Trinidad, as seen by Naipaul. There is a prevalent view of the Caribbean being a Creole society, rather than colonial. The problem to Naipaul is inherent in the 'place' itself as it is fashioned by the colonial forces. As he says: "Black Power in these black islands is protest. But there is no enemy. The enemy is the past, of slavery and colonial neglect and a society uneducated from top to bottom; the enemy is the smallness of the islands and the absence of resources" (250).

Naipaul envisages the power of individual and collective forces and the future of the Caribbean. *A House for Mr Biswas* belongs to the transitional era—the transition of Trinidad from a colonial state to an independent state. The novel reveals Naipaul's idea that an individual's growth is embedded in social and cultural anatomy, while any development in the social sphere requires co-operation of self-decolonized and grounded subjects, a vicious cycle that seems to be unbreakable in the Caribbean. The lack of resources for growth and the possibility of rebellion against the status-quo are projected when Mr. Biswas considers breaking away from the restraint of the Tulsi family to follow his ambitions: "But go where? And do what? What could he do? Apart from being a bus conductor, working as a labourer on the sugar-estates or on the roads, owning a shop" (162). All the enthusiasm and motivation for progress dissipates because it has no clear focus. To Naipaul, Mr. Biswas, as a colonial subject cannot be 'unhomed', in the sense that he may live in the borderlines of the home and the world and turn 'unhomeliness' into an opportunity for creative initiations.

Works Cited

Bhabha, H. *The Location of Culture*. London: Routledge, 1992.

Conner, S. *The English Novel in History, 1990-1995*. London: Routledge, 1996.

Malpas, J.E. *Place and Experience: A Philosophical Topography.* Cambridge: Cambridge University Press, 1999.

Massey, D. *A Place Called Home? New Formations*. Web. July 17 2013.

Naipaul, V.S. *A House for Mr Biswas*. London: Picador, 1961.

Nasta, Susheila. Ed. *Writers Across Worlds*. Oxfordshire: Routledge, 2004.

Nixon, R. *London Calling: V.S. Naipaul, Postcolonial Mandarin*. New York: Oxford University Press, 1992.

Rohlehr, G. "Character and Rebellion in *A House for Mr Biswas*." *Critical Perspectives on V.S. Naipaul,* Ed. Robert D. Hamner. London: Heinemann, 1977. 84-93.

Warner-Lewis, M. "Cultural Confrontation in *A House for Mr Biswas*." *Critical Perspectives on V.S. Naipaul*, Ed. Robert D. Hamner. London: Heinemann, 1977. 96-99.

Wright, E. *Psychoanalytic Criticism*. Cambridge: Polity Press, 1998.

15

Anguish and Defeat of Unhoused and Unnecessary: A Critical Study of V.S. Naipaul's *A House for Mr Biswas*

Deepak Kumar and *Shagufta Naj*

> Nor fame, nor power, nor love, nor leisure.
> Others I see whom these surround
> Smiling they live, and call life pleasure:
> To me that cup has been dealt in another measure.
> (Shelley CCXXVII 24-27)

The sense of alienation and fragmentation in these lines is bred and articulated from that of detachment and division of personal feelings of the poet which he observes around his surroundings. What Shelley felt in romantic age has become more acute in the modern age with man's inner inconsistencies and existential incompatibilities exacerbating the schism. The sense of isolation, alienation and loss that was born in sensitive writers of the twentieth century, informs the literature of that age. West Indian fiction is distinctive for its intense social consciousness faced by a society formed through slavery and colonialism whose values have never been defined before. Chakrabharti considers that it reflects the general disillusionment that besets the two post-war generations and deep spiritual isolation felt by man in a universe in which he felt himself to be inconsequential and stranger (Chakrabarti 46).

At present, the most rational debate characterizes West Indian literature as a tradition within a tradition, an outgrowth and extension of the Western mode of writing. This creates an environment of literature just like the colonial experiences of the West Indian writers who are striving to find an identity for themselves and their dexterity that's distinct from the borrowed forms of the colonial authorities. West Indian fiction is distinctive for its intense social consciousness faced by a society formed through slavery and colonialism whose values have never been defined before, the novelists in the West Indies must recreate experience and simultaneously create the standards against which such experiences must be judged.

One of the best-known writers of post imperialism society is V (idiadhar) S (urajprasad) Naipaul, the accomplished novelist from the English speaking Caribbean, once commented on the contents of his literary works, "I feel that any statement that I make about my own work would be misleading. The work is there: the reader must see what meaning, if any the work has for him" (James 102-03). Naipaul is an expatriate from Trinidad whose primary business as a novelist is to project carefully the complex fate of individuals in "cross-cultural society" (Parag 135). He is unique in the history of English literature. He contributed many works which more or less are related to Indian identity. He is the most significant practitioner of art of fiction where he blends myth, reality, multiculturalism, Hinduism, modernism traditionalism and much more to give a full vent to his emotions which crave for identity. In *Hopes and Impediments: Selected Essays*, Chinua Achebe accuses Joseph Conrad and Naipaul of racism on the grounds that in certain respects, they use their remarkably powerful creative myth of the African as pathologically primitive (1988: 2). His novels bring to life the complexities of understanding, the nature of mankind against the backdrop of social influences that interact to give vent to such actions and activities. Chikodiri Okpara submits that Naipaul's fiction captures the minutest aspects of the sterile life of his society in his works in such a manner that leaves the reader with a raw account of life using customary fictitious characters to shed realities (2005: 160).

Fragmentation, alienation, and exile are common terms associated with postcolonial literature. Needless to say,

"Imperialism played a key role in bringing a sense of alienation and disorder to the countries where imperialists ruled" (Parag 135). Homi K. Bhaba states that "there is structural non-equivalence, a split between superior and inferior which explains why any group of people can dominant another at all" (Huddart 59). The struggle for domination, as Foucault shows, can be both systematic and hidden. There is an unceasing interaction between classes, nations, power centers and regions, seek to dominate and displace one another [...] (Ashcroft 85). Homi K. Bhaba also describes the effect of colonization as a result of "mimicry" he continues to argue that mimicry does not merely "rupture" the discourse, but becomes transformed into an uncertainty which fixed the colonial subject as a "partial" presence (Huddart 60-61).

Naipaul has unseverable emotional bond with Indian which remains for him an area of pain, an ache for which one has a great tenderness yet from which "fragmentation and rootlessness" are viewed in his works in the form of "anguish and defeat". The fragmented society "demonstrates a disorder which originates from within" (Freed 69). Naipaul's fiction thus acquire a three dimensional significance, historical, social and psychological and understandably Naipaul is at once a chronicler, historian and biographer (Iyer 17).

Naipaul uses variety of techniques to explore his own former status as colony, as margin to the centre of dominant imperial powers. Undoubtedly, the 'colonial experiences' is the theme that confronts each West Indian writer, and his attempt is a resolute confrontation between himself, his inner needs and his history. For Naipaul, the West Indies consists of races that have been uprooted from their original societies and have not produced a new culture, to replace, what was lost. Naipaul has written extensively about different aspects of post-colonial society, viewed from post-colonial perspective Naipaul's novels become a fascinating study of the diasporans, "their sense of loss and gloom leading to unhappiness" (Mishra 45). He presents "psychic and symbolic sense of homelessness" (Ball 90) because of which it was impossible to return for them to any pure cultural and historical origin or wholeness (Boxhill 81). He deals with shifting identities, roots, homes and changing realities of migrants. He describes the people who had to abandon their own countries and found themselves in strange places, without friends with few loyalties and with the feeling that they are trespassing.

Naipaul's writing is suffused with a great melancholy and loneliness for these people, and he also feels about himself that he is "under the volcano, homesick for homesick" (Meyers 56). Naipaul himself is split into his characters in whom are manifested subtle shades of his "emotions and traits" (Adams 74). Writing in the New York Reviews of books about Naipaul, Joan Didion said: "[...] the world Naipaul sees is of course no void at all": it's a world dense with physical and social phenomena, brutally alive with the complications and contradictions of actual human endeavours [...] (Handibag 1).

The constituents such as dislocation, confusion, disorder, mimicry, despair and utter rootlessness form the content of Naipaul's fiction. The first three indicate a preliminary state of fragmentation. The second set, building upon the first, leads to an irreversible alienation from all previous ties. The phrase from "fragmentation to rootlessness" can easily be rephrased as "from disorder to rejection of all order" (Deodat 69). Fragmentation and rootlessness are viewed in his works in the form of "anguish and defeat". The fragmented society "demonstrates a disorder which originates from within" (Freed 69). The under lying theme of the research paper is the disorder and despair which fragmentation and rootlessness have spawned (Deodat 70).

In Naipaul, the sense of fragmentation comes across his deep and unshakable sense of loss, of being perpetual outside. As fragmented (they could not go back to the sources of their realities) thus they were continually in the process of searching for a sense of their own self, of coming to some senses of completion of themselves. But "arriving is a process which can not come to an end" (Cooke 140). In addition, the harsh conditions of colonialisms have left the West Indian crippling burdens of physical condition correspond so closely, the unhoused, poverty-stricken. West India is often culturally and spiritually dispossessed as well (Boxhill 49).

V.S. Naipaul's *magnum opus*, *A House for Mr Biswas* (1961) can rightly be called a work of art that deals with these problems, i.e. isolation, frustration, anguish, disgust and defeat of an individual. *A House for Mr Biswas* is Naipaul's unforgettable third novel, often regarded as his masterpiece, which tells the tragi-comic story of the search for independence and identity of a Brahmin Indian living in Trinidad. *A House for Mr Biswas* displays a unique affection for the homeland of his birth. It deals with historical period of colonialism and indenture and the expression of migration and displacement with respect to Trinidad. However, a rereading of *A House for Mr Biswas* suggests that it is an extra-ordinary narrative which evokes the memory of indenture and the post-indentured unaccomodated man with psychological acuteness and emotional truth. Naipaul describes *A House for Mr Biswas* in his non-fiction book, *Finding the Centre*, saying that it was very much my father's book (Parag 136). Similarly, in his Nobel Award Ceremony acceptance speech, Naipaul alludes to *A House for Mr Biswas,* saying that "intuition led me to a large book about our family life" (136).

Partly autobiographical, *A House for Mr Biswas* delineates the traumas of a tainted and troubled past and Mr. Biswas's attempts to find a purpose in life; the novel beautifully analyzes the sense of alienation and the pangs of exile experienced by the characters (Parag 135). The stagnant, decaying Hindu world; the poverty and chaos of the Creole society; and the painful struggle of one man to rise above both, are all rendered with the authenticity that only historical truths will allow, and the artistry that only a truly talented writer can generate (Deodat 53). *A House for Mr Biswas* is Naipaul's most profound attempt to dramatize his own integrated society. It is seen to concern with the lives of the poverty-stricken and riddled with the frustration and despair (Meyers 27).

As Kenneth Ramchand notes, *A House for Mr Biswas* is the West Indian novel of rootlessness par excellence and part of Naipaul's re-achievement is that these themes work at a number of levels for various subjects simultaneously (Ramchand 102). In this novel, Naipaul presents a space in which his characters move and feel a sense of unease, a sense of not belonging at home or in the vocabulary of novel a "familiar temporariness" (Naipaul 2003: 201). He found them haunted by the indenture syndrome of ancestors of "unnecessary and unaccommodated" (Naipaul 8). Similarly, his characters inherit a kind of 'neuroses' of the past insecurity, madness, anguish, out of placement, defeat and rootlessness (Clemens 71).

Naipaul presents this vicious circuit in *A House for Mr Biswas* as "self disgust led to anger, shouts, tears something to add to the concentrated hubbub of the evening, the nerve torn helplessness" (Naipaul 463). *A House for Mr Biswas* deals with the historical period of colonialism, indenture and the experiences of migration and displacement with respect to Trinidad. However, a re-reading of the novel suggests that it is an extraordinary narrative which evokes the memory of indenture and the post-indentured "unaccomodated and unhoused" man with psychological acuteness and emotional truth (Ramchand 20). By a blind accident of history they all find themselves "unnecessary and unaccomodated" and various painful feelings with futile attempt to save themselves from this. The condition of Mr. Biswas was so pitiable that he found himself totally dipped into the ditch of frustration and disgust: "Everything he now saw becomes sullied by his fear, every field, every house, every tree, every turn in the road [...] so that by merely, looking at the world, he was progressively destroying his present and his past" (Naipaul 281).

Naipaul concentrates on the struggle between the individual will or desire for a separate identity and the compelling will of the milieu, its anonymity of stifling corporate identity (74). He also realizes that their full creative potential is highly indicative of the colonial retardation with which the writer's environment seems to afflicted, and which in Naipaulian formula reads: "Ought oughts are ought, ought twos are ought" (Naipaul 43). Naipaul addresses the problem of alienation, exile and displacement with a positive approach. He presents Mr. Biswas relentless struggle against the forces that he tries to subdue his individuality.

From the very beginning, Mohun Biswas is depicted as marginalized individual in the limited world of Trinidad. Biswas flawed and inauspicious birth renders his childhood a travesty of the title, this phase of his life bears "Pastoral". His entrance has been described in the world as "six fingered, and born in the wrong way" (Naipaul II). He is fated to have an unlucky sneeze; he is warned never to go near water, etc. Pundit also characterizes Biswas: "First of all, the features of this unfortunate boy. He will have good teeth but that will be rather wide, and there will be spaces between them. I suppose you know what that means" (Naipaul 12).

Biswas is acutely aware of his lack of physical endowment and is not sufficiently secure psychologically to survive without a support and identity offered by a family group, yet he constantly reels against the Tulsi household. He becomes a lonely individual who is trying to get a new social role but fails to find it. Aware of his loneliness and dilemma, Mr. Biswas tells his son, "I am just somebody. Nobody at all" (Naipaul 284). Unlike, his father and brothers who have inherited the social identity of labourers, this can not be claimed by Mr. Biswas.

He looks after his uncle's shop while his brothers work as labourers. After leaving his uncle's shop, he takes up a job as sign painter, where he meets Shama, a daughter of the Tulsis, whom he later marries. His marriage makes him realize that life is not romance, but an act of responsibility. Without money and without dowry, Mr. Biswas has no choice, but to move in at Hanuman House. Hanuman House provides shelter to Mr. Biswas but wants total dilution of his identity in return. In a novel dominated by the Hinduism, "Hanuman House" is actually described in military terms:

> [...] Hanuman House stood like an alien white fortress. The walls looked as thick as they were and when the narrow doors of the Tulsis store on the ground floor were closed the House became bulky, impregnable and blank. The side walls were window less and on the upper floor the window were more slits in the facades. (*AHFMB* 81)

In Trinidad it is not merely "alien" but crumbling. The bulky impregnable walls are deceptive. They are not made of concrete at all, but hollow clay block (94). The Tulsis are vainly attempting to keep in act a culture which has been battered by transplantation and colonialism and which is now reduced in hollow rituals. While the "fortress" offers some protection to its older members who are incapable of dealing with the "new world" (Clemens 54). Mr. Biswas finds out that he is unwanted in Hanuman House, where he was treated with indifference rather than hostility. As a hero, Mr. Biswas is never truly free of the Tulsis and whenever he seeks his freedom has to be bailed by members of the Tulsis clan, intensifying his subservience and sense of gratitude to them.

In the section entitled "The Chase", Mr. Biswas begins his independent life with Shama. From the beginning, however, Mr. Biswas has the feeling that in Chase, he is unnecessary and unwanted. But he also thinks that life in Chase will help him to discover his own identity, but it's the sense of isolation that looms large and he fails to find his authentic selfhood. Mr. Biswas now feels that despite hostility, he is recognized as a mimic man in Hanuman House. At Chase, he feels 'alienated' (Parag 138).

Naipaul seeks to convey that a person's social identity depends on the society to which he belongs and that the family is sustaining and stabilizing experiences for marginalized individuals like Mr. Biswas. For Mr. Biswas, life is meaningless without Shama, his children, and even the Tulsis. So Mr. Biswas visits to Hanuman House more frequently.

Life at Green Vale is more distressing experience. Although Green Vale gives him a sense of freedom and importance, his actions in Green Vale are motivated by excessive insecurity both physically and mentally:

> He waved the stick. He moved to the window and, looking at her, waving the stick, began to draw the bolt. 'Don't touch me, he bawled, and there were sobs mixed with his words [...]. He began screaming and crying. He pressed his palms on the window sill and tried to hoist himself up [...]. (*AHFMB* 288)

His dream to build a house begins to shape into reality somehow, he starts building his house in Green Vale but it's nowhere near the house of his dream. So the intensity of alienation and displacement continues and here too, he fails to gain acceptance as an individual.

The second part of the novel focuses on Port of Spain, a place that opens new avenues for Mr. Biswas. The city provides him with opportunities to establish him professionally, something he has long searched for. He becomes a reporter for the *'Trinidad Sentinel'*, with a salary of fifteen dollars a month, a job that helps him to earn some respect from the Tulsis too. His relations with Mrs. Tulsi gradually improve. There is no hostility from either side. For the time being, he forgets his wish to have space of his own and enjoys his success and family life. His happiness however is short lived. The takeover of the Trinidad Sentinel by new authorities, Seth's break up with the Tulsis and Mrs.Tulsi's decision to live in Shorthills; all come as a blow upsetting the family hierarchy upon which the Tulsi's family has used to run. Domestic situation after the return of Owad also changes, who slaps Anand for answering him back; in humiliation, Anand argues his father that "they must move. He can not bear to live here another day" (Naipaul 551). Mr. Biswas, who has himself faced such humiliation innumerable times during his childhood, is deeply moved by his son's appeal.

The vivid correlation between his own lack of accommodation and that of the Hindu and Creole world of Trinidad becomes powerfully apparent during this period of his life. Mr. Biswas manages to get loan from Ajodha and buys a house in Port of Spain. He describes his house: "The sun came through the open window work and frosted glass was hot to touch. The inside brick wall was warm. The sun went through the home and laid dazzling strips on the exposed staircase" (Naipaul 572). Naipaul uses words like "sun" and "dazzling" in his description of the house, words that clearly reveal Mr. Biswas's happiness and sense of fulfillment (Deodat 140).

At forty-six his battles are over, this cultural orphan, this history-less man has achieved all the success which his limited talent and sterile environment will allow. He must now give way to his children and await their successes: "there was nothing Mr. Biswas could do but wait. Wait for Anand, wait for Savi; wait for the five years to come to an end, wait, wait" (Naipaul 76). Wait for death; it's a tragic, stunning testimony of life in a rootless, disordered society that the achievement of a single, real victory drains the life blood of the soul. Biswas dies enjoying the company of his daughter, Savi and admiring the mystery and romance of life, he was never destined to share: "the shade was flowering again; was not it strange that a tree which grew so quickly could produce flowers with such a sweet scent?" (77).

It's by no means a happy ending while his hopes for his children may be justified in Savi, the son who was closet to him, Anand, is morose and moody. He has inherited the psychic fragmentation which frustrates and darkens many of his father's active years (Deodat 78). As Kumar Parag also underlines "a house is not just a matter getting a shelter from heat, cold or rain. In fact, it is both an imposition of order and a carving-out of authentic selfhood within the heterogeneous and fragmented society of Trinidad" (139). The novel portrays not only Mr. Biswas as a man who stays put struggling against the hostile environment but also another characters such as Shekhar, Owad and even the children.

Naipaul presents the "Youngs and Children" struggle to survive in this alien "new world" pathetically. The "childish multitude" of "readers and learners" feel the immediate results of their new state. They are housed and feed like cattle. Many have been separated from their parents and are now merely anonymous units under Bandai's frenzied supervision and exhortations, "Read; Learn; Learn; Read" (Clemens 56).

Mrs. Tulsi's two sons are seen as proof of the success and security. But Owad and Shekhar are not as content and complete as their little emulators are led to believe. After his marriage into a rich family, Shekhar does not bring his wife in his home, but leaves his own home to live with his wife's family. So Shekhar now finds himself in the same emasculated role as Biswas and the other poor husbands who married into the Tulsi's clan.

Marriage and money are poor substitutes for a thwarted ambition. Materially Shekhar has gained much; culturally and psychologically, he has lost just as much. On other hand, a clearer demonstration of Owad's petty, self-centered mind, his heartless and cruel belittling of Anand before the entire family; his agony condemnation of what he terms Anand's conceited "selfishness and egocentricity" is pure irony. It takes him very little time to find his "right place" in society. He becomes part of the "new elite" released from both the Hindu and Creole world of Trinidad. The main changes which are recorded are the decline of the Hindu culture and rituals as they undergo the process of 'creolisation,' and the accompanying changes in attitude. Mr. Biswas himself is caught between the old culture from India and the emerging cross-fertilizations which are shown in many ways culminating in Mr. Biswas's own children, Anand and Savi. Mureen Warner Lewis takes a long hard look at the situation and expresses: "...the conflict in the story has strong bearing on clash of culture which accounts for the background to and explanation of many events, in the novel as well as Mr. Biswas difficulty of adjustment in his relationship with Tulsidom" (Warner 94).

The *"readers and learners,"* Owad and Shekhar, and even Anand are caught in a wretched dilemma to remain within the traditional fold is to stagnate and decay; to succeed in the "new world" is to betray one's origin and deny the very basis one's personality. Mr. Biswas's quest for integrity and his ardent struggle to attain "accommodation and necessity" are the central movements of the novel (Deodat 59). Ramchand expresses that the hero's achievement (for he is indeed a hero in spite of all his apparently unheroic qualities) lies in the attempt made with faith and ever-returning courage to interpose a human institution (the family) and a humanized object (the house) between himself and a universe threatening annihilation on every side (78-79).

Although Mr. Biswas is an ordinary man with no outstanding features, Naipaul succeeds in giving him a heroic status. He is in many ways an archetypal figure. In him, Naipaul embodies a universal theme—the search of identity and meaning in life. The effort to achieve the ownership of the house reflected in the very little of the novel becomes his passion and motive of life. The elements of vulnerability and lack of certainty help to take Mr. Biswas into a human and sympathetic whose identity crisis is never ending story.

Mr. Biswas symbolic victory in finally gaining his house does not alter the many limitations his past and unaccommodating societies have placed on him, and will place on his descendents. Even when the material conditions have changed, real integrity still evades the rootless East Indian, West Indian. In Anand's character are the seeds for Naipauls's exploration of the West Indian who has achieved educational and financial success but who is still psychologically burdened by his broken, inglorious heritage (Greenberg 78).

A House for Mr Biswas emphasizes the theme of freedom, loss of freedom and humiliation. It should also be taken into account that the society and culture in which the novel takes place is much concerned to the issues of caste and class-conscious. Mr. Biswas never has an opportunity to develop a sense of self. He finds himself in situations that made him feel powerless. He is always in situations where he is having people tell him what to do. He never has any personal power. Mr. Biswas realizes that with money and possessions a person tends to have move power in society. As Cooke also explains that Isolation is far more damaging than the insulation of those who fail (59). Ramchand argues that Naipaul's *A House for Mr Biswas* gives life to the vision of "the broken individual in the West Indies" (5) who suffer from deprivation, longing and rootlessness (6). *In a Way in the World,* Naipaul presents the homelessness of Trinidadian Indians Post-Indenture: "these people were without money, job, without anything like a family, without the English language; without any kind of representation. They were utterly destitute" (Parag 135). So Naipaul's language consists of the races that have been uprooted from their original society (Ball 54). There is the recurrence of images of destruction and disintegrated like "empty houses," "chaotic dining room," "offending brick wall," "sinking floor amidst the squalor" of disintegration, all serving to reemphasize futility and hopelessness (Clemens 17).

For these alienated and displaced people of the colonized countries, Naipaul seems to suggest that searching for creativity (as Mr. Biswas does and never gives up) relying on their own originality is one of the basic means to find their lost and alienated identity (TAS 4). Naipaul accepted the colonial culture when he was a little, but he had no access to transcend the regional barrier in the course of literature creation. By mean of memory and re-experience, he reproduced the true life of Trinidad: the hopeless struggle of marginalized people; person with multicultural in limbo, the disorder democracy and freedom. In the study of *A House for Mr Biswas,* "processing a house" is rather symbolic of having an identity of one's own in the society (Chandrapradhan 28).

To conclude, Mohan Biswas's love for natural human liberty and individuality inspire him to fight against the lifeless rotten rituals, myths and customs of degenerated Brahmin cultural systems represented by the Tulsis in the novel. During his forty-six short years, Mr. Biswas has always struggled to seek and define his sense of self but to no avail. *A House for Mr Biswas* masterfully evokes a man's quest of autonomy against the backdrop of postcolonial Trinidad. Despite being buffeted by economic, social and cultural forces, he tries to emerge from the trauma of life. Owning a house may be the symbol of rehabilitation, as in the case of Mr. Biswas, but it seems tasking, if not Herculean process (Deodat 96). It seems to illustrate his ability to realize a self identity and gain personal power to control of his personal life. Ultimately Naipaul's vision is sorely affected by a majority of the underprivileged class whose progress and existence are naturally stifled by the paleness of the society.

Works Cited

Achebe, Chinua. *Hopes and Impediments: Selected Essays: 1965-1987.* London: Heinemann, 1988.

Adams, Robert Martin. "V.S. Naipaul." *Hudson Review* 33 (1989): 474-78.

Ashcroft, Bill and Pal Ahluwalia. *Edward Said.* London: Routledge, 1999.

Ball, John Clements. *Satire and the Post Colonial Novel: V.S. Naipaul.* New York: Routledge, 2003.

Boxhill, Anthony. "The Paradox of Freedom: V.S. Naipaul's *In a Free State.*" *Critique: Studies in Modern Fiction* 18.1(1976): 81-91.

Chakrabarti, Santosh. "Alienation and Home: A Study of A House for Mr. Biswas." *V.S. Naipaul, Critical Essays.* Ed. Mohit K. Ray. 3 (2005): 41-48.

Pradhan, Prakash Chandra. "Search for Identity: Ideology and Social Conflict in V.S. Naipaul's 'A House for Mr Biswas'". *V.S. Naipaul, Critical Essays.* Ed. Mohit K. Ray. 3 (2005): 28-31.

Clemens, Walter C. "The Third World in V.S. Naipaul." *Worldview.* 25 Sept. 1982.

Conrad, Joseph. *Heart of Darkness.* London: Penguin, 1999.

Cooke, John. "A Vision of the Land: V.S. Naipaul's Later Novels." *Journals of Caribbean Studies.* 1 (1980): 140-61.

David, Ormerod. "In a Derelict Land: The Novels of V.S. Naipaul." *Wisconsin Studies in Contemporary Literature* 9 (1968.): 74-90.

Deodat, Ravindradat. *V.S. Naipaul's Fiction, 1954-71, Fragmentation and Rootlessness*, Simon Frarer University, 1979.

Freed, Lynn. "The Critical is Personal." *The New York Times Book Review* (2004): 11.

Gourevitch, Philip. "Naipaul's World." *Commentary* 98.2 (1994): 27-31.

Greenberg, Robert M. "Anger and the Alchemy of Literary Method in V.S. Naipaul's Political Fiction: The Case of The Mimic Men." *Twentieth Century Literature: A Scholarly and Critical Journal* 46.2 (2000): 74-80.

Handibag, Y.S. *et al.* "Towards the Centre: A Critique to V.S. Naipaul's The Enigma of Arrival." *International Refereed Research Journal.* 2.15 (2010): 1-12.

Huddart, David. *Homi K. Bhaba.* London: Routledge, 2005.

Hughes, Peter. *V.S. Naipaul.* London: Routledge, 1988. Web. 19 August. 2009.

Iyer, N. Sharma. "A House for Mr. Biswas A Study in Cultural Predicament." *V.S. Naipaul, Critical Essays.* Ed. Mohit K. Ray. Vol. 3 (2005): 28-31.

James, Vinson and Kirkpatrick. Ed. *Contemporary Novelists*. London: St. James Press, 1976.

Meyers, Jaffery. "V.S. Naipaul: Essays, Stories, Reviews, and Interviews, 1948-1992." *Bulletin of Bibliography* 50.4 (1993): 17-29.

Mishra, Pankaj. "*The Writer and the World.*" *Times of India*. Apr 14, 2009.

Naipaul, V.S. *A House for Mr Biswas*. 1961. India: Picador, 2003.

——. *A Transition Interview by Adrian Rowe-Evans*. Transition 8 No. 47. 1971.

——. Nobel Award Ceremony Acceptance Speech. Web. 20 Dec. 2012.

Okpara, C.M. "Fraud and Recompense: The Symbolism of Ganesh Ramsumair in V.S. Naipaul's *The Mystic Masseur.*" Ed. A. Akpuda. *The Black Presence in Caribbean Literature*. Enugu: Sandrew PTD Press, 2005. 156-66.

Parag, Kumar. "Identity Crisis in V.S. Naipaul's *A House for Mr Biswas*." *Neither East nor West: Postcolonial Essays on Literature, Culture and Religion*. Ed. Kerstin W. Shands. Sweden: Södertörns högskola, 2008. 135-42.

Pathak, Sunil, *et al*. "V.S. Naipaul in the Line and Light of Colonial Culture." *International Journal of Recent Research and Review.* 2 (2012.). Web. 27 July 2012.

Ramchand, Kenneth. *From Street to House*. Intrd. "A Discussion of Naipaul's Later Fiction". New Brunswick: Rutgers, 1996. Web. 16 Nov. 2012.

Shelley, P.B. *The Golden Treasury*. Ed. Francis T. Palgrave. 1875. Web. 12 March 2013.

Spivak, Gayatri Chakravorty. *In Other Worlds: Essays in Cultural Politics*. London: Routledge, 1993.

TAS, Mehmet Recep. "Alienation, Naipaul and Mr. Biswas." *International Journal of Humanities and Social Science*. 1.11 (2011): 115-19. Web. 14 March 2013.

Warner, Lewis M. "Cultural Confrontation, Disintegration and Syncretism in *A House for Mr Biswas*." *Critical Perspective on V.S. Naipaul*. Ed. R. Hammer. Washington DC: Three Continued Press, 1977. 94-103.

16

The Theme of Marriage in V.S. Naipaul's *A House for Mr Biswas*

Mujeeb Ali Murshed Qasim

V.S. Naipaul's writings are heavily loaded with Western impacts, the colonial and postcolonial elements. He writes unsentimentally and cruelly about the Third World countries. It is also noticed that Naipaul forms preconceived notions to misrepresent his ancestral homeland along with their sociocultural traditions. His satirical attitudes towards India, the Caribbean, and the Islamic world are understood as uncouth and uncompromising.

The theme of marriage is one of the major themes in V.S. Naipaul's *A House for Mr Biswas* (1961). Naipaul's vast knowledge about the socio-cultural life of the Hindu migrant community in the Caribbean along with his childhood memories has been greatly depicted in this novel. Naipaul has closely recorded several customs and traditions that the Hindu migrants have preserved and practiced in their day-to-day life. His masterpiece *A House for Mr Biswas* is considered as an 'epic' about his Hindu family's socio-cultural life. Marriage has a big space in this novel; but, unfortunately, the term carries traditions which are unclear for non-Indian or Caribbean readers to fully comprehend the novel. This paper aims to manifest and spell out the ambiguity of such customs and traditions. Naipaul stresses on understanding the social life of the Caribbean in order to grasp his work. He explains this fact in *The Overcrowded Barracoon* (1972):

> I live in England and depend on an English audience. Yet I write about Trinidad, and more particularly about the East Indian community there.... The social comedies I write can be fully appreciated only by someone who knows the region I write about. Without that knowledge it is easy for my books to be dismissed as farces and my characters as eccentrics. (11)

Naipaul has introduced the concepts and issues related to marriage in *A House for Mr Biswas*. This diversity of marriage related patterns include arranged marriage, love marriage, elopement marriage, dowry, living in wife's family, caste system, widowhood and divorce, wedding presents, Hindu wedding season, and child marriage, which are discussed respectively, providing several examples of Hindu customs and traditions performed on those occasions. As far as arranged marriages are concerned, Naipaul demonstrates how the groom's family plays an important role in picking up the marriage partner. Unlike the profound Indian traditions, it is the responsibility of the Hindu migrant groom's parents to make the initial move toward marriage, seeking eligible females and ensuring that their son is marketable. To put it somewhat differently, when a match is found and arrangements met, the two families meet to discuss dowry, time, and location of the wedding, male and female's birth astrology and education: "Details—the bridegrooms and dowries had been easily settled, and now the puzzling estate was forgotten and all energy went to preparing for the weddings" (*HMB* 425). Naipaul, through Mr. Biswas, criticizes the traditional way in which Hindu youths get married without being familiar with or even seeing each other before the day of their wedding. Naipaul has, absolutely, given a comic term to such marriages, i.e. "cat-in-bag marriage." Mr. Biswas shows his independence of such traditions. He tells Shama "that is all your family do for you.... Marry off the whole pack of you cat-in-bag.... As a matter of fact, I didn't get married cat-in-bag. I did see the girl first" (*HMB* 123-24).

Some people suffer from their parents' choice of the partner and the way the parents arrange such marriages. In the novel, Misir, an Arien Movement guide, said: "The present system is nothing more than cat-in-bag" (*HMB* 123). In his book *Marriage: The Family and Women in India*, V.V. Prakasa Rao and V. Nandini Rao comment: "Marriage is treated as an alliance between two families rather than a union between two individuals" (15). Arranged marriages have been in practice since the fourth century. Rao and Rao also highlight six functions of the arranged marriages in the Indian community:

> (1) Helps maintain the social satisfaction system in the society. (2) Gives parents control, over family members. (3) Enhances the chances to preserve and continue the ancestral lineage. (4) Provides an opportunity to strengthen the kinship group. (5) Allows the consolidation and extension of family property. (6) Enables the elders to preserve the principle of endogamy. (17)

However, love and understanding between the couple may not exist because they do not get used to each. The following example is an argument between two Arabian parents, who arranged marriage for their son, who had no idea about his bride. Absolutely, harmony, passion and love found no way in their life. As a result, the son divorced his pregnant wife shortly after the wedding: "I'll tell you what we've done. We've done wrong to the mother and to the child. You and I decided that our son should marry the girl despite the fact that he didn't want her and felt nothing for her. We forced her onto him with as much dignity as we force-feed stalks to cattle" (Mutahar 83).

On the other hand, Naipaul points to the fact that Hindu wedding is a very special occasion which has its own traditions. In ancient India, the most popular form of marriage was *Swayamvara*: "it can be translated as self-selection of one's husband, *Svayam* = self, *Vara* = husband. Instances of *Swayamvara* ceremony are found in our national epics, the *Ramayana* and the *Mahabharata*" (Padhy 135), where the grooms assembled at the bride's house and the bride selected her spouse. Explicitly, Hindu marriage is not a legal act, but a religious and social one. In other words, marriage procession starts with the bride's family inviting many people, including their relatives, friends, neighbors...etc. to their house to witness the wedding. When Shama's seven nieces are to be married: "Days before the ceremony guests and relatives and dancers, singers and musicians came from Arwacas. They slept in the tent, the verandah, the garage the cover space between the kitchen and house" (*HMB* 425-26). All the same, unlike Islamic or Christian cultures, Hindu marriage does not grant the two parties any official contract. In Islam, for example, marriage is a religious, legal, and social act as well. A Muslim groom will "get the girl engaged, draw up the marriage contract, and take her off after a wedding ceremony" (Mutahar 200). In Muslim arranged marriages in India, the actual marriage ceremony (*nikah*) consists of both individuals being asked if they are in agreement for marriage, settling the dowry and drawing up a marriage contract. With regard to Christianity, "marriage is a contract, an argument between the partners to assumed specified responsibilities toward each other" (Green 4).

Nonetheless, the first party is held at the groom's house. Then, the groom goes with his family, relatives, friends...etc. on parade to the bride's house. They are warmly received by the people there. The ceremony often takes place early in the morning, with the male leading the female around a fire (*agni*) seven times. Furthermore, when there are several grooms, there should be a welcoming ceremony and a separate party for each groom: "The seven bridegrooms came in seven cavalcades with seven teams of drummers, followed by stupefied villagers. At the concrete steps there were seven ceremonies of welcome... seven wedding ceremonies went on all night...there was singing, dancing and feasting" (*HMB* 426).

Naipaul criticizes the way Hindu family pays more attention to marry its son than to marry its daughters, who "Notwithstanding the chancy haste of their own marriages" (*HMB* 426). When the Tulsis want to marry Shekhar, the elder son, they put some conditions for the desirable daughter-in-law. They search for a beautiful and educated girl to match his education, provided she is from a rich family: "The search among the eligible families had failed to provide someone beautiful and educated and rich enough to satisfy Mrs. Tulsi or her daughters" (*HMB* 239).

Apart from arranged marriage, Naipaul presents love marriage, which results from affectionate love between a male and a female, who know each other before getting married. When the lover and the beloved decide to get married, there is no compulsion on the daughter's family to offer a big dowry to the groom. This is true when Mr. Biswas works with the Tulsis, he falls in love with Shama. To reveal his love, he writes a letter to Shama, which is discovered by her mother, Mrs. Tulsi. As a consequence, Mrs. Tulsi traps him into marrying Shama without appropriating a dowry for him. After marriage, Tara, Mr. Biswas's aunt, has learned about the way Mr. Biswas got married and she immediately goes to the Tulsis to settle down his dowry. She comes back and tells Mr. Biswas with a reproaching tone "They said you didn't want any dowry or big wedding and they didn't offer because it was a love match…. They showed me a love letter" (*HMB* 102).

As love marriage does not offer a big dowry as in Mr. Biswas's case, the couple might face some problems. The novelist suggests that a respected dowry would help the couple to open a new house with all its requirements. Mr. Biswas lives in a bad psychological situation because he has not been given sufficient dowry, which could have helped him open a house and live away from his in-laws. He is extremely scathing about love marriage and the way some families trap sons-in-law into marrying their daughters. Mr. Biswas tells Shama: "I'll tell you what your philosophy is. Catch him. Marry him. Throw him in a coal barrel. That is the philosophy of your family" (*HMB* 546).

Naipaul introduces a third kind of marriage, in which the bride and groom, due to money deficiency or other problems, may certify between themselves that they would marry each other without the consent of their parents. Naipaul shows how a Hindu family is strict about issues, concerning its honour and dignity. If a daughter elopes with her boy-friend, showing ingratitude and disgrace to her family, she is considered to be dead for that family. For instance, when Mr. Biswas's sister, Dehuti elopes with the yard boy, "Tara had vowed never to mention her name again" (*HMB* 57). Rather, "Dehuti had been ostracized since her marriage" (*HMB* 546). Therefore, such disrespectful marriage is not accepted by the Hindu community and it becomes a social stigma attached to the girl's family. This is clear in the dialogue between Mr. Biswas and Seth: "So", Seth went on. "You want to see girl children educated and choosing their own husband, eh? The same thing that your sister does...picking up boy-friends?" (*HMB* 126). Similarly, this kind of wedding is known as "orfi marriage" in some Arabian countries like Egypt, for example. However, such marriage is not accepted in the Muslim society and is regarded as a scandal. In Islam, this kind of marriage is prohibited. According to Prophet Muhammad's (PBUH) saying: "If a woman marries without the consent of her guardian, her marriage is null and void, is null and void, is null and void; then, if her marriage hath been consummated, the woman shall take her dower; if her guardians dispute about her marriage, then the king is her guardian" (Hughes 314).

Naipaul also depicts the Hindu fundamental responsibilities of paying a heavy dowry to the groom in order to get its daughter married happily. Unlike Islamic Arabian culture, in Hinduism dowry has to be given by the bride's family to the groom at the time of her marriage. In fact, the groom's dowry expectations are according to his in-laws' status, i.e. if the family is rich and has much landed property, the groom expects to obtain a respected dowry. Traditionally, dowry consists of goods and cash payments, or more than that. When Mr. Biswas is to marry Shama, he "assumed that they had decided to give more than a dowry that they would help with a job or a house, or both" (*HMB* 97).

In Hinduism, dowry is regarded as a woman's wealth and property that she gets in advance from her family. In other words, the woman has no claim on her parents' inheritance. When Shama gives birth to her fourth child, a third daughter too, Anand's aunts congratulate him: "You are lucky. You are still the only boy. But wait. One day you will get a brother, and he will cut off your nose" (*HMB* 315). On the contrary, in Islamic culture, the bridegroom has to offer a dowry to his bride. Further, Islam also grants the right to a woman to inherit not only from her parents but also from other members of the family (in some specific cases). According to the Holy *Qura'n*: "Allah commands you as regards your children's (inheritance); to the male, a portion equal to that of two females; if (there are) only daughters, two or more, their share is two thirds of the inheritance; if only one, her share is half" (*Qura'n* 4.11).

Naipaul has sarcastically indicated the status of a woman in the Hindu culture, where she is considered as the goddess Lakshmi (the goddess of wealth). But, unfortunately, for a poor family, the unmarried daughter is regarded as a burden, particularly when the family is not able to offer her dowry. For example, after the death of Biswas's father, Raghu, his mother, Bipti does not care much about the future of her three sons, but she pays more attention to and takes care of the future of her daughter, Dehuti. Being unable to offer her daughter's dowry, Bipti decides to give her daughter to her rich sister, Tara, to help her in the housework and for the purpose that "in four or five years Dehuti would have to be married and it was better that she would be given to Tara. She would learn manners, acquire graces and, with a dowry from Tara, might even make a good match" (*HMB* 32).

We can observe that Naipaul has displayed one of the social problems in the form of dowry. He states that because of poverty and disappointing economic conditions, some poor families cannot offer dowries to marry their daughters. Therefore, they intend to kill their female infants as soon as they are born. However, this tradition is not present in the Hindu migrant family. Mr. Biswas remembers this fact that "Mrs. Tulsi had said in the hall of Hanuman House when Savi was born, they would survive: they wouldn't be killed" (*HMB* 563). Nowadays, with the help of ultrasonic waves they can abort the embryo: "This age also perpetuated customs like Sati and looking upon the birth of a female baby as an ill omen, even killing newly born baby girls by drowning them in a tub of milk. Amidst the feeling of insecurity, the presence of young unmarried girls was a potential invitation for disaster" (Birodkar). This same case of killing baby girls was committed in the pre-Islamic period. However, people used to kill female babies not because of dowry but being afraid that ladies may be taken as captives after war and face dishonor at the hands of the victorious enemy, being jealous that they are married to other men, or because of poverty that they cannot feed or dress them. Nowadays, collecting dowry is a social problem some poor Arabian families, who find it difficult to marry their sons: "Thanks be to God, we managed to collect money for the bride price and the wedding with a lot of effort and through sweating blood, and we're still in debt to other people" (Mutahar 80).

The main theme of the novel, in several ways, is based on the custom of *ghar jamaei* (the case of a man marrying a girl and living with her family) and Mr. Biswas's struggle of getting a house of his own. That is to say, since his childhood, Mr. Biswas has been going from one house of strangers to another due to poverty. Even after marriage, he faces a lot of problems because he marries Shama hastily and he is compelled to stay with his in-laws due to his hopeless living status: "He had not had time to think about the problems marriage would bring...where would he live? He had no money and no job" (*HMB* 97). We see him struggling for a long time to live in a separate house of his own. In the final reckoning, when he becomes very old and has four children, he is able to buy a house.

Traditionally, after marriage, the groom brings his bride home, where she would live in what is called a joint family. And "Traditionally, the husband/father would be responsible for being the breadwinner, financial planner, and household mechanic. The wife/mother would be the homemaker and the childcare provider" (Georgas 488). If, otherwise, the groom lives in the bride's house, this is socially considered very bad, especially when the family is not rich. Seth attacks and humiliates Mr. Biswas's being a *ghar jamaei*: "This is a helluva man. When a man is married he shouldn't expect other people to feed him. In fact, he should be feeding his wife" (*HMB* 110). This is the psychological conflict and flaw in the character of Mr. Biswas. He struggles all over his life to free himself from his in-laws and to build his own house. But, with the temptations of food and cloth, provided by Mrs. Tulsi, we can see his conscience shrivelling for a while. Although he dislikes living with his in-laws, he finds: "He was more fortunate than most people.

His children would never starve; they would be sheltered and clothed. It didn't matter...if he were alive or dead" (*HMB* 317).

Although it is not socially accepted, the groom, in some other cases, would be respected and treated as a member of the bride's family, when he gets married to a rich family daughter and lives with his in-laws. Besides, he might work with them and maintain their property. An example in the novel is that when Shekhar marries Dorothy: "Contrary to Hindu custom and traditions of his family, [Shekhar] did not bring his bride home, but left Hanuman House for good...to look after the lorries, cinema, land and filling station of his wife's family" (*HMB* 240). In the case of Mr. Biswas, the reader of the novel feels pity for Mr. Biswas, who does not feel comfortable, being in his in-laws' house. We notice that Mr. Biswas has a lot of troubles and quarrels with his wife and almost all members in that house. Naipaul is of the opinion that a newly married couple should live in a separate house, as a nuclear family to be comfortable. This is clear when Mr. Biswas, after trials and tribulations, manages to live in the house at Sikkim Street, where his life changes totally and his relationship with Shama undergoes a positive transformation:

> He didn't now care to do anything against his wife's wish. He had grown to accept her judgment and to accept her optimism. He trusted her. Since they had moved to the house Shama had learned a new loyalty to him and to their children; away from her mother and sisters, she was able to express this without shame, and to Mr. Biswas this was a triumph almost as big as the acquiring of his own house. (*HMB* 2)

At the same time, Mr. Biswas's children are fascinated by the new house. They think they have never lived anywhere but in this house and "From now their lives would be ordered, their memories coherent..." (*HMB* 614). Shama is also excited and she welcomes living in the new house. She wishes they could have lived there a long time ago and "She did not want this to happen after a quarrel and a humiliation" (*HMB* 600). The same is true in the Arabian culture, which considers it shameful when a boy marries a girl and lives with her family. And the joint family system let the groom marry the bride and bring her to his parents' house. However, nowadays such marriage scarcely exists. Moreover, the bride's family insists on the groom to have a separate house. They think the bride may face troubles in the house of her in-laws as the case of Mr. Biswas: "But I told you that you should have insisted she had a separate house before marrying her off, while we were in a position to make a decision" (Mutahar 50).

Naipaul exposes the fact that caste plays an important role in the Hindu marriage traditions. Hindu society, to start with, has traditionally been divided into four groups called castes, based on heredity, which determine a person's occupation and status. First, the *Brahmins* are those, who keep engaged in sacrifices and priestly functions. Second, the *Kshtriyas* are the rulers and warriors. Third, the *Vaishyas* are the merchants, farmers and tradesmen. Finally, the *Shudras* are laborers, craftsmen, and service professions. Among those layers, however, there are sub-castes and subcategories. The essential function of the caste is that a girl from a high caste cannot marry a boy from a low caste. For instance, Mr. Biswas's family gets angry because his sister, Dehuti, runs away with and gets married to the yard boy. They are upset not only for this reason, but also "for the yard boy is the lowest of the low" (*HMB* 57). Another example is of the Tulsi's daughters whose marriages are, "based solely on caste" (*HMB* 239). So the bride's family has to check the groom's caste before letting him marry their daughter. Mrs. Tulsi has married Shama to Mr. Biswas "simply because he was of the proper caste, just as they had married the daughter called C to an illiterate coconut-seller" (*HMB* 99).

On the other hand, a boy from a high caste may marry a girl from a low caste. When the Tulsis want to marry their son, Shekhar, they search among many families, regardless what caste or religion the bride belongs to: "The oil families, whatever their original condition, were too grand. So they searched among the families in soft drinks, the families in ice ...And at last, in a laxly Presbyterian family...they could find a girl" (*HMB* 240). Naipaul criticizes the orthodox-Hindu-Tulsi family, who married their son to a Christian girl. Such a marriage is not traditionally accepted. Rather, the groom is considered an outcaste. So some migrant families are not stuck to their inherited culture.

The novelist presents widowhood in an arresting way that makes the reader deeply grieve at widows' conditions. Hindu traditions allow a woman to marry only once during her life time; even if her husband dies at an early age, she would remain a widow forever. Strangely enough this logic was never applied to widowers. After the death of Mr. Biswas's father, his mother:

> Bipti was bathed. Her hair still wet.... Then the henna was scooped out and the parting filled with charcoal dust. She was now a widow forever. Tara gave a short scream and at her signal the other women began to wail. On Bipti's wet black hair there were still spots of henna, like drops of blood. (*HMB* 29)

The use of the words "charcoal dust, scream, wail and blood" suggests how critical Naipaul is. Furthermore, his resentment of this tradition is reflected in the way he describes the widow's life in the novel. Naipaul distinguishes between two kinds of families, regarding widow's life: nuclear family and joint family. In the former, the widow suffers more. For instance, Bipti, a nuclear family widow, has no source of support after the death of her husband. Above all, she is prohibited from remarrying. Consequently, the family splits off; her two elder sons work away on sugarcane fields; Dehuti is sent to serve her aunt Tara; and her youngest son, Mr. Biswas remains homeless most of his childhood. And Bipti lives alone suffering from loneliness. In the latter, Naipaul expresses the importance of the joint family system as a solution to the problem of widowhood in Hindu society. Unlike nuclear family, joint family takes care of all its members under any circumstances. We can observe Tulsi family as the best example of a joint Hindu family. When any of their daughters becomes a widow, for instance, she immediately goes to live with her parents, where she is being cared of and respected by all. Even when Mrs. Tulsi, the great grandmother, gets sick, everybody in the family takes care of her. This is the explicit structure of a family in Trinidad, India as well as most countries in the East.

Throughout the novel, the word divorce is not used but mentioned once by one of Tulsi's daughters, Suniti, who expresses her fears of hearing such a word. As far as divorce is concerned, and according to Hindu traditions, it is strictly considered to be shameful for a woman to be divorced. So the Hindu family does its best to keep its daughter married: "After quarrel and reconciliations with her husband, and [Suniti] attempted to shock by talk of getting a divorce" (*HMB* 542). Likewise, no Yemeni family likes its daughter to be divorced.

Naipaul shows the importance of some social customs, which strengthen the relationships as well as mutual social links among people. Wedding present is not only an Indian custom but also international; it is practiced by many communities all over the world. Traditionally, and still modern, relatives, friends... etc. usually give presents to a newly married couple. The gifts could be either cash or in kind. When Mr. Biswas gets married, his aunt, Tara "undid the knot at the end of her veil and took out a twenty-dollar note" (*HMB* 101) and gives it to him. The present could be given after the wedding, too. Shama is given a Japanese coffee-set "by Seth as a belated wedding present" (*HMB* 147).

Socially, people who have once given presents to a spouse, expect similar or different presents to be returned on such occasions or on their children's marriages. This is clear in the argument between Shama and Mr. Biswas, who is angry at her as she borrows a lot of money to buy wedding presents, usually water-sets. Shama logically argues: "I know what I am doing. My children are going to be married one day too" (*HMB* 240). However, Mr. Biswas critically replies: "And when they give back all the water-sets poor Savi wouldn't be able to walk, for the glasses and jugs. If they remember, that is" (*HMB* 166).

Hindu marriage season is present in the novel as part of the wedding traditions. To a great extent, Hindu migrant society in the Caribbean preserves and follows the possible days on which they could marry. The best months for marriage, in accordance with the Hindu calendar, are November, December, January, February, April, May and June. Further, marriage is held on specific days of those months, especially when there is a *lagna*, i.e. the most suspicious and appropriate days for marriages: "Shama got invitations in her own right and during the Hindu wedding season she borrowed deeply from the rent money..." (*HMB* 366).

Child's marriage has been common among Hindus. According to their beliefs, if a nine-year-old girl, for example, gets married, she will come to her in-laws with an instinctive behaviour. Therefore, at this age, the girl could adopt her mother-in-law as her own mother. The most important thing to note is that the girl, who comes from a different background or village, could culturally and socially be easily moulded and trained into the traditions and customs of her in-law's family. Upon her arrival, her husband's mother is put in charge of her, where she is to learn the inner workings of the house. During this time she is not allowed to interact with the males of the house, because she is considered pure until the marriage is consummated. By way of comparison, when a grown-up girl gets married, it will be difficult for her to adopt and adopt herself to her in-laws' customs and traditions. Further, she might not be able to adopt her mother-in-law and vice versa. Although child's marriage seems to have its own advantages, it is fought by intellectuals and movements: "Misir [an Arient Movement guide] was keen on the discussion and resolutions, and under his guidance they passed resolution that education was important, that child marriage should be abolished, that young people should choose their own spouses" (*HMB* 123).

To conclude, the socio-cultural customs and traditions concerning marriage do greatly emerge in *A House for Mr Biswas*, in which Naipaul has presented them in a very clear picture. Although Hindu migrants were removed from their native land and culture for many generations, they still perform and practice their inherited religious rituals with almost no changes. Similarities between such Hindu traditions and customs in India and the Caribbean exceed the differences in spite of the fact that Hindus in the Caribbean have completely cut their roots from their forefather's land, India. On the other hand, they have not transformed all traditions and customs with them to the Caribbean. For example, the unfavorable tradition of female infant killing, which is still common in some parts of India, is not practiced by the Hindu migrants in the Caribbean. Further, we have seen that Hindu and Islamic cultures share some similarities regarding marriage traditions and principles. This is due to the fact that these two cultures are contagious and are not affected by the Western cultures.

Works Cited

Birodkar, Sudheer. "Child Marriage (*Baal Vivaaha*)." Web. 10 May 2012.

Georgas, James et al. Eds. *Families Across Cultures: A 30-Nation Psychological Study*. London: Cambridge University Press, 2006.

——. *Marriage and Family: A Basic Self-Introductional Guide*. USA: McGraw Hill Book Company, 1977.

Hughes, Thomas Patrick. *A Dictionary of Islam*. New Delhi: Asian Education Services, 2001.

Mutahar, Abd al-Rahaman. *Social Issues in Popular Yemeni Culture*. Trans., Ed. and Annotated. Janet C.E. Watson. Yemen: Sana'a, 2002.

Naipaul, V.S. *A House for Mr Biswas*. London: Picador, 2002.

——. *The Overcrowded Barracoon*. New York: Andre Deutsch, 1972.

Padhy, Prafullah. *Social Legislation and Crime*. New Delhi: Isha Books, 2006.

Rao, V.V. Prakasa and V. Nandini Rao. *Marriage: The Family and Women in India*. Printox: South Asia Books, 1982.

The Noble Qura'n, "Surah 4, An-Nisa." Part 4, Ayat 11.

17

Fossilized Folks: Women in Naipaul's *A House for Mr Biswas*, *The Mystic Masseur* and *Half a Life*

Shalini

> ...A little boy who dashes up a tree, while his sister hovers uncertainly on the ground; an older man plunges in to a life of adventure and travel while his wife or mother anxiously waits at home hoping and praying for his safety. (Geetha 127)

In any Indian community, the roles of male and female are decided even before the child is born. The society about which V.S. Naipaul chooses to write is no exception to these norms. Naipaul writes about the Indian community in the Caribbean and Africa which live through the rotten old customs and rituals. Female oppression, orthodoxies regarding women's status in the society and family, lack of education and hindrances in their progress are inseparable parts of these customs rigidly followed by them. A modest attempt to explore and analyze the myth of masculinity in Naipaul's *A House for Mr Biswas* (1969), *The Mystic Masseur* (2001) and *Half a Life* (2001) has been made in the present paper.

These texts are largely set in the Indian communities of Trinidad and India. A huge segment of population in these communities believes in age old customs of treating men and women differently. The characters in these novels are highly prejudiced and archetypes of Indian masses. There is a range of female characters—widely categorized in major slots of dominating and the dominated types. Both the categories exist in the same culture, with slight difference in their overall condition. They dominate and hold power to dictate terms in their families yet they bear scorn and sometimes are severely beaten by their men. They, despite coming from affluent backgrounds are given only primary education and are later confined to their homes.

The world of a woman ends with her family which reduces her merely to a component in the household machinery. Her world shatters if her family suffers. The women in Naipaul are ignorant. Most of the time, they stay at home minding their family responsibilities. Men on the contrary, move outside according to the expectations of the society. Simone de Beauvoir's observation in *The Second Sex* seems quite appropriate to illustrate their place in society:

> ...she is the one who waits, submits, complains, weeps, makes scenes: an ungrateful role that in daily life leads to no apotheosis; as a victim she is looked down on; as a shrew detested; her fate seems the prototype of rapid "recurrence": life only repeats in her, without going anywhere; family set in her role as a housekeeper, she puts a stop to the expansion of existence, she becomes obstacle and negation.... (322)

Women, generally shut themselves in the confines of domestic affairs and remain ignorant, thus they put an end to all the possibilities which could bring them to the light of the new world. They become handicapped as they depend on their husbands for their personal needs and rely on them more than themselves.

People like Pt. Ganesh, Mohun Biswas and Willie Chandran, who have stepped out of their finite worlds of orthodoxies, desperately feel the need to change the thinking of the women of their families and want their partner to be their equal. The irony lies in the fact that they would never make an effort instead they expect the change by itself. These men want educated wives who would understand them well and would also accompany them in the course of life. Though they understand the need, they cannot deny their tradition of patriarchy, which in many ways satisfies their ego and covers most of their shortcomings. They laugh at their women's families and ridicule them intentionally which is consequential to their male chauvinism. They derive a sadistic pleasure by tormenting their wives physically and mentally. It allows them to feel happy and content despite being inferior in some respects.

A House for Mr Biswas discusses at length, the ups and downs of Mr. Biswas's life in a typical migrated Hindu community. Mohun Biswas is an exiled Indian "modeled after Naipaul's father" (Ray 19). For Mr. Biswas life and "success means the wonder and audacity of having a house and portion of earth all his own" (*A House* back cover). *A House for Mr Biswas* is basically a diasporic text where an exiled protagonist tries to establish his identity in an alien world. For him search for a house is the ultimate aim of life.

In this saga of a "man's world", women are thrown to the periphery. Women do not stand as the prominent figures, yet they minimally affect the general course of the story. People in such a society believe nature grants superiority to men over women who try to crush them under the patriarchal system. They relegate women to the status of mere "entity" that can be owned or disowned. They are treated as the pieces of property, therefore have become an object of possession.

Bipti, Mr. Biswas's mother, serves a perfect example of stereotypical Indian woman. She depends on her husband when she lives with him and on her mother's family when deserted by her husband. A comparison could be drawn between Bipti, as a feeble character, and her sister Tara, an assertive housewife. But the society does not appreciate Tara for her authoritative nature. Bipti willingly gives her children's responsibility to Tara, and sets herself free from the burden of caring. It is evident because Bipti, "who had not been consulted" for anything after her husband's death, feels "very grateful to Tara" and Mr. Biswas gets "thrilled at the thought of earning money" by being nurtured by his affluent aunt (*A House* 59).

In medieval India "sati system" was followed with a pure religious dedication. The society had no guilt in burning the widowed wife on her husband's pyre. Bipti, is born in modern times is not burned but she has to suffer the painful phase of widowhood. She leads the life of alienation and seclusion devoid of all the pleasures after the death of her considerably incompetent husband. Now she was to be avoided in all pious ceremonies of her family and could not perform any ritual as she is seen as the inauspicious sight in her very house.

Bipti is a weak widow and the mother of four—three sons and a daughter. She has to suppress the mother inside her before others due to her dependence on her sister. She could not express the grief of losing her daughter Dehuti post her elopement with Tara's low caste yard boy Ramchand. Instead of grieving she sheds tears in empathy with Tara who is stripped of her honour by her act. Dehuti's "shameless" act is well contrasted with Mr. Biswas's quest for identity as a sign of self pride. This highlights the difference between the expectations from a boy and a girl child. Simon De Beauvoir in *The Second Sex* writes about the liberty granted to both sexes:

> The mother, as we shall see, is secretly hostile to her daughter's liberation...but the boy's effort to become a man is respected, and he is granted much liberty. The girl is required to stay at home; her comings and goings are watched.... If they roam the streets, they are stared at and accosted. (351-52)

A certain sort of feminism and environmentalism has been utilized in categorical thinking to the advancement of women, throughout history. This mode of thinking has worked to keep women away from male preserves: higher education, intellectual life and art and power. It has effectively confined women to the cramped spaces of the home, to low-paying jobs, denying their mobility, curtailing their desire to go about the world, meet new people and experience life in its magnanimity. Shama in *A House for Mr Biswas*, Leela in *The Mystic Masseur,* and Sarojini in *Half a Life* are a few such examples.

Sarojini in *Half a Life*, in comparison to Willie is better in adjusting and equally intelligent. Her father sends Willie abroad for further studies and thinks of an "international marriage" for her. Men have derived a great deal of advantage from "the simple and irrefutable logic of categorization" (Geetha 46). A similar distinction is visible between Mr. Biswas and his sister Dehuti. Mr. Biswas gets an opportunity to go to the school and later on for a training to become a proper "pundit". Whereas, his sister is given to his aunt Tara to learn some "grace" which would help her in getting a match.

"Shyness" and wearing heavy jewelry is a sign of their feminine nature. Dehuti was liked by Tara because she "smiled shyly, not looking up" (*A House* 35). In Indian society, identity of a girl is always associated with the identity of her husband. His role in her life is that of a "provider". Caste is a matter which is applied to men only; women ethically belong to their provider's caste regardless of their inborn strata. They, as V. Geetha writes, are "feminized in a derogatory sense". The state of women is as demeaning as a "*shudra*", she argues: "In Hinduism both untouchables and women are polluting—a menstruating woman is literally an untouchable for the days that her period lasts. Gender and class differences are likewise mutually linked…" (50).

The above statement fits Dehuti's stature suitably. Dehuti by her impassioned elopement degrades herself completely and consequently excommunicated by her high-caste family. Naipaul presents the attitude of her family post-elopement through Mr. Biswas who visits her place by chance. He feels "to Dehuti marriage had brought no joy" (*A House* 71). She was uneasy at being caught among her household possessions which was embarrassing for both of them. Dehuti's mental struggle is overpowered by Mr. Biswas's repulsion. Her poor status and low caste become a reason of shame for Mr. Biswas because he is linked with the affluent and high caste Tulsis, the reputed household of Port of Spain.

The novelist too seems to be prejudiced as he doesn't bother to give an insight in her mental struggle; instead, the repulsion of her brother is highlighted. Dehuti's words and mind do not hold any value for him. It is not so with this demeaned girl only but the rest of the female characters in the text suffer from this servitude and attitude of inferiority. They are conditioned. Shama is taught servitude although she belonged to a "rich" family and lived in the big house famous as "Hanuman House".

Mr. Biswas is married to the youngest daughter of Hanuman House, Shama and started behaving like an adult. Their marriage was like "make-believe" as a "child's game". He had "little idea of the problems" that marriage in a patriarchal system would bring to a jobless man. Mr. Biswas was already haunted by his nostalgic quest for a home. The questions that startled his mind now were: "where would he live...what would happen to his mother?" (*A House* 95). His condition was pathetic because "he had no money and no job, for sign-writing, while good enough for a boy living with his mother, was hardly a secure profession for a married man" (*A House* 95).

Naipaul presents Shama as a properly trained woman by the patriarchy. She displays her discomfiture for Mr. Biswas's status as a dependent of Tulsis. She considers herself inferior to her brothers and other sisters due to her husband's incompetence to provide them bread and butter. Shama by her looks enamored Biswas in the first glance but her childish behaviour was enough to make his "disenchantment complete" (85). Leela in *Mystic Masseur* appeals Pt. Ganesh initially when he saw her peeping from behind the curtain. Willie's mother in *Half a Life* was a medium of sacrifice for Chandran; an excuse to live according to Gandhi's ideology. They commonly lack sense of aesthetics. They are either "frankly ugly" or tolerably common. They are never attributed exceptional traits so that they could attract men permanently towards them. It is a man's world where women have a very little say and importance. Mr. Biswas is powerful only for Shama otherwise he is a failure. He is beaten by everyone in the Hanuman house due to his ill behaviour and bad temper. His shame and defeat is exerted in the form of his frustration and angst on Shama. His masochistic obsession over her is a camouflage for his inferiority and failure.

Wives in Naipaul take their husband's habit of beating as a matter of "pride". Sushila, Shama's widowed sister "regarded them as a necessary part of her training and often attributed the decay of Hindu society in Trinidad to the rise of timorous, weak, non-beating class of husbands" (*A House* 148). Sushila and Leela in *The Mystic Masseur* are a case in point. The society has assigned roles for them befitting their gender. In India, a woman as a wife is expected to be "patient, understanding, emotionally expressive and compassionate" (Geetha 35). The women conceive their passive roles as the sign of dignity. Women in Indian society hardly take initiative in sexual matters and often condemn women of "other race" for their "sexual appetite". Padma condemns Dorothy for her allegedly "insatiable" desires.

The women in Mr. Biswas's life are his mother, aunt, wife and his daughters, Savi, Myna and Kamla. Savi was perfect like any Indian girl as she was "dispirited and submissive" and "afraid" of her father (222). The only thing which "gave him comfort" was that "he had claimed Savi" (*A House* 227). Savi as a daughter is a source of comfort because she satisfies her father's male ego by listening quietly to him. She does not argue with him like Shama.

Children are given toys according to their gender. It prepares them for their roles in the society in future. Mr. Biswas gifts a "doll house" to Savi, but a toy car to his son Anand. In Savi, thus, her girlhood is invoked by her parents and the people around her. The daughters despite their sharp intellect are left with nothing in their lives. Their father never thought of sending them abroad for further studies. They follow the "natural" way of life like their mother and aunts. Most of these girls have never been to college. Their knowledge is limited to writing and reading letters in a funny way, be that Shama or Leela or Sarojini in *Half a Life*. There is a wide difference in the level of education of Willie and Sarojini, Leela and Ganesh, and Mr. Biswas and Shama.

Comparing the women of *A House for Mr Biswas* and of *Half a Life*, there lurks a marked difference between the two. Willie's mother and his wife Ana are graduates and understand their men to a certain limit, yet they are considered as obstacles. Willie's mother always falls short of his father's expectations. Willie's father borrows the idea of marrying a low caste girl without understanding the motive. Therefore, he regrets after "marrying" an ugly and insensitive girl. He repents his choice because he could neither accept her against the will of his Brahmin parents nor he could disown her due to her firebrand uncle's fear. He makes his life hell by living with a low born girl without comprehending the real purpose of Gandhi's idea of "life of sacrifice". They are a complete mismatch in all respects. She was hardly impressive, as he observes, "Her thin black feet in her cheap slippers" (H) and thinks that "this was the girl I thought I should go and make declaration to and in her company live out a life of sacrifice" (*Half a Life* 12).

Chandran without taking her emotions into consideration proposed to her timorously. Chandran felt "repelled, ashamed, moved" and instead of love "there came a little sympathy" (12) in his heart for her. The idea of sacrifice is imposed on her by Chandran. She is often accused and abused by Chandran for her low caste etiquettes, because for him she is "uneducated inherently". She is shown as a rough and insensitive woman as the mark of her low caste. Chandran's incompetency to contemplate relegates their married life to a tragedy.

Naipaul narrates the story from Chandran's point of view; therefore, she becomes an object of subordination. Chandran's making all the important decisions of his family without her consent leads to family feuds. She serves Chandran throughout her life willingly, yet she is not given a proper place in his life. She loves her son Willie beyond the fact that he was entirely different from her and never felt associated with her. Willie is the only hope to his mother, yet he deserts her like his father. He always had negative thoughts for his mother even during his college time in England. He associates her with everything ugly; his friend Percy's bad taste of colours reminds him of his mother's colour choice (*Half a Life* 64).

All these men desert their wives at a certain point of time-some literally and some stop talking to them. Willie used and deserted Ana just because he was "fed up living her life". He gave words to his desire of living alone while taking the best of her life as he narrates to his sister that, "when she came back later I said to her, "I am forty one. I am tired of living your life" (*Half a Life* 227). Willie shows his selfishness by ignoring Ana's point of view. His acknowledgement of her services and love at the time of departure is delivered in the form of a favour:

> I know, you did everything for me. You made it easy for me here. I couldn't have lived here without you. When I asked you in London I was frightened. I had nowhere to go. They were going to throw me out of the college at the end of the term and I didn't know what I could do keep afloat. (*Half a Life* 227)

Willie was an out and out failure. With the help of Ana he could achieve the confidence to live on his own. In case of Ana, the relationship is different, as Willie is financially and prestigiously dependent on her. In spite of her dominating status she never overpowered him. Ana suffered Willie's selfishness post-marriage. Ana, in spite of belonging to non-Indian community, has to accept Willie's treachery and deception. She witnessed Willie and Graca's increasing incestuous relations, without a sign of agitation on her face. She bore all the insult to save her marital life. Despite the despotic nature of their husbands, they do not revolt against them as they continue to live with them.

Willie's sister Sarojini is seen in the image of his mother as he calls her the "little ugly Sarojini". Sarojini epitomizes Chandran's failure and poses a threat to his reputation. Sarojini is not sent abroad for higher education like her brother. For her father Sarojini is a constant cause of worry. The only better prospects he could devise for her is an "international marriage". He finds a lame German war photographer, an already married man with two children, for her. Due to her marriage, she manages to visit England once and her brother too in his hostel. Willie feels ashamed of her presence in his hostel room in England. He disliked her Indian way of cooking and dressing. He avoids introducing her to his college friends. It is important to note that girls are seen as a burden and are dispensed with no sense of regret. This German photographer deserts Sarojini in Germany and has no feelings for her.

After leaving Ana, Willie seeks support from his sister. She is comfortable even in adverse situation. She had no complications, no fabricated lies, and no unreal conceptions to lead in her problems like her brother Willie. She adjusts naturally and never feels awkward for her 'Indianness'. Willie scorns at his poor adjustability in awkward situations when he sees Sarojini living a comfortable life. Willie also guesses about her being in love with many other men besides her German husband. Willie, as Naipaul presents him would have probably been lost in nothingness if the women in his life, like Ana, June, and Sarojini would not have supported him. He narrates the role of Ana in his life to Sarojini: "I drew comfort from Ana, her strength and authority. And just as now, as you may have noticed, Sarojini, I lean on you…I leaned on Ana. I believed in a special way in her luck, some of this had to do with the very fact that she was a woman who had given herself to me" (*Half a Life* 141).

Willie had always been "protected" and "guided" by one or the other woman "in some essential way". Naipaul here draws a difference between two women from different communities. Both of them have different ideas—Sarojini follows her "firebrand" maternal uncle's "radical genes" and is furious in nature; whereas Ana is different in her thinking due to her racial and social difference. Ana was "important" for him because he depended on her "for his idea of being a man" in his beginning years but Sarojini becomes the need for his survival in his later life (*Half a Life* 142).

Leela in *The Mystic Masseur* has to face her fate of being a childless woman due to which her husband loses interest in her. As Naipaul writes, "there was another disappointment in his life. After a year it was clear that Leela could not have children. He lost interest in her as a wife and stopped beating her" (*The Mystic* 63).

Chandran is worried for his daughter's marriage to the extent that he closes his eyes to the general good of her. Thus he does not hesitate to wed her to an undeserving man without seeking her consent. As Naipaul shows in the above incident girls can not have their choice in the most private decisions like their own wedding. This instance is not only painful but also highly condemnable that a father may overlook his daughter's emotions and defy the bond of affection. They lack efficiency to stand on their own; therefore, they can not rebel. The men in the family limit their needs to clothing and food. They forget their emotional aspect very comfortably.

She is a "doll" to be decorated and showcased; a plaything and an object of possession. She has to dress up the way men like them to dress. Simon de Beauvoir gives way to her angst on this issue in *The Second Sex*:

> ...paralyzed by inconvenient clothing and by the same rules of propriety—then woman's body seems to men to be his property, his thing. Make-up and jewelry also further this petrifaction of face and body. The function of ornamental attire is very complex; with certain primitives it has a religious significance; but more often its purpose is to accomplish the metamorphosis of woman into idol. (167)

Naipaul's "classic comedy" *The Mystic Masseur* sarcastically narrates the struggle of a failed pundit in Trinidad. Like Mr. Biswas and Willie, he tries his hand upon various jobs—first of a school teacher, writer, masseur, and finally of a politician which lasts till the end. His hobby of writing survives the ups and downs of life. Pt. Ganesh lives mainly in the Hindu community and is influenced by the Indian ethics and theology. He marries an Indian "good girl" who shyly peered "through the grimy lace curtain" (22). She is looked as burden or the "debts of previous life" which her father wants to shed. Ramlogan's attempt to trap Ganesh for his under educated girl, with the temptation of dowry serves a fine example to this: "Ramlogan had a sixteen year old daughter he wanted to married, and wanted to married to Ganesh. It was an open secret in the village. Ganesh was always getting little gifts from Ramlogan—a special avocado pear, whenever he passed the shop Ramlogan was sure to call him in..." (*The Mystic* 22).

In spite of knowing all he agrees to marry her because he has nothing to do with her academics. He needs her for the domestic requirements.

Traditionally, these men have ethical ways to escape matrimony. They can choose celibacy and live a life of honour and respect; but for girls there is no redemption from the institution of marriage. Ganesh is taught by his aunt "the great belcher" that it is necessary to "whip" the wife all the time to keep her under control. Naipaul highlights that it is the elderly women who keep the patriarchy alive. He writes about domestic culture seasoned with patriarchy practiced by females:

> Whether arising out of a love marriage or an arranged marriage, it was the eternal conflict of Hindu family life, a ritualized aspect of the fate of women, like marriage itself or childbirth or widowhood. To be tormented by a mother-in-law was part of young woman's testing, part, almost, of growing up. Somehow the young woman survived; and then one day she became mother-in-law herself, and her own daughter-in-law to torment, to round off a life, to balance pain and joy. (*Mutinies* 49)

Leela herself feels proud that she is mature enough to have a husband who beats her every now and then. Leela always runs behind Pt. Ganesh and keeps on shifting the residence as per his convenience. She cooks food for Ganesh, washes his clothes and waits after him and also bears his frustration. These male protagonists have a very masculine way of showing their affection to their wives—they beat them to express their interests. It is sardonic to note that society very efficiently understands that husband loses interest in his wife if he stops beating her.

It is after nine years of her marriage when she gets a chance to have her will. She opts for the social work and contributes in the paper *The Dharma* published by her husband. A century before, J.S. Mill had closely observed condition of women and wrote in his *On the Subjection of Women*, that they love their oppressors and work tirelessly for them without gain. Years have passed but men are still rigid and do not to accept any other role for their wives other than of servants. The condition of women has minimally changed down the ages. In 19th century, J.S. Mill spoke for the pathetic condition of women regardless of the national and political boundaries. Mill's effort to bring equality of gender has been futile for these societies in Naipaul as the condition has changed minimally for them. The same standards are maintained even today years after the movement was initiated by Mill. Women are still uneducated, mentally subordinated and psychologically unstable. These women especially are fit only for the roles of wives, and sisters, daughters and selfless dedicated mothers. V. Geetha observes in *Gender*: "Women practice a great deal of denial: whether it is food, leisure time, questions of health or sexual desire. Women learn to put them by and attend to tasks that await them as wives, sisters, daughters and mothers" (48).

Shama before doing anything has to seek her husband's permission. Ana in *Half a Life* is deprived of her status of a wife due to Willie's sexual adventures. These men go by their patriarchal ethics which argue that, "(...) woman's innate nature is bad...their passions are insatiable, for they act according to their inborn nature. Thus, the very nature of woman demands that they be controlled and disciplined by men" (Geetha 13).

When men come under stress they exert it on their subordinate women because in their view women are responsible for the stress. The unconditional love and devotion is rewarded by promising them food and security for life time. In Naipaul's texts love is not rewarded with love, instead it is used to arouse anger. Willie sleeps with several women including prostitutes. Coetzee says that through these encounters with child prostitutes in Africa he "is able to free himself from the ghosts of London" (Panwar 175).

It is against the feminine ethics that such woman should suffer through the hands of a powerless man. It is obvious that women help men in their worst times yet they are discarded in their good times. Leela too accompanies Ganesh in his struggle like a dutiful loyal Indian wife but during the celebration of his victory she is almost absent from the scene. Ganesh takes all the credit to the self. Leela and Ana both accompany their husband's during life's bitter experiences but seldom are they found in the moments of celebration.

Indian communities practice patriarchy and therefore always expect from its women to be docile, obedient and tolerant of her master's harshness. If they fail to follow him, there is no space for her. They marry her for her obedience and carnal joy but when she proves her stuff beyond that, she becomes a cause of irritation for them. They seldom tolerate her standing equal or demanding space for herself. Simon de Beauvoir thinks that the problem is deep rooted as, "it is among the psychoanalysists in particular that man is defined as a human being and woman as a female wherever she behaves as a human being she is said to imitate the male" (II 53). The male-dominated society in Naipaul's works fails to understand the psyche of "Other" sex. If Naipaul's protagonists live on the periphery and remain segregated from the mainstream of Europe due to the racial discrimination, then his women suffer doubly since they live under oppression of the oppressed.

They have adopted patriarchy as a natural law, without questioning their suppression. Chandra Talpade Mohanty argues that:

> To speak of the patriarchal family or the tribal kinship structure as the origin of the socio-economic status of women is to again assume that women are sexual-political subjects prior to their entry into the family. So while on the one hand women attain value or status within the family, the assumption of a singular patriarchal kinship system (...) is what apparently structures women as an oppressed group in these societies. (Mohanty 181)

They are week, ignorant, unattractive, and submissive who submit to their men to save their family. They depend on their men entirely for their needs. They are incapable of creating a place in the society on their own. Ana shares the sensibility and Willie's mental status, but at her ancestral house, she, too, submits to his will. Naipaul shows a visible dichotomy between male and female characters both.

Ana satisfies Willie's male ego by accepting his supremacy. She makes him feel extraordinary. Willie's assertion, "...I found there was no special reaction to me. It was curiously deflating. I was expecting some recognition of my extraordinariness and there was nothing..." (*Half a Life* 144) clearly shows his disappointment. He understands very well that no other African feels the way Ana feels about him. She respects him and treats him specially despite being aware of his ordinariness. She still treats him the same as she used to do in London. Willie shrinks to think of his rejection by Ana. He leaves her due to his insecurity and fear only. To Sarojini he reveals that how crucial it was for him to spent time in matrimony with Ana as it undid his fear to be lost. He expresses his gratitude for her "for the luck and liberation" which "she had brought" him, as well as for "granting" him "full manhood" (*Half a Life* 145). He lived in Africa not solely because he loved Ana but because he had no other way to survive. After sucking the essence of her life he deserts her like an "invader".

Women in Naipaul are weak, submissive, fragile and mentally backward and subordinate therefore dependent on men. They are wives, mothers and sisters but never the soul-mates and confidants. It is distressing to witness their plight in these novels for no one cares for their sentiments. There is hardly any male character that after "using" a woman ever thinks of her reactions or after-effects. But, if women withdraw themselves from the household and do not conform to their so-called "legal subordination" their whole universe collapses. Pathetically no one, in these societies, is ready to acknowledge the importance of their mutual bonding.

If they are looked, conclusively, separate from their men, women are ignorant individuals. Being a realist, Naipaul shows the true state of women. In these novels it is the struggle of male protagonist who the story ahead and sustains the interest. Women remain indifferent and sidelined. Females in Naipaul are "flat characters" and lack life as well as development. They live on the extremes of existence. Indeed equality of status is on alien term not only for men but also for women in Naipaul. Women are left apart; they ramble in another sphere, which definitely co-exist with men's world but are entirely different. Male individuality crushes conjugal relationship and thus brings estrangement to the institution of marriage. The acceptance of identity of both the genders cannot be expected from these people; subsequently clashes between them increase. As women don't develop, the only way to survive for them is to adopt the male-oriented atmosphere and remain stereotypes forever.

Works Cited

Beauvoir, Simon de. *The Second Sex*. London: New English Library, 1970.

Geetha, V. *Gender: Theorizing Feminism*. New Delhi: Stree, 2001.

Iyer, N. Sharda. "*A House for Mr Biswas*: A Study in Cultural Predicament." Ed. Mohit K. Ray. *V.S. Naipaul: Critical Essays*, Vol. III. New Delhi: Atlantic Publishers and Distributors (P) Ltd., 2005. 16-25.

Mongia, Padmini. Ed. *Contemporary Postcolonial Theory*. New Delhi: Oxford University Press, 2009.

Naipaul, V.S. *The Mystic Masseur*. London: Picador, 2001.

——. *A House for Mr Biswas*. Harmondsworth: Penguin, 1969.

——. *India: A Million Mutinies Now.* London: Vintage, 1998.

——. *Half a Life*. London: Picador, 2001.

Sharma, S.S. "Identity and Sensuality in V.S. Naipaul's *Half a Life*." *V.S. Naipaul: An Anthology of Recent Criticism*. Ed. Purabi Panwar. New Delhi: Pencraft International, 2000. 173-78.

Contributors

Ajay K. Chaubey: Ph.D. on Naipaul; Uttarakhand-SLET (2012), and Rajasthan-SLET (2012). Assistant Professor of English, Department of Sciences and Humanities, National Institute of Technology (NIT), Uttarakhand.

Aju Mukhopadhyay: Bilingual poet, author and critic; author of 30 books and recipient of several poetry awards, besides other honours from India and abroad. Many of his works have been translated in Indian and foreign languages and anthologized.

Amod Kumar Rai: Assistant Professor, Dept. of English, Buddha Post Graduate College, Kushinagar (UP); author of five books (including three edited) on different but contemporary issues.

Asis De: M.Phil; Assistant Professor and Head, Department of English Language and Literature, Mahishadal Raj College (Govt. Sponsored), Mahishadal, West Bengal; Doctoral Research Scholar in the Department of English of Jadavpur University, Kolkata; awarded the Teacher Fellowship by the University Grants Commission.

Balkar Singh: Research Scholar, Dept. of English, Bharathiar University, Coimbatore (TN). He is presently discharging his onus as a translator in Parliament, New Delhi.

Bishun Kumar: Ph.D., UGC-NET; Assistant Professor, Department of English in BBDNITM, a constituent college of Babu Banarasi Das University, Lucknow. He has co-edited two books entitled *Major Voices in New Literatures* and *Mahesh Dattani: Themes, Techniques and Issues*.

Chandan Kumar Panda: Ph.D. Scholar in the Department of American and Caribbean Literature, English and Foreign Language University, Hyderabad; currently working on "V.S. Naipaul's Vision of History".

Deepak Kumar: Associate Professor of English, H.N.B. Garhwal University, Srinagar, Garhwal (Uttarakhand); trainer in Communicative Skills, Soft Skills, Creative Writing Programmes and Teaching Methodologies.

Madhu Sharma: Assistant Professor, Department of English, S.D. Girls College, Narwana (Haryana). She has a few articles and papers to her credit.

Mujeeb Ali Murshed Qasim: Ph.D.; Assistant Professor of English Literature. He is translator, academic administrator, and author of a number of significant articles in international refereed journals. He has worked at King Saud University, KSA (2008-10) and Sana'a University, Yemen (2005-08).

N.D.R. Chandra: Vice Chancellor of Bastar University, Jagdalpur (Chhattisgarh); former UGC Visiting Professor, H.S. Gour University, Sagar (M.P.). He was Fulbright-Nehru Senior Research Fellow in Wisconsin University, Madison and Brown University, Providence, USA in 2010-11.

Paramita Ghosh: M. Phil; Assistant Professor and Head, Department of English, Maynaguri College, Jalpaiguri, West Bengal. Her doctoral research is based on a comparative study of Naipaul and Amitav Ghosh in the post-colonial context and the way they have incorporated travel writing in their fiction.

Prakash Chandra Pradhan: Professor of English at Dept. of English & MEL, Banaras Hindu University, Varanasi; has published forty-eight research papers and reviews in the journals and anthologies of reputation. He has also published four books including *D.H. Lawrence's Novels: A Stylistic Approach* and *D.H. Lawrence's Novels: A New Historical Approach*.

Satendra Kumar: Associate Professor and Head, Dept. of English, Govt. P.G. College, Lansdowne, Pauri Garhwal, Uttarakhand. He has authored many books. He has had a UGC Minor Research Project titled "A Study of Lexical

Categories of Languages and Sounds: Switching of Hindi and English Words". He was honored with Michael Madhusudan Award (2010) by the M.M. Society of West Bengal. He was also honored with Bharat Shiksha Ratan Award (2012) by GSHEG, New Delhi.

Sayantan Pal Chowdhury: M.A. English, Lingusitics; Assistant Teacher in English, Siliguri Baradakanta Vidyapith (H.S.), Siliguri, Darjeeling (WB). His papers were selected in World Shakespeare Conference in Banaras Hindu University, SALA Conference 2013, and International Conference on Literature to Cinema.

Shalini: Ph.D.; Lecturer in English at Govt. Girl Inter College, Unnao (UP). She has actively participated in seminars and conferences in her area of research.

Shashank Shekhar Sharma: Assistant Professor, Department of English, Bodofa U.N. Brahma College, Dotma, Kokrajhar; Research Scholar at Nagaland Central University, Kohima Campus.

Shagufta Naj: M. Phil; former Assistant Professor in Techwords College of Engineering, Roorkee. Presently she is doing her research work on comparative study of Canadian and South Asian Literature.

Vineet Kashyap: Ph.D.; teaches Professional Communication at Govt. Girls Polytechnic, Lucknow. Her doctoral thesis "The Portrayal of the First Nations in the Plays of George Ryga" has been published in the book form by the leading International publisher, Lambert Academic Publishing Gmb H & Co. Landstra Be, Germany.

Valiur Rahaman: Assistant Professor in the Department of English, Central University of Rajasthan, Bandasindari, Rajasthan, India; author of many books; Executive Editor of international journal, *Avant Garde Responses: An Interdisciplinary Journal of Humanities & Social Sciences*.

Vishnupriya Sengupta: Ph.D. on V.S. Naipaul; former postdoctoral research fellow at the Universita degli Studi di Milano, in Milan, Italy; Special Editions Editor for a volume on Naipaul in the *Journal of Caribbean Literatures*, brought out by the University of Central Arkansas, USA.

